THE LATER ROMAN EMPIRE

THE LATER
ROMAN EMPIRE

AD 284–430

AVERIL CAMERON

Harvard University Press
Cambridge, Massachusetts

Library of Congress Cataloging-in-Publication Data

Cameron, Averil.
  The later Roman empire / by Averil Cameron.
    p. cm.
  Includes bibliographical references and index.
  ISBN 0-674-51193-X. — ISBN 0-674-51194-8 (pbk.)
  1. Rome—History—Empire, 284–476. I. Title.
  DG311.C36 1993   92-41000
  937'.06—dc20   CIP

Preface

THE MAIN IDEAS and emphases expressed in this book and its companion volume, *The Mediterranean World in Late Antiquity, AD 395–600*, Routledge History of Classical Civilization (London, 1993), have evolved over twenty or so years of teaching and lecturing. Although during that period the later Roman empire has become fashionable, especially in its newer guise of 'late antiquity', there is still, strangely, no basic textbook for students in English. I am very glad therefore to have been given this opportunity to attempt to fill that gap. My own approach owes a great deal to the influence over the years of my colleagues in ancient history, especially to those who have been associated with the London Ancient History Seminars at the Institute of Classical Studies. Not least among them is Fergus Millar, who initiated the seminars, and who both encouraged a broad and generous conception of ancient history and insisted on the great importance of lucid and helpful presentation. Most important of all, however, have been the generations of history and classics students, by no means all of them specialists, who have caused me to keep returning to the old problems, and to keep finding something new.

This book was written at speed, and with great enjoyment, partly as a relief from more difficult and recalcitrant projects. Though of course infinitely more can be said than is possible in this limited compass, I hope that it will at least provide a good starting point from which students can approach this fascinating period.

The Later Roman Empire is published in London as part of the Fontana History of the Ancient World. I am grateful to the editor of the series, Oswyn Murray, for wise guidance, and to several others for various kinds of help, notably to Dominic Rathbone and Richard Williams. But they, needless to say, had no part in the book's defects. Following the principles of the Fontana series the book contains numerous translated excerpts from contemporary sources; in the case of Ammianus Marcellinus, such translations are taken from the Penguin edition by W. Hamilton.

London, August 1992

Contents

List of Illustrations		ix
Maps		xi
I	Introduction: the third-century background	1
II	The Sources	13
III	The New Empire: Diocletian	30
IV	The New Empire: Constantine	47
V	Church and State: the legacy of Constantine	66
VI	The Reign of Julian	85
VII	The Late Roman State: Constantius to Theodosius	99
VIII	Late Roman Economy and Society	113
IX	Military Affairs, Barbarians and the Late Roman Army	133
X	Culture in the Late Fourth Century	151
XI	Constantinople and the East	170
XII	Conclusion	187
Date Chart		195
List of Emperors		197
Primary Sources		199
Further Reading		209
Index		229

List of Illustrations

1. *Notitia Dignitatum*, insignia of *dux Arabiae*. MS. Canon. Misc. 378, fol. 118r, Bodleian Library, Oxford. Page 34.

2. Head of colossal statue of Constantine, Rome, Palazzo dei Conservatori. Courtauld Institute of Art. Page 50.

3. Arch of Constantine, Rome, AD 315. Courtauld Institute of Art. Page 51.

4. *Largitio* dish, silver, with the name of the Emperor Licinius. Trustees of the British Museum. Page 52.

5. Greek dedication to Constantius II and a Caesar (name missing), by Eros Monaxius, governor of Caria, ? AD 355–60, Aphrodisias. Mossman Roueché. Page 70.

6. Sarcophagus with scenes from the story of Jonah. Trustees of the British Museum. Page 77.

7. S. Maria Maggiore, interior. Courtauld Institute of Art. Page 80.

8. Head of Socrates, from mosaic floor showing Socrates and six sages, Apamea, Syria. J. Balty. Page 96.

9. Chair ornament in the form of a City Tyche, Esquiline Treasure. Trustees of the British Museum. Page 104.

10. Villa mosaic, Tabarka, North Africa. Musée National du Bardo. Page 120.

11. Leaf of ivory diptych showing a priestess performing religious rites; the inscription at the top reads 'of the Symmachi'. Trustees of the Victoria and Albert Museum. Page 160.

12. Leaf of ivory diptych apparently showing the *consecratio* of an emperor, perhaps Julian, though the monogram at the top may refer to the Symmachi family. Trustees of the British Museum. Page 161.

13.   Head of youthful beardless Christ (labelled Cristus), from gold-glass bowl. Trustees of the British Museum. Page 163.

Maps

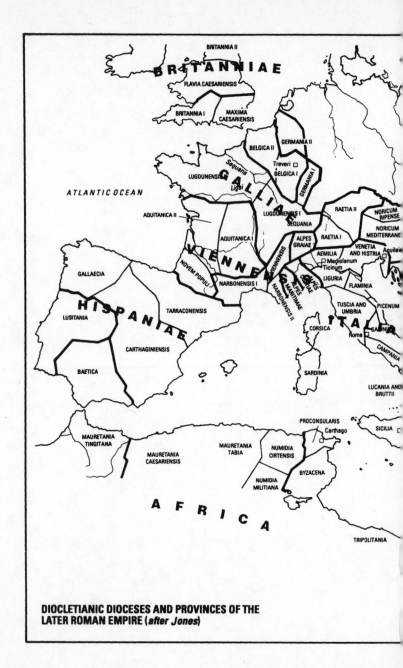

**DIOCLETIANIC DIOCESES AND PROVINCES OF THE
LATER ROMAN EMPIRE (*after Jones*)**

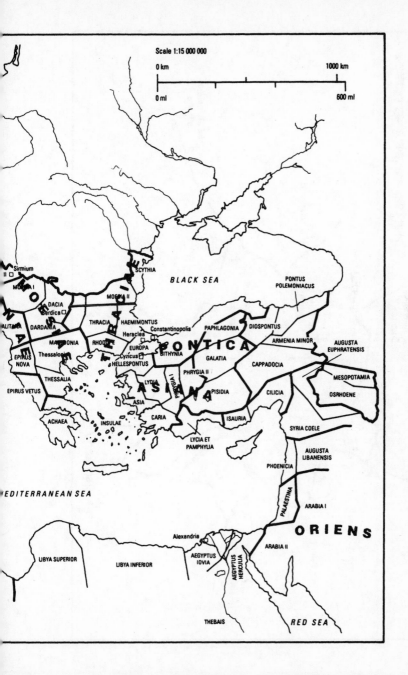

Scale 1:15 000 000

0 km   1000 km

0 ml   600 ml

Sirmium

MOESIA I

DACIA

Serdica

ALITANA

DARDANIA

EPIRUS NOVA

Thessalonica

THESSALIA

EPIRUS VETUS

ACHAEA

INSULAE

SCYTHIA

BLACK SEA

MOESIA II

THRACIA

HAEMIMONTUS

Heraclea

Constantinopolis

EUROPA

Cyzicus

HELLESPONTUS

MACEDONIA

RHODOPE

PONTICA

PAPHLAGONIA

DIOSPONTUS

PONTUS POLEMONIACUS

ARMENIA MINOR

AUGUSTA EUPHRATENSIS

BITHYNIA

GALATIA

CAPPADOCIA

PHRYGIA II

LYDIA

PHRYGIA I

ASIANA

PISIDIA

CARIA

ASIA

ISAURIA

CILICIA

MESOPOTAMIA

OSRHOENE

LYCIA ET PAMPHYLIA

SYRIA COELE

AUGUSTA LIBANENSIS

PHOENICIA

MEDITERRANEAN SEA

ARABIA I

PALAESTINA

ORIENS

Alexandria

LIBYA SUPERIOR

LIBYA INFERIOR

AEGYPTUS IOVIA

AEGYPTUS HERCULIA

ARABIA II

THEBAIS

RED SEA

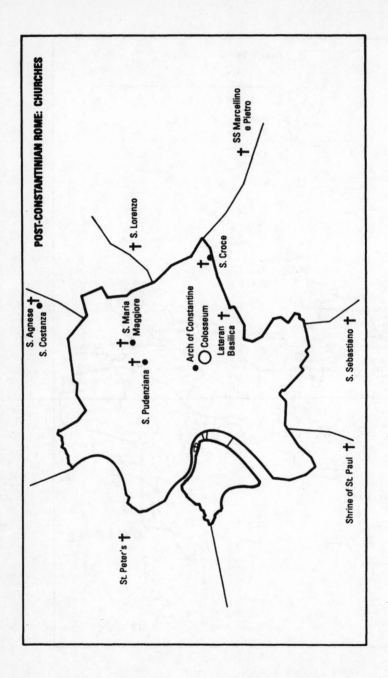

POST-CONSTANTINIAN ROME: CHURCHES

St. Peter's ✝

S. Agnese ✝
S. Costanza •

✝ S. Maria
• Maggiore

S. Pudenziana ✝
•

S. Lorenzo ✝

Arch of Constantine
• ○ Colosseum
Lateran ✝
Basilica

✝ S. Croce
S. Croce

SS Marcellino
✝ e Pietro

S. Sebastiano ✝

Shrine of St. Paul ✝

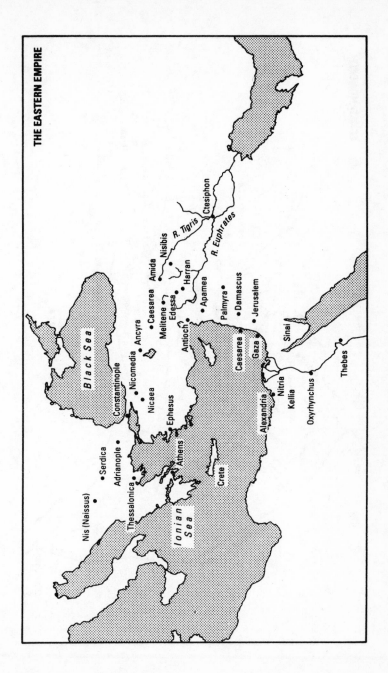

THE EASTERN EMPIRE

Nis (Naissus)

Serdica

Adrianople

Thessalonica

Athens

Ionian Sea

Crete

Black Sea

Constantinople

Nicomedia

Nicaea

Ancyra

Ephesus

Melitene

Caesarea

Antioch

Edessa

Harran

Amida

Nisibis

R. Tigris

Ctesiphon

R. Euphrates

Apamea

Palmyra

Damascus

Jerusalem

Caesarea

Gaza

Sinai

Alexandria

Nitria

Kellia

Oxyrhynchus

Thebes

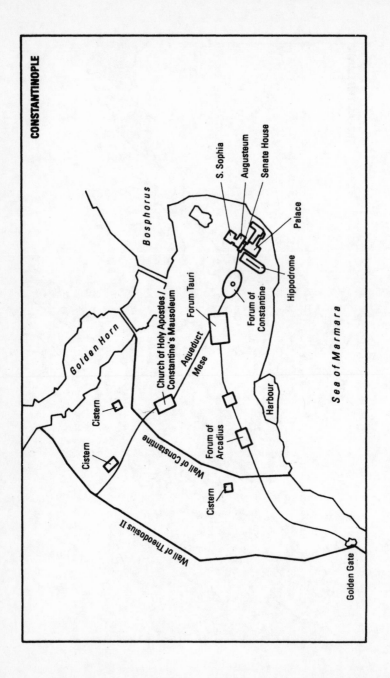

CONSTANTINOPLE

Bosphorus

Golden Horn

Sea of Marmara

S. Sophia

Augusteum

Senate House

Palace

Hippodrome

Forum of Constantine

Forum Tauri

Aqueduct

Mese

Church of Holy Apostles /
Constantine's Mausoleum

Harbour

Forum of Arcadius

Cistern

Cistern

Cistern

Cistern

Wall of Constantine

Wall of Theodosius II

Golden Gate

THE LATER ROMAN EMPIRE

I

Introduction

THE THIRD-CENTURY BACKGROUND

IT IS A MARK OF the dramatic change that has taken place in our historical perceptions of the ancient world that when the new Fontana series was first launched, the later Roman Empire, or, as it is now commonly called, late antiquity, was not included in it; now, by contrast, it would seem strange to leave it out. Two books of very different character were especially influential in bringing this change about, so far as English-speaking students were concerned: first, A. H. M. Jones's massive *History of the Later Roman Empire. A Social, Economic and Administrative Survey* (Oxford, 1964), and second, Peter Brown's brief but exhilarating sketch, *The World of Late Antiquity* (London, 1971). Of course, the subject had never been neglected by serious scholars, or in continental scholarship; nevertheless, it is only in the generation since the publication of Jones's work that the period has aroused such wide interest. Since then, indeed, it has become one of the major areas of growth in current teaching and research.

The timespan covered in this book runs effectively from the accession of Diocletian in AD 284 (the conventional starting date for the later Roman empire) to the end of the fourth century, when on the death of Theodosius I in AD 395 the empire was divided between his two sons, Honorius in the west and Arcadius in the east. It is not therefore so much a book about late antiquity in general, a period that can plausibly be seen as running from the fourth to the seventh century and closing with the Arab invasions, as one about the fourth century. This was the century of Constantine, the first emperor to embrace and support Christianity, and the founder of Constantinople, the city that was to become the capital of the Byzantine empire and to remain such until it was captured by the Ottoman Turks in AD 1453. Edward Gibbon's great work, *The Decline and Fall of the Roman Empire*, carries the narrative to the latter date, regarding this, not AD 476, when the last Roman emperor in the west was deposed, as the real end of the Roman empire. Few would agree with Gibbon now, but historians are still quarrelling about when Rome ended and Byzantium began, and in their debate Gibbon's highly-coloured perception of the moral decline which he thought had set in once the high point of Roman civilization under the Antonine emperors in the second century AD was passed remains highly influential. All writers on the fourth century must take a view about what are in fact highly subjective issues: was the regime of the later empire a repressive system which evolved in response to the chaos which had set in in the third century? Can we see in it the signs of a decay which led to the collapse and fragmentation of the Roman empire in the west in the fifth century? Did Constantine's adoption of Christianity somehow assist a process of decline by finally abandoning earlier Roman values, as Gibbon thought?

All these views have been and still are widely held by historians, and permeate much of the writing on the period. It will soon be clear that this book takes a different approach. Preconceptions, and especially value judgements, cannot be avoided altogether in a history, but they certainly do not help either the historian or the student. Moreover, we are much less likely today, given the challenge to traditional values which has taken place in our own society, to hold up the Principate as the embodiment of the classical ideal, and to assume that any deviation from it must necessarily represent decline. Finally, we are perhaps more wary than earlier generations of historians of the power and the dangers of rhetoric, and less likely than they were to take the imperial rhetoric of the later Roman empire at face value. The period from Diocletian onwards is sometimes referred to as the 'Dominate', since the emperor was referred to as *dominus* ('lord'), whereas in the early empire (the so-called 'Principate'), he had originally been referred to very differently, simply as *princeps* ('first citizen'). But the term *dominus* was by no means new; moreover, what the fourth-century emperors wanted, and how they wanted to appear, was one thing; what kind of society the empire was as a whole was quite another.

To gauge the difference, we must start not with Diocletian or the 'tetrarchic' system which he instituted in an attempt to restore political stability – according to Diocletian's plan, two emperors (*Augusti*), were to share power, each with a Caesar who would in due course succeed him. We must start rather with the third century, the apparent watershed between two contrasting systems. Here, traditionally, historians have seen a time of crisis (the so-called 'third-century crisis'), indicated by a constant and rapid turnover of emperors between AD 235 and 284, by near-continuous warfare, internal and external, combined with the total collapse of the silver currency and the state's recourse to exactions in kind. This dire situation was brought under at least partial control by Diocletian, whose reforming measures were then continued by Constantine (AD 306–37), thus laying the foundation for the recovery of the fourth century. In such circumstances, for which it is not difficult to find contemporary witnesses, it is tempting to imagine that people turned the more readily to religion for comfort or escape, and that here lie the roots of the supposedly more spiritual world of late antiquity. But much of this too is a matter of subjective judgement, and of reading the sources too much at face value. Complaints about the tax-collector, for instance, such as we find in rabbinic sources from Palestine and in Egyptian papyri, tell us what we might have expected anyway, namely that no one likes paying taxes; they do not tell us whether the actual tax burden had increased as much as they seem at first sight to imply. While there certainly were severe problems in the third century, particularly in relation to political stability and to the working of the coinage, nearly all the individual components of the concept of 'third-century crisis' have been challenged in recent years. And if the crisis was less severe than has been thought, then the degree of change between the second and the fourth centuries may have been exaggerated too.

'The third-century crisis', 'the age of transition', 'the age of the soldier-emperors', 'the age of anarchy', 'the military monarchy' – whatever one likes to call it, historians are agreed that the critical period in the third century began with the murder of Alexander Severus in AD 235 and lasted until the accession of Diocletian in AD 284. The first and most obvious symptom to manifest itself was the rapid turnover of emperors after Severus – most lasted only a few months and met a violent end, often at the hands of their own troops or in the course of another coup. Gallienus (253–68) lasted the longest, while Aurelian (270–5) was the most successful, managing to defeat the independent regime which Queen Zenobia had set up at Palmyra in Syria after the death of her husband Odenathus. But Valerian (253–60) was captured by Shapur I, the king of the powerful dynasty of the Sasanians who had succeeded the Parthians as the rulers of Persia in AD 224, while from AD 258 to 274, Postumus and his successors ruled quasi-independently in Gaul (the so-called 'Gallic empire').

This turnover of emperors (the distinction between emperor and usurper became increasingly blurred) was intimately linked with the second symptom of crisis, constant warfare, which furnished an even greater role for the army, or armies, than they had already played under the Severans. The Sasanians presented a serious and unforeseen threat to the east which was to last for three hundred years, until the end of their empire after the victories of Heraclius in AD 628. Conflict with the Sasanians was to exact a heavy toll in Roman manpower and resources. Their greatest third-century king, Shapur I (AD 242–c.272), set a pattern by invading Mesopotamia, Syria and Asia Minor in AD 253 and 260, taking Antioch and deporting thousands of its inhabitants to Persia; he recorded his victories in a grandiose inscription at Naqsh-i-Rustam, with reliefs showing the humiliated Emperor Valerian. To the north and west Germanic tribes continued to exert the pressure on the borders which had caused such difficulty for Marcus Aurelius, and, before Valerian's capture by Shapur, Decius had already been defeated by the Goths (AD 251). The underlying reasons for the continued barbarian raids and the actual aims of the invaders are still far from clear. It is a mistake to think in apocalyptic terms of waves of thousand upon thousand of barbarians descending on the empire, for the actual numbers on any one occasion were quite small. Nevertheless, there is no doubt that in these incursions the third century saw the prototype of another problem which was to assume a great magnitude in the later empire, and to which was to be accorded, by many historians, primary responsibility for the fall of the western empire. At one time or another virtually all the northern and western provinces suffered barbarian invasion, as did Cappadocia, Achaea, Egypt and Syria, and Italy itself was not exempt under Aurelian. Contemporaries could be forgiven for seeing this as the beginning of the end.

The army had already assumed far more importance than before as a result of Septimius Severus's reforms, and the critical situation in the third century gave it a dangerous preeminence. Not surprisingly, each provincial army put forward its own candidate for emperor, and as quickly murdered him if they so chose. There was nothing to stop the process being repeated: the senate had never controlled armies directly, and even if there was an emperor in Rome he had little chance in such disturbed conditions of controlling what happened on the periphery of the empire. It was not so much that external military threats caused internal instability (though they certainly contributed), but rather that they fell on an empire which was already highly unstable, as had been vividly shown in the civil wars which broke out from the reign of Marcus Aurelius onwards. In the third century, however, further consequences soon appeared: the army necessarily increased in size, and thus in its demands on resources, and in contrast to the peaceful conditions of the early empire when soldiers were on the whole kept well away from the inner provinces, they were now to be found everywhere, in towns and in the countryside, and by no means always under control. When a more stable military system was reintroduced by Diocletian and Constantine, the situation was in part recognized as given, and the army of the later empire, instead of being largely stationed on the frontier, was dispersed in smaller units inside provinces and in towns.

Not surprisingly in such circumstances, the military pay and supply system broke down under the strain. The army had been paid mainly in silver *denarii*, out of the tax revenues collected in the same coin. The silver content of the *denarius* had already been reduced as far back as the reign of Nero, but from Marcus Aurelius on it was further and further debased, while the soldiers' pay was increased as part of the attempt to keep the army strong and under control. The process was carried to such lengths that by the 260s the *denarius* had almost lost its silver content altogether, being made virtually entirely of base metal. It may seem surprising that prices had not risen sharply as soon as the debasements had begun in earnest. But the Roman empire was not like a modern state, where such changes are officially announced and immediately effected. Communication was slow, and the government, if such a term can be used, had few means open to it of controlling coins or exchange at local levels even at the best of times, and certainly not in such disturbed conditions. The successive debasements, which were to have such serious consequences, were much more the result of *ad hoc* measures taken to ensure continued payment of troops than of any long-term policy. But naturally prices did rise, and rapidly, causing real difficulties in exchange and circulation of goods. This is not inflation in the modern sense; rather, it was the result of very large amounts of base-metal coins being produced for their own purposes by the fast-changing third-century emperors, and of the gradual realization by the populace that current *denarii* were no longer worth anything like their face value. The inevitable effect of this was to push older and purer coins out of circulation, and indeed a large proportion of the Roman coins now preserved derive from hoards apparently deposited in the third century. Gold and silver disappeared from circulation at such a rate that Diocletian and Constantine had to institute special taxes payable only in gold or silver in order to recover precious metals for the treasury. Once the spiral had been set in motion, it was even harder to stop, and despite Diocletian's efforts at controlling prices, papyrological evidence shows that they were still rising dramatically under Constantine.

This is the background to the return to exchange in kind which many historians have seen as a reversion to a primitive economy and therefore a key symptom of crisis. Not merely were the troops partly paid in goods instead of in money; taxes were collected in kind too, the main drain on tax revenue having always been the upkeep of the army. But especially in view of the experience of our own world, we should be less struck by the the retreat from monetarization than by the success with which an elaborate system of local requisitions was defined and operated, and needs matched to resources. It is also relevant to note that direct exactions had always been part of Roman practice in providing for the *annona militaris*, the grain supply for the army, and the *angareia*, military transport; it was not the practice itself that was new, but the scale. But conditions were extremely unstable, especially in the middle of the century, and local populations were liable to get sudden demands without warning which caused real hardship; it was left to Diocletian to attempt to systematize the collections by regularizing them.

If the army was, if only partly, being paid in kind (money payments never ceased altogether) other consequences followed, for instance the need for supplies to be raised from areas as near as possible to the troops themselves, for obvious reasons connected with the difficulty of long-distance transport. We find the fourth-century army, therefore, divided into smaller units posted nearer to centres of distribution. Again, there were changes in command: the praetorian prefects, having started as equestrian commanders of the imperial guard, had gradually taken on more general army command functions; with these changes in the *annona* and requisitions generally, they effectively gained charge of the provincial administrative system, and were second in power only to the emperor. In a similar way equestrians in general acquired a much bigger role in administration, for instance in provincial governorships, traditionally held by senators. Later sources claim that Gallienus excluded senators by edict from holding such posts (Aur. Vict., *Caes.* 33.34), but it is clear that there was never a formal ban, and some did continue; the change is more likely to have been the natural result of decentralization and of the breakdown of the patronage connection necessary for such appointments between the emperor in Rome and the members of the senatorial class. It was more practical, and may have seemed more logical, for emperors raised in the provinces and from the army, as most were, to appoint governors from among the class they knew and had to hand.

The Senate's undoubted eclipse in the third century is partly attributable to the fact that emperors no longer resided or were made at Rome; the close tie between emperor and Senate was therefore broken, and few third-century emperors had their accessions ratified by the Senate according to traditional practice. Meanwhile the Senate itself lost much of its political role, though membership continued to bestow prestige and valuable fiscal exemptions. Rather than owing their elevation to the Senate, therefore, emperors in this period were often raised to the purple on the field, surrounded by their troops. The legacy of this dispersal of imperial authority can still be seen under Diocletian and the tetrarchy, when instead of holding court at Rome the Augusti spent their time travelling and residing at a series of different centres such as Serdica and Nicomedia, some of which, in particular Trier and Antioch, had already acquired semi-official status in the third century. Rome was never to become a main imperial residence again. Moreover, Rome and the Senate had always gone together. But Constantine now put the senatorial order on a new footing by opening it more widely, so that membership became empire-wide rather than implying a residence and a function based on Rome itself.

In fact, the mid-third century did not see a dramatic crisis so much as a steady continuation of processes already begun, which in turn led to the measures later taken by Diocletian and Constantine that are usually identified with the establishment of the late Roman system. How therefore should the evidence of monetary collapse be assessed in this context? This is one of the most difficult questions in trying to understand what was actually happening. We need to ask how far rising prices were due to a general economic crisis and how much they were the result of a monetary collapse caused by quite specific reasons. One phenomenon often cited in support of the former argument is the virtual cessation of urban public building during this period. The local notables who had been so eager to adorn their cities with splendid buildings during the heyday of Roman prosperity in the second century no longer seemed to have the funds or the inclination to continue. The kind of civic patronage often known as 'euergetism' from the Greek word for 'benefactor', that had been so prominent a feature of the early empire, now came to a virtual halt. From the fourth century onwards the economic difficulties of the town councils become a major theme in the sources. But a drop in the fortunes of the upper classes is only one possible explanation for the cessation of building; it is clear that the upkeep of existing public buildings, which fell on the city councils, was already a problem by the late second century. Further additions to the stock might be an embarrassment rather than a cause for gratitude. By the mid-third century the uncertainty of the times in many areas also made the thought of building, as of benefactions in the old style, seem inappropriate; in cities which felt themselves vulnerable to invasion or civil war, the first interest of town councils was simply in survival or indeed repair. Some cities showed considerable resilience even after severe attack. Antioch and Athens were badly damaged by the Sasanians and the Heruli respectively, yet both were able to recover. By contrast, the cities in Gaul which suffered during the third-century invasions were more vulnerable than those in the more prosperous and densely populated east, and when rebuilding and fortification took place their urban space typically contracted, as at Amiens and Paris. While in the early empire cities had not needed strong defences, they now started to acquire city walls, and to change their appearance into the walled city typical of late antiquity. At Athens itself the area north of the Acropolis was now fortified. But in North Africa the situation was different again. There, the third century saw continued building and urban growth. Protected to some extent from the insecurity elsewhere, the North African economy profited from increased olive production, and the cities of North Africa in the fourth century were among the most secure and prosperous in the empire.

It is evident that given the rapid turnover of emperors, smooth functioning of relations between centre and periphery must have been seriously disrupted. The empire had been a balancing act from the beginning, and the equilibrium was now endangered. Formerly a balance of imperial and local interest had obtained, and had been at its steadiest during the age of the Antonines. In the third century, local cultures became much more visible. From Gaul to Syria and Egypt, local styles are more evident in visual art, and local interests had an opportunity to make themselves felt, most obviously in the so-called 'Gallic empire' and in Zenobia's bid for independence at Palmyra. Another important development in the third century was the extension of Roman citizenship to all the inhabitants of the empire under the Emperor Caracalla by the so-called *Constitutio Antoniana* of AD 212; though Caracalla's motives may have had more to do with getting in more taxes than with idealism or generosity, this measure extended the notion of what was considered 'Roman' to cover a multitude of ethnically and locally divergent cultures. Though the balance of power shifted back somewhat towards the centre under Diocletian and the tetrarchy (AD 284–305), the political and military fragmentation during the middle and later third century also had long-term implications for the cultural pattern of late antiquity. From now on, both Syriac and Coptic emerged as major literary languages used by large numbers of Christians in Syria, Mesopotamia and Egypt. The Christian church also profited: despite persecution under Decius (AD 249–51) and Diocletian (AD 303–11), it was able to develop a solid institutional structure which stood it in extremely good stead when it found favour with Constantine.

The third century was certainly a difficult period. Nor were its problems all man-made. The plague which struck the empire in the reign of Marcus Aurelius was much less serious than the attacks of bubonic plague which hit the eastern empire in the sixth century and western Europe in the fourteenth, and indeed, plague and disease were endemic in the ancient world at all periods, but it may nevertheless have been a factor, with the effects of invasion and war, conducive to a reduction in population, and with it (since land needs labour in order to produce wealth) to a diminution in the economic base. The question is highly controversial; though shortage of manpower has been adduced as a reason for the alleged decline of the empire, the case has been argued on poor grounds. Nevertheless, general considerations, together with evidence of urban contraction, especially in the western provinces, do support a cautious hypothesis of a reduction in population. But it is essential to see this over a longer period; the eastern empire at any rate was well able to recover, and there is good evidence of an actual population increase from the late fourth and certainly during the fifth century.

Modern historians, for various reasons, have been quick to emphasize the negative aspects of the period. But it is less obvious that contemporaries saw it in those terms. To our eyes, the social and legal distinctions between *honestiores* ('upper class') and *humiliores* ('lower class') are a striking feature of the later empire; yet they had been developing well before the period of the 'third-century crisis'. Again, it is probably a modern idea to see the Gallic emperors as forming a separatist regime, for, as Tacitus had remarked, it had long been one of the 'secrets of empire' that legitimate emperors could be made outside Rome. Furthermore, the negative views expressed by contemporaries, on which many modern accounts rely, usually have a specific explanation. Bishops such as Cyprian of Carthage, who was himself martyred in the persecution under Valerian in AD 258, very naturally emphasized the evils of the age. On the other hand, cultural activity flourished. The philosopher Plotinus continued to lecture on Platonism in Rome and to attract fashionable crowds to hear him, besides pupils from far afield. P. Herennius Dexippus, who had led the citizens of Athens in their resistance to the Heruli, wrote a history of the Gothic and Scythian invasions, which unfortunately only survives in fragments. We tend to be misled in judging the period by the fact that no good contemporary narrative survives for the critical middle fifty years of the third century, so that we must depend on the often fanciful and trivializing *Historia Augusta*, which reads rather like a gossip column in a tabloid newspaper, and once read, is hard to forget.

Especially when looking back from the vantage point of modern rationalism, it is very tempting to suppose with E. R. Dodds and others that the 'age of spirituality' (as late antiquity has been called) grew out of the insecurity experienced in the third century, or, in other words, that people turned to religion, and perhaps especially to Christianity, in their attempts to find meaning, or to escape from their present woes. The persecuting emperors, Decius, Valerian and Diocletian, certainly believed that neglect of the gods endangered the empire's security, and that deviant groups such as Christians must therefore be brought into line. In the same way, Constantine saw himself as specially charged by God to make sure that worship was properly conducted and properly directed. But it is one thing to suppose a general connection between religion and the desire for comfort, reassurance and explanation of suffering, and quite another to imagine that difficult times always call forth religious movements, or, to put it the other way round, that a religious development is always to be explained by reference to adverse social factors. Whether late antiquity was really more an age of spirituality than the periods that had gone before is itself now in question; it is an assumption which tends to hang together with the notion that paganism was discredited or somehow in decline, and that Christianity rose to fill the resultant gap. But this Christianizing view does not stand up to recent study of the lively and diverse religious life of the early empire, and the reasons for the growth of the Christian church and the spread of Christianity can only be located by a broad analysis, not simply by appeal to an alleged decline of paganism.

Christianization, and the profound consequences for the empire and for society of Constantine's espousal of Christianity, form one of the strands which make late antiquity different from the early empire. But there were many others, among which we must give a special place to the series of reforms and administrative, economic and military changes which evolved during the fifty years (AD 284–337) covered by the reigns of Diocletian and Constantine. Though there were of course striking differences between them, which are vividly reflected in the surviving source material, we should also attempt to take a broad view, and to see their reigns as marking, when taken together, a fifty-year period of recovery and consolidation after the fifty-year 'age of anarchy', in Rostovtzeff's phrase. Contrary to the usual emphasis, however, it was not so much Diocletian and Constantine themselves as personalities who managed to stabilize the situation, but rather a combination and convergence of factors, from which many of their 'reforms' in fact emerged piecemeal and *ad hoc*. Seen in this light, the mid-third century looks less like a time of 'crisis' from which the empire was dragged by the efforts of a strong and even a totalitarian emperor (Diocletian is often termed an 'oriental despot' because of his adoption of elaborate court ceremony in the Persian style), and more like a temporary phase in a developing and evolving imperial system.

II

The Sources

IN SHARP CONTRAST with that for the third century, the available source material for the period starting with Diocletian's reign, and more especially for the late fourth century onwards, is extremely rich and varied. This is attributable not only to the large amount of Christian writing but also to the sheer quantity of secular writing in both Latin and Greek. The amount of Latin writing surviving from the late fourth century in particular is such as to surpass even the age of Cicero, and to make this one of the best-documented periods in Roman history. Ammianus Marcellinus, the one great Latin historian after Tacitus, completed his *Res Gestae* in Rome in the early 390s, while the voluminous letters of Q. Aurelius Symmachus, a latter-day Pliny, give us an idea of the priorities and the constraints on a pagan senator of wealth and position, even if not one of the super-rich who are unforgettably described by Ammianus (see below). In addition, this is the age of the great Christian writers, men such as Jerome, Ambrose and, above all, Augustine, whose Greek counterparts were Basil of Caesarea, his brother Gregory of Nyssa, Gregory of Nazianzus, and John Chrysostom, the twice-exiled bishop of Constantinople. All bishops, and all highly educated in the traditional secular style, these men carried on the great tradition of classical rhetoric, which they turned to Christian purpose in speeches such as the funeral oration which Ambrose delivered in honour of the Emperor Theodosius I (AD 395). Another example, the funeral speech on Basil, bishop of Caesarea, by Gregory of Nazianzus (AD 379) has been described as probably the greatest piece of Greek rhetoric since the death of Demosthenes. The fourth and fifth centuries represent the golden age of what is termed 'patristic' literature, works written by the great Fathers of the Church, men who, released from persecution during the reign of Constantine, now often took on the public role of statesman as well as that of bishop.

This is just to give a preliminary idea of the richness of the available literary material. Not surprisingly, it took some time to flower, given the apparent dearth of writing in the third century and the degree of social change which took place under Diocletian and Constantine. From the middle of the fourth century, however, we begin to see an upsurge of writing of several different kinds under the stimulus of a more settled social order which offered great opportunities to those with literary talent. Ausonius, a poet and rhetor from Bordeaux, rose to the very top and became praetorian prefect and consul after gaining the post of tutor to the future Emperor Gratian, while Claudian, a Greek-speaking Alexandrian, made his fame and fortune in Rome writing Latin panegyrics, highly elaborate and rhetorical poems in praise of the Vandal general, Stilicho, and Honorius, who succeeded his father Theodosius I as emperor in the west. The fourth-century emperors tried to curb social mobility by legislation, in the interests of securing the tax revenue; but a rhetorical, that is a classical, education was a path by which one could readily climb the social ladder.

In most cases the great churchmen of the day had also had a training in classical rhetoric. Accordingly, the relation of secular to Christian culture is not easy to define (see in particular Chapter X below), and sometimes the two came very close. The pagan philosopher and rhetor Themistius, for instance, served Christian emperors apparently without difficulty, and was actually out of favour during the reign of the pagan Julian (AD 361–3). The Emperor Julian, the only pagan emperor after Constantine and an interesting writer himself, had been brought up in early youth as a Christian. He became a pagan when he was effectively exiled as a boy after his older male relatives had been murdered by their rivals, the sons of Constantine, and when he was, rather surprisingly, allowed to come under the influence of Athenian Neoplatonism. Once emperor, he produced a number of offbeat works, all in Greek, including a satire called *The Caesars*, partly directed at Constantine, an invective against 'the Galilaeans', as he called the Christians (mostly in fact concerned with Moses and the Old Testament), a hymn to the sun-god ('King Helios') and a lampoon called 'The Beard-Hater' in which he defended himself against his unpopularity with the citizens of Antioch. Earlier, he had composed a panegyric on his hated Christian patron and predecessor, Constantius II (AD 337–61) in which he still kept his paganism concealed.

We must look at certain writers in more detail before turning to the non-literary sources. For the reign of Diocletian we are badly served by contemporaries, for no connected history survives, and it is necessary to rely to a large extent on the venomous Latin pamphlet *On the Deaths of the Persecutors* by Lactantius, a Christian convert and formerly a rhetor at the court of Nicomedia. Writing probably about AD 314, shortly after Licinius and Constantine had declared toleration for all religions in the so-called Edict of Milan, Lactantius's object was to make an example of the horrible deaths that had befallen the persecutors of Christians, which he does in great detail, especially in the case of Galerius. This of course makes him a highly unreliable witness to the secular aims of Diocletian, who had initiated the persecution in AD 303; unfortunately the chapter which he devotes to Diocletian's administrative and military reforms (*De mortibus persecutorum* 7) is too often taken at face value. The relevant part of the Greek *New History* by Zosimus, the late fifth or early sixth-century pagan writer from Constantinople, is missing, but had it survived, it would of course have been equally misleading, since in direct contrast to Lactantius the pagan Zosimus praised Diocletian and blamed Constantine for every ill the empire had subsequently suffered.

For Constantine, it is a somewhat different story, for we have a number of important works by Eusebius, Bishop of Caesarea in Palestine, a great Christian writer and scholar. Eusebius established the new Christian genres of church history and chronicles, and still more important, is the major source for our understanding of Constantine. He did not suffer himself in the persecution of Christians, but knew and visited many senior clergy who did, and his later work was coloured by that experience. His *Ecclesiastical* or *Church History*, now in ten books, may have been begun before persecution broke out again in AD 303, though this is controversial; either way, it went through several rewritings as the situation literally changed all around him. The first change was when persecution was called off in AD 311, the next when Constantine defeated Maxentius in the name of Christianity at the Battle of the Milvian Bridge in AD 312; Constantine then went on to fight two further campaigns against Licinius, culminating in his victory in AD 324. The *Church History* received its final touches after this victory but before the Council of Nicaea which Constantine summoned in AD 325 and which Eusebius describes in his later work, the *Life of Constantine* (*VC*, *Vita Constantini*), completed after Constantine's death in AD 337. Manuscript variants in the *Church History* make it clear that the author himself went over his earlier versions and touched them up in order to write out Licinius (previously presented in neutral or even favourable terms as Constantine's ally) and defend and glorify Constantine as the champion of Christianity.

The *Life of Constantine*, in four books, is less a biography than an extended and extremely tendentious panegyric, whose exaggerations and distortions have led many scholars in the past to doubt whether it could be the work of Eusebius. Some still suspect that certain passages are later in date, but by detailed comparison with the techniques of Eusebius's other writings on Constantine it has been convincingly demonstrated that the work as a whole is consistent with Eusebian authorship. Eusebius also composed official speeches for the dedication of Constantine's church of the Holy Sepulchre in Jerusalem in AD 335, and a highly rhetorical panegyric of Constantine for the thirtieth anniversary of the emperor's reign in AD 335–36, known as the *Tricennalian Oration*, or *LC* (*Laus Constantini*, *Praise of Constantine*).

There are some obvious problems about Eusebius' reporting about Constantine. In the first place, it is extremely one-sided; he wishes to persuade us that Constantine was a model Christian emperor in everything that he did. Yet it is clear that the *Life of Constantine*, doubtless written with an eye to the unstable situation which followed the emperor's death in May, AD 337, takes what Eusebius had said in his *Church History* much further, embellishing and adding details of a highly tendentious kind. Thus the famous story of Constantine's vision before the Battle of the

Milvian Bridge is told for the first time by Eusebius only in the *Life* (I.28), being entirely absent from the account in the *Church History* of the same battle (*HE* IX.9), which is clearly in general the foundation of Eusebius's later narrative. The theme of Constantine's youth, and his father's alleged sympathy for Christianity, is similarly taken further than in the earlier work, the campaign against Licinius written up as though it were a holy war, and the role played in it by Constantine's eldest son Crispus, which is recorded in the *Church History*, is here entirely omitted, so as cover over the awkward fact that he had been executed at his father's orders in AD 326. All this certainly makes one suspicious of Eusebius's honesty as a reporter. The situation is not helped by the fact that a high proportion of what we know about Constantine is dependent on Eusebius's *Life*, which (like Book X of the *Church History*) includes a large number of imperial letters and edicts, either allegedly transcribed from official copies or translations of Latin originals, or summarized by Eusebius himself. In most cases there is no other evidence from which to check his accuracy, and it has been shown that the range of such material known to him was actually rather narrow; he met the emperor personally only at the Council of Nicaea in AD 325, and before that would have had limited access to documents and information from the western half of the empire, Constantine's portion at the time. Eusebius' is also the only eye-witness account of the Council of Nicaea, of which no official *Acts* survive, and is notoriously disingenuous, since he himself, as an Arian sympathizer recently formally condemned by another council, had much to explain away; he therefore glosses over the actual doctrinal issues so far as he can, and focuses instead on the unprecedented phenomenon of Constantine's appearance as patron of the church:

> he passed through the assembly like a heavenly angel, giving out a bright radiance as if by shafts of light, gleaming with fiery rays of purple, and adorned with the bright light of gold and precious stones. So much for his physical appearance. He could also be seen to be adorned in his character by fear of God and downcast eyes, his ruddy complexion, his gait and the other aspects of his appearance, including his height, which surpassed all those around him (II.10).

Eusebius's deficiencies as a sober historian vividly illustrate however his ideological purpose as a Christian apologist, in which he was followed by many later Christian writers. His *Church History*, the first of its kind, was a pioneering work, taking the history of the church from the time of Jesus up to Eusebius's own day. Though it is by no means devoid of stylistic pretensions, it differs from classical history in that it has a point to prove, and it includes verbatim documents in order to help its case. His *Chronicle*, surviving in Syriac and in the Latin version by Jerome, was essentially a chronological table beginning with Creation, and presenting the ancient kingdoms of the Old Testament as well as all Greek and Roman history as part of a linear progression which would eventually culminate with the Second Coming and the end of the world. Eusebius's own linear thinking was further worked out in his apologetic works, the *Praeparatio Evangelica* and the *Demonstratio Evangelica*, which propounded the view that all previous history was in fact a preparation for the coming of Christ and the establishment of Christianity, and his *Chronicle* was to provide the basis for the later Christian world chronicle, which became a standard medieval historical form in both Greek and Latin. Unlike the *Life of Constantine*, which had a more obviously topical relevance, the *Church History* and the *Chronicle* immediately became standard; the former was translated into Latin and continued in the late fourth century by Rufinus and became a model for later church historians such as Socrates and Sozomen, both lawyers who wrote in Constantinople in the fifth century.

The audience for such works was no doubt largely if not entirely Christian; but there was also a need for historical works of a secular kind, and this may be the explanation for the series of short historical compendia in Latin which date from the middle of the fourth century and include Aurelius Victor's *De Caesaribus* and the *Breviarium* of Eutropius. With the social and cultural changes of the third century, especially the decline of the Senate and shift of focus from Rome, senatorial history in the manner of Tacitus had apparently ceased to be written, while a Greek history of Constantine's reign written by one Praxagoras, a pagan, has failed to survive intact. But from the end of the fourth century secular history in Greek underwent a considerable revival, which was to continue until the time of Theophylact Simocatta, writing in the seventh century; Zosimus's *New History* falls into this category, though it is by no means one of the best examples. We ought also to include here the Latin *Res Gestae* of Ammianus Marcellinus, by far the most important historical work of the fourth century, deserving to rank with the classic writers of the republic and early empire, and a work with a vigour and power all its own.

As he signs off his work, Ammianus tells us that he had begun it with the year AD 96, the reign of Nerva, which is also the point at which both Tacitus and Suetonius had ended:

> This is the history of events from the reign of the emperor Nerva to the death of Valens, which I, a former soldier and a Greek, have composed to the best of my ability. It claims to be the truth, which I have never ventured to pervert either by silence or a lie. The rest I leave to be written by better men whose abilities are in their prime. But if they choose to undertake the task I advise them to cast what they have to say in the grand style.

As he tells us here, he ended with the disastrous Roman defeat and death of the Emperor Valens at Adrianople in AD 378. Since the part we have, beginning at the year AD 354, late in the reign of Constantius II, comprises eighteen books in itself, and is written on a very large scale, the first part (probably up to the section on Constantine, which is unfortunately lost) must have been considerably abbreviated by comparison; some scholars have believed that he wrote two separate works, but this is unlikely. In any case, Ammianus's focus of interest changed in the last six books, which deal in famous detail with Rome and the vices of its late fourth-century senatorial class; though he was a pagan himself, the scathing vehemence with which he condemns the love of luxury among these Roman grandees makes it unlikely that he was the recipient of their patronage, or a spokesman for a supposed senatorial 'pagan reaction' (see Chapter X); book 28 includes a lengthy excursus on the vices of the nobility (28.4; cf. also 14.6), in the course of which Ammianus remarks that 'some of them hate learning like poison but read Juvenal and Marius Maximus with avidity. These are the only volumes that they turn over in their idle moments.' There seems to be a personal note here, but his actual milieu while in Rome remains a mystery, as does the identity of his patrons, if any; there are many other details about him which remain equally obscure, for instance his exact relation to contemporary Latin writers, including the author of the mysterious *Historia Augusta* (see below). Nor is it clear when he began writing, or how far his conception of the work changed during a long period of travel, which lasted from the death of the Emperor Julian (AD 363) until his arrival in Rome some time before AD 384. Completion of the work came in the early 390s.

Ammianus describes himself as 'a Greek', and it is generally believed, though not on conclusive evidence, that he came from Antioch, a major seat of imperial administration in the east, where Latin would have been used in official and military circles. His inspiration was certainly the Emperor Julian, on whose ill-fated Persian expedition he served himself as an officer, and his books about Julian (20–25) are masterpieces of writing. Julian's death during this campaign from an unexplained arrow shot (25.3; cf, Ammianus' obituary of Julian, 25.4) must have been a severe blow to Ammianus himself; somehow, however, the material he had evidently collected while serving on this campaign became the basis of a grand imperial history, stretching backwards in time to AD 96 and forwards to AD 378.

Ammianus is an original. A staunch conservative in his views, he admired Julian not only for his personal qualities as a leader, but also for his attempt to revive the independence of cities. Like Julian, Ammianus disliked the centralist policies of Constantine, and his account of Constantine, which would have been a major counterpart to that of Eusebius, is a great loss. As a pagan, Ammianus was no great lover of the Christian church, and his Roman books emphasize the unseemly conduct of ecclesiastical parties in Rome in the 370s and 380s, but his judgement remained independent, and Julian's idea of preventing Christians from teaching as a means of reducing their influence earned his criticism:

> the laws which he enacted were not oppressive, and what they enjoined or prohibited was precisely stated, but there were a few exceptions, among them the harsh decree forbidding Christians to teach rhetoric or grammar unless they went over to the pagan gods. (25.4)

In general, though, even a hasty look at his choice of vocabulary and his frequently expressed personal opinions shows that he had strong prejudices; while professing to abhor any form of excess and to commend moderation in all things, he himself saw the world, and especially human beings, in lurid terms, as is shown in his famous judgement on the Emperor Valentinian (29.3), where he remarks that he had 'two savage man-eating she-bears, called Gold-dust and Innocence, to which he was so devoted that he had their cages placed near his bedroom'.

Ammianus has often been criticized for his supposedly uncouth Latin, which many scholars have attributed to his having been brought up as a Greek-speaker, but though often clumsy, his Latin is vivid, even melodramatic, and his highly-coloured vocabulary, which shows through even in translation, gives it a unique flavour. Comparison with contemporary writers shows that what has often been attributed to Ammianus's poor Latin is in fact standard late Latin usage. Because of the vividness of Ammianus's own writing, and his sharp eye for the bizarre, he has been seen as an essentially unclassical writer. However, this view is actually a disguised value judgement, which goes together with the notion of a qualitative 'decline' from the classical to the medieval. With the revaluation of late antiquity we can at last take Ammianus on his own terms (as Edward Gibbon did) and recognize in him one of the great writers of antiquity.

This is hardly the case with the author of the *Historia Augusta*, who seems to have composed his strange work in Rome very close in date to the completion of Ammianus's *Res Gestae*. Purporting to be the work of six authors writing under Constantine, this is a collection of imperial biographies beginning with Hadrian in the early second century, which become progressively more fanciful and scandalous and less historical as they reach the middle and later third-century emperors. Its purpose hardly seems to have been that of serious history, and indeed, as we have seen, Ammianus writes scathingly about the contemporary taste for such biographies, so different from the serious purpose of his own work (see above on his reference to Marius Maximus, 28.4). Though some scholars have seen the *Historia Augusta* as a document of anti-Christian propaganda, it is hard to regard it as anything but light reading. As regards the Constantinian date, there are in fact many apparent anachronisms, of which enough are convincing to make it almost certain that this is a late fourth-century work; moreover, stylistic analysis aided by computer techniques suggests that it is the work of a single author ('the joker', as Syme calls him). It is our own misfortune that we have to rely so heavily for third-century history on what was no more than a bow to prevailing popular taste.

A final Latin work of the late fourth century must be mentioned in connection with the so-called pagan revival. This is the lost *Annales* by Nicomachus Flavianus, the pagan senator who committed suicide after the defeat of the usurper Eugenius by Theodosius I at the River Frigidus in September, AD 394. Like the *Historia Augusta*, this work, known from contemporary inscriptions, has been made into a cornerstone of the theory of a heavily ideological pagan revival among the senatorial class of the period, which it is assumed would have extended to its view of the Roman past. But while Nicomachus Flavianus himself evidently saw the battle at the River Frigidus as representing the confrontation of Christianity and paganism, and indeed is said by Christian authors to have cited oracles promising a pagan victory and the suppression of Christianity, we know hardly anything about the nature of the work itself. Nicomachus himself did however translate from Greek into Latin the tendentious *Life* of the pagan holy man Apollonius of Tyana by the second-century writer Philostratus. It would have been strange indeed if the literary productions by pagans written in so tense a period as the 390s, when Theodosius I's anti-pagan legislation had stirred up violence in a number of cities, did not somehow reflect their ideological stance; after all, as we have seen, Christian writers constantly interpreted historical events in such a way as to demonstrate the triumph of Christianity or to explain away its setbacks. The greatest work of this kind was Augustine's *City of God* (*De Civitate Dei*), a work of twenty-two books written in part at least to explain why God had allowed the sack of Rome by Alaric the Visigoth in AD 410. There is no likelihood however that Nicomachus's *Annales* was a similarly philosophical or meditative work. Indeed, a number of fundamental problems have been exposed in the general theory of pagan revival insofar as it has been based on specific literary sources; these will be discussed further in Chapter X.

The genre of biography, the *Life*, plays an important role in the literary sources of this period. The encomium, or panegyric, had always had elements of biography in it, and Eusebius's *Life of Constantine* combined both these forms, while also owing something to the existing tradition of lives of philosophers and holy men. Later in the fourth century both Christians and pagans developed such writing further. The classic work on the Christian side was the *Life of Antony*, the Egyptian hermit (d. AD 356) , often held to be the first example of Christian hagiography (saints' lives) and attributed to Athanasius, bishop of Alexandria since AD 328 and a central figure in the religious controversies of the fourth century. The work exists in Syriac as well as Greek, and some uncertainty surrounds its origins. The Greek text which survives presents Antony as being above such worldly concerns as rhetorical education; this was also a stance adopted by Athanasius himself, but rejection of culture was a matter of degree – the *Life* does not hesitate to have Antony delivering elaborate speeches or receiving imperial letters from Constantine. Whether or not by Athanasius, the *Life* was quickly translated into Latin and transmitted to Christian circles in Rome by Jerome, where it became the key text in the promulgation of the ascetic lifestyle. Augustine writes in the *Confessions* of its role in the process of his own spiritual development (see below). The *Life of Antony* set a moral and literary pattern: it emphasizes ascetic renunciation (symbolized by the desert) at the expense of worldly knowledge, and presents the life of the Christian holy man in terms of the progress of the soul towards God. The saint is marked out by his holiness, and indicated to others by the miracles he can perform (in Antony's case, taming wild animals). This literary pattern, often influenced by the secular rhetorical encomium, was followed in countless later works from the fourth century into the Middle Ages. Hagiography can and does vary greatly in the extent of its historical content, from the virtually non-existent to the heavily circumstantial; each work has to be taken on its own merits, but it was certainly the *Life of Antony* which provided the classic model, and it would be hard to overestimate its importance. Jerome, characteristically, tried to go one better, himself composing Latin lives of rival hermits, Hilarion and Paul, as well as the *Life of Malchus*, all three of them essentially literary imitations of the *Life of Antony*.

Two other interesting *Lives* may be cited, both of women.

First, the Greek *Life of Macrina* written by her brother Gregory of Nyssa. This is also a highly literary and indeed philosophical work, drawing on Plato's *Phaedrus* for its presentation of the immortality of the soul. Macrina and Gregory came from a large landowning family which also included the great figure of Basil of Caesarea. As we learn from the *Life*, as a woman Macrina had not received the secular education given to her brothers, but had stayed at home with her mother in Pontos, where she later established a kind of religious community at the family home. She, according to Gregory, had the true philosophy, not Basil, despite all the glittering prizes he had won at Athens. The other, very different, *Life* of a woman is that written about Melania the Younger (d. AD 439), who at the age of twenty persuaded her husband Pinianus, whom she had married at thirteen, to renounce their vast inherited properties in order to lead a life of asceticism and religion. The *Life of Melania the Younger* survives in both Latin and Greek versions, which are similar but not identical; the original may have been written in Greek *c.* AD 452 by Gerontius, a deacon at Melania's monastery on the Mount of Olives in Jerusalem. As we have seen, Christian works were often immediately translated, and indeed Melania herself was fluent in both languages. The evidence of the *Life* is of great importance, not simply for Melania herself and her family connections with the Roman senatorial aristocracy but also as a primary document for economic history, since it provides detailed information about Melania's estates and the sources of senatorial wealth. This is a good example of a hagiographical text which combines the ascetic theme ('the angelic life') with a large amount of hard historical material. Finally, both the *Life of Macrina* and the *Life of Melania the Younger* are witnesses to a feature of Christian writing which is hard to parallel in classical sources in their choice of a woman as the main subject. There was much in late antique Christianity that was deeply inimical to women, yet the fact that Christian women of good family like Macrina and Melania (and many others are known in the late fourth and early fifth centuries) became the subjects of works by male authors is something remarkable in itself.

One of the most famous literary productions of this period is Augustine's *Confessions*, often regarded as the first ancient autobiography. That judgement however fails to do justice to the philosophical complexities of the work, whose thirteen books discuss such topics as memory and the nature of time; it does however contain detailed accounts of Augustine's own life, background and intellectual development, which are of great importance for cultural history, as well as the unforgettable account of his own conversion experience in a garden at Milan (VIII.14–30). Feeling the call of God, Augustine resisted – 'just a little longer, please' (*Conf.* VIII.12) – until a certain Ponticianus, a baptized Christian, came to visit and told Augustine and his friend Alypius about Antony, of whom they had never then heard, and of how one of his own friends had been converted through reading the *Life of Antony*. After hearing this story Augustine went out into the garden and struggled with his conflicting feelings, especially his reluctance to renounce his sexuality and commit himself henceforth to a life of Christian chastity. Following a mysterious impulse, which he describes as hearing a child's voice, he opened his text of St Paul at Rom. 13.13–14 'put on the Lord Jesus Christ and make no provision for the flesh in its lusts', and at once feeling at peace in himself, he went inside and joyfully told his mother Monica what had happened. The most striking feature of the *Confessions* is the honesty and power of Augustine's psychological observation of himself and of human nature in general. Augustine's understanding of human feelings, human emotions and human sexuality pervades the *Confessions*, and is constantly to be found even in his most intellectual theological works. Augustine is a towering and exceptional figure; but this focus on the individual can also been seen elsewhere in the Christian literature that was now developing, and is reflected for instance in the important sets of letters written by Augustine and his contemporaries, such as Ambrose, Jerome and John Chrysostom. As for the *Confessions*, it is one of the great works of world literature, and one that is hard to imagine coming from the classical world.

Two Latin texts from the fourth and early fifth centuries are particularly important for the late Roman army. These are the anonymous treatise dating from the late 360s, known as the *De Rebus Bellicis*, and the official document setting out the military establishment of which we have an early fifth-century copy, the *Notitia Dignitatum* ('List of Offices'). The first is the work of a rather original, but unknown, author, who addressed to the reigning emperors Valentinian and Valens a memorandum outlining a series of ingenious inventions by which military performance could be improved. He was clearly a pagan, and blames Constantine for extravagant public spending; he complains both that the defence of the empire is too weak and that too much money is spent on the army. The understanding of the anonymous author leaves something to be desired, both as an economic analyst and as a military commentator, but his little work comes as a breath of fresh air, and it seems a pity that we do not know whether it was even read, let alone whether it had any effect. As for the *Notitia*, what we have is a copy of a document, illuminated, incidentally, with interesting depictions of military insignia, that purports to set out full details of the military and civil provincial establishments. It is therefore *prima facie* an extremely important source. However, it must be used with great caution, for several reasons. First, the surviving text postdates the division of the empire in AD 395, and is a western document; the eastern parts seem to relate to an earlier phase than the western, so that the document as a whole contains anomalies and discrepancies. Second, and fundamentally, the *Notitia* sets out the situation as it was supposed to be, which is not necessarily how it actually was at any given time. Like the lawcodes, it is prescriptive, not descriptive; this makes it dangerous to take its figures on trust unless they can be corroborated by other means.

Similar caveats apply to one of the most important sources of all – the *Codex Theodosianus*, a collection of imperial legislation from Constantine onwards, put together in Constantinople by a group of legal commissioners over the years AD 429 to 438 as part of a wider legislative project ordered by the Emperor Theodosius II, and a vital source for the history of the period. The constitutions are arranged thematically, according to subject, and in chronological order within the subject headings, and there are over two thousand five hundred in all. They begin in AD 311, and build on two earlier collections made under Diocletian, the *Codex Gregorianus* and the *Codex Hermogenianus*. Historians have to be very cautious when using the evidence of the Code. In the first place, it is not complete: the laws were dispersed and the commissioners had a difficult task in collecting them. Justinian's later collection includes many constitutions not in the Theodosian Code. Further, though care was taken to preserve the original wording, many constitutions were shortened, and the commissioners were at the mercy both of their sources (not always good) and their own judgement.

More generally, many constitutions were simply repeated with variants by one emperor after another, so that it can be difficult to know how far they represent a response to a real situation and how much is simply taken over from previous precedent. The constant repetition of certain laws, especially those limiting freedom of movement for decurions (members of town councils) and *coloni* (agricultural tenants), did much to encourage the view of the fourth century as a repressive, or even a totalitarian regime, until it was pointed out that constant repetition usually indicates that the laws in question were in fact ineffective.

It is essential to realize that the Code consists of a set of prescriptions; it does not tell us what actually happened. Furthermore, other sources suggest that the process of legislation itself was far less straightforward than we might imagine. Constitutions passed in the name of a certain emperor are not necessarily to be associated with him personally; drafting responsibility lay with the *quaestor sacri palatii*, a post established under Constantine, whose job it was to deploy the elaborately rhetorical style which makes the Code such tortuous reading. Getting laws to the public was also a hit-or-miss affair. Though provincial governors had the task of making them public, ignorance of the law was common, as the constitutions themselves often reveal.

The administration and the bureaucracy in the later empire were highly complicated even in theory; in practice the system was full of loopholes and the rules, such as they were, were continually evaded, at times even with the open connivance of the authorities who should have been enforcing them. The mass of legislative material in the Code reveals both the ideal and the constant departures from it.

To this ample and often contradictory evidence can be added what we can glean from other non-literary sources, including the many surviving inscriptions, papyri and coins. Among the most important inscriptions are Diocletian's *Edict on Maximum Prices* (AD 301), of which several versions are known, and his so-called

Revaluation Edict. Like the laws in the Code, of which type this is an inscribed example, the *Price Edict* adopts a heightened moral tone, laying down terrible penalties for anyone who dared to put up prices beyond what was prescribed for each item:

> Who is so insensitive and devoid of human feeling that he is unaware or has not perceived that immoderate prices are widespread in the commerce of the markets and the daily life of cities, and that uncontrolled lust for gain is not lessened by abundant supplies or fruitful years? . . . Since it is agreed that in the time of our ancestors, it was customary in passing laws to prescribe a penalty, since a situation beneficial to humanity is rarely accepted spontaneously, and since experience teaches that fear is the most effective guide and regulator for the performance of duty – it is our pleasure that anyone who violates the measures of this statute shall, for his daring, be subject to capital punishment.

Despite such rhetoric, and despite the many inscriptions and papyri which made the edict public, we know in this case that it was a dead letter within a very short time; the government simply lacked the necessary apparatus to put it into force. Many other inscriptions of the period are less dramatic – for instance the career inscriptions of the senatorial class, which increase in number with its re-establishment by Constantine, or the many inscriptions from cities of the Greek east, which now begin to use classicizing verse even for recording the careers of city officials. To these are added a new class: church dedications and Christian funerary inscriptions. As for coins, they are an important source for imperial titulature and imperial movements, especially during the tetrarchy and under Constantine. Many aspects of the late Roman bronze coinage remain obscure, but the gold *solidus*, introduced by Constantine, remained undebased and in use for many centuries.

No attempt is made at this point to describe or evaluate the archaeological and visual evidence for the period. This is partly because the range is so wide in each case that it would be impossible to summarize. But the other reason is that it is simply impossible now to write a history of this period without constantly referring to archaeological and visual evidence. Whereas Jones could base himself on an exhaustive knowledge of the literary and documentary sources, the subject has moved on dramatically in the last twenty-five years. Archaeologists have turned increasingly to this period, especially once a system had been evolved for dating late Roman pottery; general interest in urban history of all periods has focused attention on the wealth of material available from late Roman cities; and finally, as political and narrative history have lost their appeal, most historians have become much more conscious of the need to use material as well as literary evidence. As for visual art, two factors have brought about closer integration of this with the literary and documentary record; first, a growing willingness to take in Christian evidence, including Christian art, and second, the effects of a tendency in other periods of ancient history, perhaps deriving from modern comparisons, to place emphasis on the visual environment and the power of images as a means of communication. To sum up, the main writers are of course still the same, though they are in many cases viewed differently; by contrast, the scope of study has broadened out of all recognition.

III

The New Empire: Diocletian

BETWEEN THE accession of Diocletian in AD 284 and the death of Constantine in AD 337, the disturbed situation which held in the mid-third century came under control and the empire passed through a phase of recovery, consolidation and major social and administrative change. In effect, the system of government which was to prevail in the east until the early seventh century, and in the west, though with less success, until the fall of the western empire in AD 476, was put into place. It is natural to attribute the achievement mainly to the two strong emperors who ruled during the fifty-three-year period, especially since this is also the tendency of the ancient sources; but it is necessary to remember that the actual process certainly involved less forward planning and more piecemeal development than hindsight would suggest. Caution is particularly necessary in view of the tendency of the sources to draw an over-sharp distinction between Diocletian and Constantine because of their religious differences, and to let that distinction carry over into the interpretation of their secular policies.

Diocletian came to the throne in AD 284, having risen from a lowly background in Dalmatia to command the *domestici*, the imperial guard. He was thus one of the several Illyrian soldier-emperors who reached imperial power after the death of Gallienus in AD 268. The Emperor Aurelian (AD 270–5) had been able to repel an invasion of Italy by the Alamanni, defeat Zenobia at Palmyra and put an end to the 'Gallic empire' under Tetricus. Like Gallienus and so many others, Aurelian was murdered, but this time the assassins were punished, and Probus (AD 276–82) not only drove back the Germanic invaders from the

Rhine, which they had crossed in force, but concluded a treaty establishing a Roman military presence beyond the Rhine and taking large numbers of hostages and recruits for the Roman army. When Probus too was murdered by his own troops, Carus (AD 282–3) embarked on a major and successful Persian expedition, only to die suddenly with the army on the Euphrates. His son Numerian led a Roman retreat, but when he too died under suspicious circumstances while on the road, Diocles was elevated at Nicomedia in November, AD 284, allegedly accusing his rival, the praetorian prefect Aper, of having murdered Numerian and stabbing him to death on the spot in full view of the troops, quoting from Virgil as he did so (*SHA Vita Cari* 13); he then took the name Diocletian. In the following year Diocletian defeated Carus's other son Carinus in a major battle in the former Yugoslavia and found himself in total control.

Even more pressing than the question of military security was that of how to put an end to the rapid turnover of emperors. Diocletian's answer lay in the establishment in AD 293 of a system of power-sharing known as the tetrarchy (rule of four), by which there would be two Augusti and two Caesars, the latter destined in due course to succeed. Once established, the tetrarchic system lasted until it was destroyed by the ambition of Constantine, who had been raised himself on the death in AD 306 of his father, Constantius, who had first been made Caesar and then Augustus during the reign of Diocletian. Diocletian's scheme did not come into being immediately on his accession. His first step was to raise another Illyrian soldier, Maximian, to the post of Caesar, at the same time adopting him as his son, though he was only a few years younger than himself (AD 285). An *ad hoc* division of responsibility gave Maximian the west while Diocletian was in the east; the fact that a certain Carausius had been declared Augustus in Britain no doubt influenced Diocletian to make Maximian Augustus in AD 286. Even then, the further step of appointing two Caesars was not taken until March, AD 293. Constantius and Galerius now became Caesars to Maximian and Diocletian respectively; the arrangements were sealed by dynastic marriages and the adoption of Diocletian's family name Valerius, and advertised on coins and in official panegyric. Diocletian and Maximian, meeting formally at Milan in the winter of AD 290–1, had already affiliated themselves to the gods Jupiter and Hercules by taking the divine titles Jovius and Herculius, and their Caesars shared the same titulature and the same religious associations. As heir to his father Constantius, Constantine too is attested as Herculius in AD 307.

A porphyry statue group now to be seen as part of San Marco, Venice, shows the tetrarchs as squat figures in military dress, embracing each other. The surviving Latin panegyrics, like the *Historia Augusta*, emphasize unity and concord:

> Four rulers of the world they were indeed, brave, wise, kind, generous, respectful to the senate, friends of the people, moderate, revered, devoted, pious. (*SHA Vita Cari* 18)

Such heavy-handed propaganda betrays the fragility of the new arrangement: it rested on nothing more solid than consent. Carausius, who had seized power in Britain, was murdered and replaced by his rival Allectus in AD 293; Allectus was defeated in turn by Constantius in AD 296, who then entered London as a liberator (*Pan.Lat.* 8(5)). Not that the defeat rewarded legality at the expense of usurpation, as the victors naturally claimed, for Carausius had been recognized as Augustus in Britain and northwest Gaul, and had issued coins in that capacity.

The propaganda, and the religious aura claimed for the tetrarchy, no doubt helped to impress their subjects, and to reassure Diocletian and his colleagues themselves, but it was in fact military, and by extension political, success which conferred legitimacy. Diocletian's system remained in place only until it was challenged from within, after Diocletian himself retired in AD 305. Luckily for the empire, however, even though the tetrarchy was threatened in its early years by the regime of Carausius, it did ultimately succeed in providing a period of stability lasting nearly twenty years – long enough for some far-reaching changes to be introduced.

Any assessment of the nature of Diocletian's reforms is rendered difficult by two factors: the unsatisfactory nature of the surviving literary evidence for his reign, and the fact that many individual changes either came in at a later stage, or are only attested later. Another problem is caused by the exaggerated contrast between Diocletian and Constantine which prevails in the sources; rather,

Constantine's secular policies, and even some aspects of his religious ones, should be seen as continuing the general line established by Diocletian.

One of Diocletian's first priorities was military: not only had the army to be brought under central control and made into a force capable of defending the security of the empire, but it also had to be reliably supplied. The literary sources attribute to Diocletian the most fundamental changes that the Roman military system had experienced since the days of Augustus, and they have been followed by most modern scholars; however, it may be doubted whether the break with what had gone before was quite as sharp as this suggests. The way had already been prepared by earlier emperors, including Marcus Aurelius, Septimius Severus (AD 193–211) and Caracalla (AD 211–17). During their reigns army pay was doubled, donatives to the soldiers institutionalised, the army itself enlarged and openings for military men in the administration greatly increased. More units had certainly also been raised in the course of the third century. The hostile Lactantius associates the reforms of Diocletian with his establishment of the tetrarchy:

> he appointed three men to share his rule, dividing the world into four parts and multiplying the armies, as each of the four strove to have a far larger number of troops than any previous emperors had had when they were governing the state alone. (*DMP* 7.2)

But Lactantius can hardly be taken to mean that the army had quadrupled, especially as it is likely that it had already risen during the third century to something over 350,000. More probably this, like other remarks in the same chapter, is a hostile exaggeration, more a jibe than a sober estimate. Diocletian did perhaps increase numbers (new units were certainly created), but may not have done very much more in general than recognize and regularize the status quo. The backbone of the army had traditionally been the legions, well-armed and well-drilled units of about five thousand infantry. Reading back from the evidence of the *Notitia Dignitatum* (see above, Chapter II), Diocletian created new legions on a considerable scale, giving them names such as Iovia, Herculia, Diocletiana and Maximiana, while others had already come into being during the third century. But a large increase in the number

The insignia of the *dux Arabiae*. One of the illustrations from the Oxford MS of the *Notitia Dignitatum*

of legions does not necessarily imply a doubling of the actual numbers of troops. Archaeological evidence drawn from the size of legionary fortresses and literary evidence both show that legions in the later Roman empire were much smaller than their predecessors, typically comprising only a thousand or so men, while special detachments (*vexillationes*) often stood at only five hundred or less; this implies that the calculations of total size based on earlier norms will be very misleading, and suggests that the actual total was considerably less than is often supposed.

Calculating the size of the late Roman army is very difficult. We have few actual figures for its total. At least one of them (six hundred and forty-five thousand, according to the historian Agathias, writing in Constantinople in the later sixth century) is impossibly high, although it might reflect a paper figure never realized in practice. Calculations based on the figures in the *Notitia* are likely to suffer from similar limitations. It ought to be possible in theory to base overall calculations on papyrus evidence surviving from AD 299–300, which gives the levels of pay for certain regiments, but here too there are many imponderables as to the actual size of the units. Yet the total size of Diocletian's army is extremely important in assessing the economic problems which may have led to later decline, for if it really did double in size, the extra burden on the state revenues would indeed have been colossal. Current research seems however to point to an army size of not much more than four hundred thousand; even so, the implications for supply, pay and recruitment were extremely serious (for further discussion, see Chapter IX below).

Like Lactantius, the pagan historian Zosimus draws an exaggerated distinction between Diocletian and Constantine when he accuses Constantine of having damaged Roman frontier defences by removing 'most' of the troops from the frontiers, where they had been placed by Diocletian, in order to create a new field army (*New History* II.34). He adds that these soldiers thus became accustomed to the luxury of life in cities, and grew enervated as a result. But this is all part of his tirade against Constantine; we know from epigraphic evidence that the field army (*comitatus*) certainly already existed under Diocletian and indeed earlier (Constantine may simply have enlarged it), while the stationing of soldiers in or near cities was a direct function of the problems of army supply and requisitions. All agree that Diocletian strengthened the frontiers, building forts, strengthening natural barriers and establishing military roads from Britain in the west to the so-called Strata Diocletiana in the east, a road running from the Red Sea to Dura on the Euphrates. But it is unlikely that these borders were yet manned by *limitanei*, farmer-soldiers living on the frontiers, who emerge only later. Moreover, the policy of 'defence-in-depth' attributed to Diocletian and popularized in a book by the modern strategist Edward Luttwak and others, whereby the border troops were designed to hold up invaders until crack troops moved up from defensive positions further inside the empire, has been deservedly criticized by archaeologists and others who have studied the material remains in detail (see Chapter IX). The Roman army in the late empire was different from that of Augustus, and used in different ways. Ammianus gives a vivid picture of the varied and sometimes outlandish insignia in use in the second half of the fourth century. In the same period recruitment in some areas became difficult and unpopular; the place of volunteers was therefore taken more and more by conscripts and by barbarians, both as regular troops and as federate mercenaries. But like much else this took time to work through, and we should not attribute more to Diocletian than he actually did.

One of the most severe problems associated with the army was that of pay and supply. With the collapse of the silver coinage, used for the payment of taxes and the soldiers' wages, the army had to be paid and supplied partly in requisitions in kind through the *annona militaris* and the *capitus* (a fodder ration). If such a system worked at all, it was bound to be unreliable, clumsy and extremely burdensome on local populations, who never knew what was going to be demanded from them or when. Since perishable goods could not be carried far because of the extreme slowness of land transport, there were also formidable problems of supply. It is a miracle that some level of central organization was nevertheless maintained in such conditions; however, some improvement had to be sought. Diocletian effectively recognized the status quo and introduced an elaborate new tax system in kind, based both on *capita* ('heads', i.e. poll tax, *capitatio*) and land (*iugatio*). All agricultural land was divided into notional units known as *iuga*, varying in size according to the assessment of their productivity. *Iuga*, tax units, are not to be confused with *iugera*, units of area; thus in Syria, five *iugera* of vineyard made one *iugum*, which might however comprise as much as forty *iugera* if the land were of poor quality. Mountain territory was specially assessed on a local scale of productivity; a later legal textbook describes the process:

at the time of the assessment there were certain men who were given the authority by the government; they summoned the other mountain dwellers from other regions and bade them assess how much land, by their estimate, produces a *modius* of wheat or barley in the mountains. In this way they also assessed unsown land, the pasture land for cattle, as to how much tax it should yield to the fisc. (*Syro-Roman Law Book*, cxxi, *FIRA* II.791 = Lewis and Reinhold, II.118)

Not only that: what was actually to be paid also ideally had to be linked to what was produced locally. The whole was to be assessed by a regular census, organized by five-year periods, known as indictions, from AD 287 onwards.

By these means, Diocletian sought to establish for the empire something like a regular budget, and some check was placed on the *ad hoc* requisitions which had become such a burden during the third century. The system aimed at providing what the troops needed on a regular and reliable basis. A. H. M. Jones comments that its great virtue lay in its simplicity (*LRE*, I, 65). This however is a modern view; in the conditions of the late third century, the amount of work and organization needed to put it into practice was beyond all proportion to what had gone before, and the mechanisms of economic control were both crude and poorly understood. In practice there was considerable variety from province to province, and while a large amount of evidence survives to show how the reforms were carried out, it is very unevenly distributed. Thus we know something of what happened in some areas – Syria and Egypt, for example – but nothing at all about others, such as Spain or Britain. It is therefore impossible to judge how effective the system was in any detailed way, though we can assume that Diocletian's arrangements remained in force. But cash payments also remained in force for the army, as can be seen from the ample evidence of minting of coin, and the *annona* itself often took the form of compulsory purchase of goods by the state rather than transactions wholly in kind.

These were reforms of practice, not of principle: the major tax burden continued to fall on those least able to bear it, the main tax still fell on the land, and the notion that high status should carry with it exemption from certain taxes was an idea which permeated Roman attitudes to taxation at all periods, even when the empire could least afford it. Diocletian did not attempt to introduce taxation of senators or merchants, and when Constantine did so the initiative was highly unpopular. Whether the overall rate of taxation was itself actually substantially increased, as has been argued in the past, is doubtful; indeed, papyrological evidence suggests that it remained surprisingly stable over many centuries, from the early empire to the beginning of the Byzantine period in Egypt. This means that the net effect of Diocletian's innovations was much less dramatic than is often supposed. Without technological innovations there was a natural limit to productivity, even had there been no adverse factors such as population drop or damage from war and invasion. Nevertheless, the new system of assessment may have helped to ensure a higher rate of recovery of notional tax revenue, and to that extent will have been helpful to the state (and unpopular); it probably also increased, if only temporarily, the ratio of tax receipts in kind over taxes collected in cash.

But there were other problems to face, including continued inflation and a shortage of gold and silver in the treasury, which Diocletian and Constantine attempted to address by requiring the rich to commute precious metal for bronze. Matters were not helped however by the large-scale minting of bronze, or rather base-metal, coins (the bronze content was minimal) by the government in response to the collapse of the silver *denarius*, now a paper unit only; prices continued to spiral throughout Constantine's reign as well as Diocletian's. The latter's most famous measure in the monetary sphere was his attempt to prescribe maximum prices by imperial decree ('Price Edict', or *Edictum de maximis pretiis*, AD 301). With its minute attention to detail, Diocletian's edict provides us with our largest single source of information on the prices of ordinary goods. It could not succeed however in the absence both of an adequate mechanism for enforcement and of parallel regulation of supply. The disproportionate penalties it lays down conceal the fact that the means of enforcement simply did not exist. Hostile critics like Lactantius gloated when it was soon withdrawn:

this same Diocletian with his insatiable greed was never willing that his treasuries should be depleted but was always measuring surplus wealth and funds for largess so that he could keep whatever he was storing complete and inviolate. Since, too, by his various misdeeds he was causing prices to rise to an extraordinary height, he tried to fix by law the prices of goods put up for sale. Much blood was then shed over small and cheap items, and in the general alarm nothing would appear for sale; then the rise in prices got much worse until, after many had met their deaths, sheer necessity led to the repeal of the law. (*DMP* 7.5–7)

Diocletian's attempt at price control was accompanied by equally unsuccessful measures to reform the coinage. Both failed because they were imposed from above without sufficient understanding or control of the general conditions which were in fact causing the difficulties. Lactantius uses a vocabulary and reflects a lack of economic understanding ('economic rationality') shared by all sides, which put strict limits on the ability of fourth-century emperors to manage the economy in any real sense. Diocletian's measures went far beyond those of previous emperors in their imaginative perception of what was needed, and they were continued to some extent by Constantine, but modern references to a 'command economy' or a totalitarian state mistake the letter for the reality. Rather, we should read the threats of provincial governors directed against tax collectors who failed in their duty as a symptom of actual powerlessness.

By his administrative reforms, Diocletian also laid the foundations of the late Roman bureaucratic system, whose object was to achieve tighter governmental control of all aspects of running the empire – fiscal, legal and administrative. It may be doubted whether the new system achieved its aim, though the original conception cannot be blamed for that. First, provincial government was reorganized; military and civil commands were separated, and each province henceforth had both a military commander (*dux*) and a civil governor. The provinces themselves were reduced in size and greatly enlarged in number: according to Lactantius, 'to ensure that terror was universal, Diocletian cut the provinces into fragments' (*DMP* 7.4). In fact the aim was to secure greater efficiency by shortening the chain of communications and command, and in so doing to reduce the power of individual governors. Inscriptions show that the process took some time; a list in a manuscript from Verona, known as the *Laterculus Veronensis*, or Verona List, indicates how far it had gone shortly after Diocletian's abdication in AD 305. To give only two examples, Britain now had four provinces, Spain six and 'Africa' seven; the twelve larger units (dioceses) were governed by equestrian 'vicars' (*vicarii*) representing the praetorian prefects, who at the end of the reign of Constantine lost their military role and became the heads of the civil administration. Many of the laws in the Theodosian Code are addressed by the emperors to the praetorian prefects, who then had the task of passing the information on to the provincial governors. The praetorian prefects varied in number but for much of the fourth century there were three, four after AD 395. Under Diocletian the prefect was effectively the emperor's second-in-command, with military, financial, legislative and administrative responsibility; from Constantine's reign the military side was put under *magistri militum* (Masters of the Soldiers), who had command of the army and to whom the *duces* (military commanders in the provinces) were answerable. Below the prefects and vicars were provincial governors of various ranks, with titles such as *praeses*, proconsul, *consularis* and *corrector*. Rome and, later, Constantinople too, were outside the system, being governed by prefects of their own (*praefecti urbis*, prefects of the city). The system sounds neat and tidy, but as A. H. M. Jones points out, in practice it was constantly being circumvented, with constitutions addressed to ordinary governors and other direct communication not observing the theoretical chain of command. As time went on it was also circumvented by other means – patronage, bribery and less obvious forms of corruption. One should also be careful not to make too many assumptions based on modern preconceptions; the late Roman administration is scarcely comparable to a modern bureaucracy.

This system of provincial government required large numbers of officials to run it. In addition there were the so-called *palatini*, the financial officers of the *largitiones* and the *res privata*, part of the *comitatus* (the imperial entourage), along with the eunuch officials of the *sacrum cubiculum* (emperor's bedchamber), the *quaestor sacri palatii* (imperial secretary), the *magister officiorum* (Master of Offices), who originated under Constantine and had control of what may be called the secretariat (the *scrinia*, comprising the *epistolae*, the *memoria* and the *libelli*), and probably also the *agentes in rebus*, the imperial couriers, and the *comes* of the *domestici*, the palace guard – all, naturally, with their own staffs. This group, of which the above is a highly simplified and incomplete sketch, travelled with the emperor, as did the imperial mint and wagon trains of bullion and luggage of all kinds. It all sounds very impressive, but in fact it had developed piecemeal over a considerable period, so that there was much actual confusion and duplication of duties. The officials themselves were collectively regarded as belonging to a *militia* and received military rations and pay, which made imperial service highly desirable for the hard-pressed members of the town councils, especially as they then gained release from their tax burdens. The late Roman government had therefore to strike a balance that guaranteed that enough good men were recruited into the imperial service, while ensuring that a sufficient number of taxpayers remained.

There are many problems in understanding the late Roman administrative system, which maintained an uneasy balance between bureaucracy and patronage; in particular, the number of those who were actually involved, and who were thus removed from the productive base and had instead to be supported ('idle mouths', to adopt the term used by A. H. M. Jones), has often been seen as a major factor in economic decline. These questions are discussed further in Chapter VII; meanwhile, we can note that by no means all of the system later known actually originated with Diocletian, though he is usually blamed for creating a top-heavy bureaucracy, just as he is for increasing the army to a size impossible for the empire to sustain.

Many of the changes that were taking place during his reign were in fact more a matter of long-term evolution than of individual initiative. It is often suggested, for example, that senators were excluded from posts in the provincial administration under Diocletian, who, like many other third-century emperors, had himself risen through the ranks of the army. But epigraphic evidence shows that senators were never excluded altogether; the fact that they were few in number at this period is a result not so much of imperial prejudice as of the decentralized conditions of the third century, which disrupted the existing patronage system, brought military commanders increasingly to the fore, and diminished the importance of the senate as an institution by locating the centre of government elsewhere than at Rome. Large numbers of extra provincial governors were needed to run the vastly increased number of provinces under Diocletian, and it is not surprising if they were in the first instance mainly of equestrian origin; the majority of provinces were accordingly placed under equestrian *praesides*. The separation of civil and military commands also doubled the amount of personnel needed. But senators were still used, for instance as *correctores*, regional governors in Italy. The distinction of title was kept, and when senatorial governors were reintroduced into a number of provinces by Constantine they were called *consulares* to distinguish them from the *praesides*, all of which suggests that the changes came about more for reasons of convenience and circumstance than of principle.

At the same time as supposedly favouring those of bluff military origin like himself, Diocletian is credited with transforming the Roman empire into a kind of 'oriental despotism' by importing court ceremonial and titles from Sasanian Persia. Fourth-century writers state that he was the first emperor to demand homage in the form of *adoratio* (prostration), and that he wore gorgeous clothes and lived in oriental seclusion; the term *dominus* ('lord') was freely used alongside more traditional (but proliferating) Roman imperial titulature and everything to do with the emperor was referred to as 'sacred' or 'divine'. Again this development had earlier antecedents; even during the first and second centuries there had been a noticeable change in the style of imperial rule, as the stance of first citizen adopted by Augustus gave way to a more monarchic perception. Diocletian's immediate predecessors, especially Aurelian, had taken further steps in this direction, and his alleged innovations should be regarded rather as marking the culmination and recognition of an existing trend. The titles Iovius and Herculius taken by Diocletian and Maximian and their Caesars were part of a similar development; earlier third-century emperors had already associated themselves on their coins with Jupiter, Hercules, and Mars in particular, and Aurelian claimed a divine protector in Sol Invictus ('the unconquered sun'), to whom he set up a great temple in Rome. It would be quite wrong to regard this as mere packaging; all the same, concern for their public image and its presentation was certainly an important part of the tetrarchic style, and the divine titulature played an important role.

Much more significant in the long run, however, was the failure of Diocletian and the tetrarchs to reverse the decline in Rome's status as the centre of imperial rule. Though the empire was not formally divided under the tetrarchy, several 'capitals' developed in different parts of the empire, notably at Nicomedia (Izmir), Diocletian's main residence, Serdica (Sofia), Thessalonica, the main seat of Galerius, Sirmium in Pannonia, the seat of Licinius, and Trier in Germany, which was the residence of Constantius Chlorus, the father of Constantine. In practice, emperors in this period commonly spent their time moving from one residence to another: other centres which now came to prominence were Naissus (Nis), Carnuntum on the Danube, Milan and Aquileia in Italy. Rome is rarely if ever on the imperial itinerary. This travelling, together with the plurality of imperial centres (the term 'capitals' is misleading), had several important corollaries. First, it greatly weakened the hold of Roman tradition on government and administration and in a sense freed Diocletian and his colleagues and successors to introduce innovations. Second, it fostered imperial building and stimulated urban development, for each centre needed to have certain basic requirements. A typical 'tetrarchic capital' would have at the very least a palace with a substantial audience chamber and a hippodrome for the ruler's public appearances, as well as for chariot racing; Diocletian retired to Split in the former Yugoslavia to a palace built in this style, and Constantine also followed the pattern when he transformed the existing city of Byzantium into Constantinople (AD 330). Some of these cities were very substantial, especially Nicomedia, where Diocletian was proclaimed emperor, Constantine was kept as a youth at the court of Diocletian, and Lactantius employed as a rhetor, and where there was also a notable Christian church. Since laws were issued wherever the emperor happened to be at the time, imperial travels can be at least partly traced from the dates and places recorded for each law. Finally, in the reign of Diocletian, each tetrarch had his own staff of officials (*comitatus*), his own court (*sacrum cubiculum*) and his own military guard, so that Lactantius can be forgiven for resenting the total increase in posts.

On 23 February, AD 303, the church at Nicomedia was destroyed by an official party led by the praetorian prefect, and on the next day, Eusebius says, Diocletian issued an edict ordering that churches should be destroyed and Christian Scriptures burnt; Christians holding public office were to be stripped of their rank and imperial freedmen who did not recant were to be reduced to slavery. Other orders quickly followed, which were put into practice in the east, demanding that bishops be imprisoned and compelled to sacrifice to the gods. Optatus, an African Catholic bishop of the later fourth century, preserves the record of what happened at Cirta in Numidia when the local official, who was both a pagan priest and the *curator* of the city, put the first decree into practice: the bishop and his clergy brought out all their church property, which included a rather large amount of men's and women's clothing and shoes, but the commissioner had to go to the 'readers' for the Scriptures themselves, obtaining from them about thirty copies described as 'books' and twenty-two smaller volumes (Optatus, Appendix 1; Jones, *History of Rome through the Fifth Century*, no. 174). The persecution was very unevenly carried out: Maximian and Constantius Chlorus in the west evidently showed little enthusiasm for the policy, even if we disregard Eusebius's *apologia* for the latter, but in the east many bishops and clergy were imprisoned and tortured or mutilated, and the bishop of Nicomedia and others were beheaded. The persecution made a deep impression on contemporary Christians. Lactantius's pamphlet *On the Deaths of the Persecutors* (*De mortibus persecutorum*) was written when the persecution had ended and Constantine had defeated Maxentius; the work is a version of recent history designed to show beyond argument that God was indeed on the side of the Christians, and had horrible punishments in store for those who persecuted them. Soon after the ending of persecution in May, AD 311, Eusebius (who had escaped himself) wrote a moving account of what happened in his own province of Palestine, later incorporated into his *Church History* as book VIII; he had visited the 'confessors' (those who admitted to being Christians) who were imprisoned in Egypt, and saw some of them put to death. His own friend and mentor from Caesarea, Pamphilus, who was martyred in AD 310, was one of those whom Eusebius visited, assisting him to write while in prison a defence of the third-century Christian writer Origen, who had built up the great library at Caesarea. It has been pointed out that the overall numbers of those martyred during the persecution were small, and that its effects were geographically patchy, but Eusebius's memorable account leaves no doubt as to the shock that was experienced by many eastern Christians.

There seems to have been little general support for the persecution; it was called off by Galerius in AD 311, and toleration declared for all religions by Constantine and Licinius in the so-called 'Edict of Milan' in AD 313 (Eusebius, *Church History* X.5; Lactantius, *DMP* 48). The motivation for the persecution itself is far from clear, though the sources confidently blame it on the influence of Galerius. The edict of AD 303 was preceded by a purge of Christians from the army, which itself is said to have followed an incident in AD 299 when diviners at an imperial sacrifice allegedly failed to find the right omens after some Christians who were present had made the sign of the cross. But whatever the immediate reasons, the attempt to control deviant belief and practice suited the ideology of the tetrarchy very well. Diocletian's and Maximian's adoption of the styles Jovius and Herculius was part of a heavy emphasis on moral and religious sanctions for their rule, and any sign of offence to the gods, as symbolically demonstrated by the failed divination, was interpreted as extremely dangerous for the future security of the empire. Exactly the same thinking in reverse lay behind Constantine's adoption of Christianity; he presented himself as duty-bound by God to ensure correct worship throughout the empire, and as liable for personal punishment if he failed.

The style of government adopted by Diocletian and the tetrarchy was undoubtedly severe and authoritarian, at least in theory. Strict social and moral regulation was enjoined on all classes. Much legislation in the fourth century aimed at preventing *coloni* (tenants) from leaving their estates, keeping decurions (members of town councils) from abandoning their place of residence and ensuring hereditary succession in trades and crafts, and is expressed in luridly moralizing language typical of late Roman laws, and accompanied with threats of dire punishments for disobedience. If taken at face value, this legislation can look very much like the apparatus of a totalitarian state. We shall return to it later (see especially Chapter VII); for the moment it is enough to point out that there was a large gap between theory and practice, and that the motivation was something more immediate than social repression, namely the paramount need to ensure tax revenue and production in the face of actual governmental weakness. The old view, held for example by Jones, according to which Diocletian was credited with creating the institution of the 'colonate' and effectively tying the free population to the land, has increasingly come under criticism in recent years: well before Diocletian, private tenants in Egypt had paid their taxes through their landlord as intermediary, and it was perhaps this situation which Diocletian now made hereditary, thus regularizing an existing situation rather than imposing a new one. Nor did his legislation introduce a new and unified system for the whole empire; in contrast, current research emphasizes the regional variety which continued to hold in spite of the appearance of centralization sometimes given by the existence of the law codes.

The moralizing, threatening vocabulary of imperial legislation did however indeed become habitual; it is only too apparent from the pages of Ammianus, who employs the same kind of terminology for his own judgements. But the abundant evidence which is available from the reign of Constantine onwards, and especially from the later fourth century, suggests that hard though life might be, the regimentation preached by Diocletian and his colleagues did not in fact prevail.

Diocletian was nothing if not true to his aims: he abdicated together with his senior colleague Maximian on 1 May, AD 305, and retired to his palace at Split, refusing to return to political life thereafter. Lactantius, who wished to give him an exemplary death as a persecutor, claims that he starved himself to death in AD 311 or 312 (*DMP* 42), but other sources have him living longer. Diocletian had no direct heirs and the tetrarchy hardly survived his retirement. Constantine succeeded his father Constantius in AD 306, secured his position as Augustus by an alliance with Maximian in AD 307 and soon proceeded to work for the elimination of his rivals. One of those who fell victim to him was Maximian himself (AD 310), and he defeated Maximian's son, Maxentius, in AD 312. Once sole emperor, Constantine was to set great changes in motion which have invited both contemporaries and modern historians to contrast him sharply with Diocletian; but he was himself a product of the tetrarchy and was in many ways Diocletian's heir – many of the social, administrative and economic developments in his reign simply brought Diocletian's innovations to their logical conclusion.

IV

The New Empire: Constantine

EVEN MORE THAN Diocletian, Constantine suffers from bias in the verdicts of both ancient and modern commentators. The problem centres on his support for Christianity, which fundamentally changed the fortunes of the Christian church and may well be responsible for its later history as a world religion. Our main contemporary source, Eusebius of Caesarea, was the author of a *Church History* which turned into a glorification of Constantine, and later became Constantine's panegyrist in his *Life of Constantine*. Lactantius, too, sharply differentiates the virtuous Constantine from the wicked Diocletian, although in his case at least, since he was writing his tract *On the Deaths of the Persecutors* (*DMP*), on any dating, before the final victory of Constantine over Licinius in AD 324, Licinius is allowed an equal rating with Constantine. The relevant *Latin Panegyrics* naturally give maximum credit to Constantine and arrange their historical material accordingly. For the secular aspects of the reign, we unfortunately depend a good deal on Zosimus's *New History*, which is not only equally biased (albeit in the opposite direction) but also naïvely distorted. As for documentary proof, much of the evidence for Constantine's legislation is contained only in the *Life of Constantine* by Eusebius, and thereby comes under some suspicion (see Chapter II). Finally, though the imperial letters on the subject of Donatism preserved in the Appendix to Optatus's history of the Donatist controversy are now normally accepted as genuine (and if so are highly revealing of Constantine's own mentality), we have to remember that they were preserved in a Catholic milieu and represent only one side of the controversy.

As for modern historians, one must be equally on the look-out for bias, open or hidden. Sometimes it takes a very overt form: as a saint of the Orthodox church and the founder of Constantinople, Constantine is often straightforwardly and favourably presented as the founder of Byzantine civilization; his contribution to its religious development is thus what is most emphasized. Others, especially the nineteenth-century German historian Jacob Burckhardt and the twentieth-century Belgian scholar Henri Grégoire, have sought to denigrate the integrity of Constantine by attacking the credibility of Eusebius, an approach that has provoked a defence both of Constantine and of Eusebius, notably by Norman Baynes, in his essay, *Constantine the Great and the Christian Church*. Since to write about Constantine at all entails choosing between the conflicting sources, or at least, taking a view about the credibility of Eusebius, the main Christian source, it is impossible to avoid being drawn into these controversies. Constantine is one of the most important figures in the history of the Christian church; given the significance of the latter in our culture, even apparently neutral studies tend at times to reveal a hidden agenda. A critical approach is therefore needed, though not necessarily an ultra-sceptical one.

First of all, Constantine has to be seen in the context of the tetrarchy. Born in AD 272 or 273, his father was Constantius, yet another Illyrian soldier who had risen to praetorian prefect and Caesar to Maximian, and who had been made Augustus on the latter's abdication in AD 305. Constantine accompanied Diocletian and Galerius on a number of military expeditions. The Constantinian version, wishing to blacken Galerius, has it that he eventually eluded the suspicious emperor only by a ruse, escaping post-haste and finding his father already on his deathbed; in fact he found his father about to cross the Channel, and went with him to York, where on the latter's death Constantine was proclaimed Augustus on 25 July, AD 306 by his father's troops. The politics and the chronology of the events between the joint abdication of Diocletian and Maximian in AD 305 and Constantine's defeat of Maxentius at the Battle of the Milvian Bridge in late October, AD 312, are extremely confused and difficult to establish, even though the tendentious literary sources can be supplemented by the evidence of coins and papyri, as well as by a few inscriptions. Constantine's propaganda began early: an anonymous panegyrist of AD 307 shows him allying himself with Maximian (who had returned from his short-lived abdication) by marrying his daughter Fausta. The author ends by imagining that he is addressing Constantine's dead father Constantius and envisaging the joy he must be feeling in heaven that Constantine has the same adopted father (Maximian, the senior Augustus in the Herculian line), while he and Maximian now share the same son (*Pan. Lat.* VI (7).14).

Though Lactantius claims that he was already pro-Christian (*DMP* 24), the same panegyric makes much of Constantine as a Herculian, stressing his claim to the divine titulature adopted by Maximian. By AD 310, however, things had changed dramatically: Maxentius, the son of Maximian, had seized Rome and Maximian himself, having turned on both Maxentius and Constantine, had committed suicide after Constantine had taken up arms against him. A further justification of Constantine's position was now required, and an anonymous panegyric of AD 310 duly produces a novel claim to dynastic descent from the third-century emperor Claudius Gothicus, as well as crediting him with a symbolic vision of Apollo:

> you saw, Constantine, I believe, your own Apollo, accompanied by Victory, offering you a laurel crown, signifying three decades of rule. (*Pan. Lat.* VII (6).21)

In the same year Mars gave way on Constantine's coins to Sol Invictus, the sun-god, with whom Apollo was identified. This new step looked back to the pre-tetrarchic precedent set by Aurelian (AD 270–5), who issued coins commemorating his immediate predecessor, the deified Claudius Gothicus, and associated himself with the sun-god. Constantine now claimed legitimacy on grounds of dynastic descent in order to defend himself against charges of having broken away from the tetrarchy.

The truth was that the tetrarchy had already broken down, and that Constantine was looking to the future. In AD 311, the eastern Augustus Galerius called off the persecution on his deathbed and expired in great pain, to the satisfaction of Lactantius and other Christian writers. Maximin (Maximinus Daia, nephew of Galerius), who had been declared Augustus by his own troops,

Head of a colossal statue of Constantine (Rome). Only the head, hands and feet remain.

now seized Asia Minor from Licinius, who had been appointed Augustus at the Conference of Carnuntum in AD 308. Constantine had now to protect his position; in 312 he marched down through Italy, besieging Segusio, entering Turin and Milan and taking Verona. Maxentius came out from Rome to meet his army and Constantine inflicted a heavy defeat on his troops at the Milvian Bridge over the Tiber on 28 October, AD 312. Many of Maxentius's soldiers drowned in the river and his own head was carried on a pike through Rome. Constantine entered Rome in triumph and addressed the anxious senators, many of whom had supported Maxentius, promising clemency. The battle was depicted as a great defeat of tyranny by justice, as is recorded on the inscription on the the Arch of Constantine, still standing near the Colosseum in Rome and erected for Constantine's *decennalia* (tenth anniversary) in AD 315. Dedicated in honour of Constantine by the senate and people of Rome, the inscription reads:

> by the inspiration of the divinity and by the nobility of his own mind, with his army he avenged the republic by a just war at one and the same time both from the tyrant and from all his faction.

The Arch is decorated with reliefs depicting the campaign and the entry to Rome: the siege of Verona, the defeat of Maxentius, with his soldiers drowning in the Tiber, Constantine's address to the Senate and his bestowing of largess.

The defeat of Maxentius left Constantine in control of the west. In February, AD 313, he and Licinius met at Milan, where Licinius married Constantine's sister Constantia; a few months later Licinius defeated Maximin, leaving himself and Constantine as sole Augusti, based in the east and west respectively. Maximin had renewed persecution in AD 312 (Eusebius, *Church History* IX.9), but like Galerius is alleged by Christian writers to have called it off again before his death (IX.10). The so-called 'Edict of Milan' (X.5; Lactantius, *DMP* 48), confirming religious toleration, is often attributed to Constantine alone, but is in fact an imperial letter sent out by Licinius in the east and issued by convention in joint names.

The Arch of Constantine, erected near the Colosseum in AD 315, showing the inscription recording Constantine's victory over Maxentius, *instinctu divinitatis* ('by the inspiration of the divinity'). Each side has roundels reused from earlier imperial art, with new heads of emperors added and, below them, newly carved panels representing scenes from Constantine's campaign and his arrival in Rome.

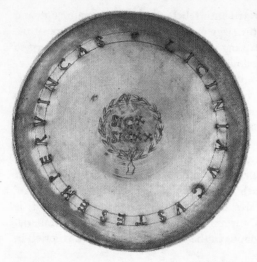

Silver dish made to be distributed as largess to commemorate the twentieth anniversary of Licinius as Augustus.

Not until AD 324, therefore, when he finally defeated Licinius at Chrysopolis, did Constantine become sole emperor. A preliminary and inconclusive clash took place at Cibalae in AD 316, after which the two Augusti patched up their alliance, declaring their three sons Caesars on 1 March, AD 317. Since Lactantius wrote his pamphlet *On the Deaths of the Persecutors* before the battle of Cibalae, and since Eusebius was living in the east under Licinius, his coverage for this period is thin; moreover, in Eusebius's account of the campaign of AD 324 in the *Life of Constantine* biblical allusion and tendentious rhetoric take the place of factual detail. In AD 324 he hastily touched up his *Church History*, removed or altered as many of the favourable references to Licinius as possible and added a brief description of the final victory. For the rest of the reign the main source is the *Life of Constantine*, written much later and completed only after Constantine's death in May, AD 337, which it describes. The character of the *Life* itself also changes when it reached this point in the narrative: so far it has followed, supplemented and subtly reshaped the narrative in Book IX of the *Church History*, but from now on the work (which is expressly described as a portrait of Constantine as a Christian emperor rather than a complete history of the reign) becomes a repository of information of very varied type and origin, all of which needs careful and detailed analysis.

Before turning to the subject of Constantine and Christianity, however, the extent of continuity between this period and the previous one first needs to be stressed. We are badly informed about Constantine's secular policies; here too the evidence is more readily available for the period between AD 324 and 337. As we have seen, on the military front Constantine was blamed by pagan authors, especially Zosimus (II.34), for having weakened the frontier defences by taking troops away to serve in the field army. Clearly the military needs of the years AD 306–24 did imply the development of strong mobile forces, but this was in fact no innovation. In other respects too, for instance in the idea of a Persian campaign that he entertained in his last years, Constantine followed precedent. He also continued and consolidated Diocletian's provincial and administrative arrangements, with the significant alteration that the praetorian prefects now lost their military functions. The reasons for, and the details of the change, which did not take place until the end of the reign, have been much disputed; it is probably attributable to the assignment of territorial areas to Constantine's remaining sons and to two sons of his half-brothers in AD 335, but in any case it was a perfectly logical extension of Diocletian's reforms. Similarly, the chief treasury minister henceforth, the *comes sacrarum largitionum* (literally 'Count of the Sacred Largesses'), is first attested only in the latter part of the reign, and probably evolved in a similarly *ad hoc* fashion. Inflation continued under Constantine just as it had earlier. He was able to issue a new gold coin, the *solidus*, which was never debased and which remained standard until late in the Byzantine period; however, this does not indicate any fundamentally new economic measures so much as the fact that he had the necessary gold at his disposal. In part this came from the treasures of the pagan temples, which Eusebius tells us were confiscated, but it also derived from new taxes in gold and silver which were imposed on senators (the *follis*) and merchants (the *chrysargyron*, 'gold-and-silver tax'):

he did not even allow poor prostitutes to escape. The result was that as each fourth year came round when this tax had to be paid, weeping and wailing were heard throughout the city, because beatings and tortures were in store for those who could not pay owing to extreme poverty. Indeed mothers sold their children and fathers prostituted their daughters under compulsion to pay the exactors of the *chrysargyron*. (Zos. II.38, writing after the tax had been abolished in AD 499)

The recent reforms were still working themselves through during the reign of Constantine, and if there was some sense of recovery, it was doubtless partly because the changes then introduced were now gradually being felt. The wars of Constantine's early years also eventually gave way to his sole rule, which in itself brought respite and consolidation. One way however in which he seems at first sight to have dramatically departed from Diocletian's precedent is in his use of senators in high office. According to Eusebius (*VC* IV.1), Constantine greatly expanded the senatorial order, bestowing senatorial rank without the obligation to reside in Rome and attend meetings of the Senate itself. Later, a second Senate was founded at Constantinople, which had to be filled largely by new appointments. The role played by the new senators was however significantly different from that of senators in the early empire (see Chapter I). Interestingly, in view of their eclipse during the third century, Constantine used members of the great Roman families in his administration, as senatorial governors (*consulares*), as *correctores*, governors of provinces in Italy, as prefects of the city of Rome, and in the now largely honorific office of consul. Emulating their early imperial predecessors, these men were proud to record their offices on inscriptions, though the offices themselves were often different. The consul of AD 337, the year of Constantine's death, was Fabius Titianus, who had been *corrector* of Flaminia and Picenum, *consularis* of Sicily, proconsul of Asia, *comes primi ordinis* (in Constantine's *comitatus*), and was prefect of the city from AD 339–41 (*ILS* 1227, see Barnes, *New Empire*, 109). One of the consuls of AD 335 was Ceionius Rufius Albinus, son of Rufius Volusianus, who was himself consul in 311 and 314; the son survived exile for magic and adultery by Constantine in the fateful year 326 to become *consularis* of Campania, proconsul of Achaea and Asia, consul and prefect of the city (Barnes, *New Empire*, 108; for his father's career, see 100).

This development gives the lie, incidentally, to the commonly held theory of estrangement between Constantine and the Roman Senate. It would be natural to suppose that Constantine surrounded himself with Christians, but few of his appointees, to these posts at least, are provably Christian. An exception is the famous Ablabius (cos. AD 331), a Cretan of humble birth who came to Constantine's attention, rose to become praetorian prefect and had the honour of having his daughter betrothed to the emperor's son Constans (see Barnes, *New Empire*, 104); but most were from the new aristocracy which emerged in Rome out of the third-century confusion. Constantine's expansion of the senatorial order was extremely important; it was to provide the foundation of a further enlargement over the next two centuries, in the course of which the equestrian order effectively disappeared. But it can be seen as supplying a need rather than as an act of deliberate social policy, and it seems less of a reversal of Diocletianic policy when it is recognized that the latter had no provable animus against senators as such; nor is it likely that it was part of a deliberate effort by Constantine directed at conciliating the still-pagan Roman aristocracy.

Constantine's legislation continued the tendencies already apparent under Diocletian, by further restricting the freedom of movement of decurions and *coloni*. The financial burdens on the former were considerable, as is clear from the difficulties Constantine had in enforcing his law exempting Christian clergy from service on the town councils (Euseb., *Church History* X.7) – their disgruntled fellow-townsmen, with their own burdens correspondingly increased, kept trying to enrol them and had to be repeatedly restrained. Ironically, Constantine also found himself legislating to control the numbers of those who now flocked to be ordained and gain these privileges for themselves; ordination was to be permitted only when a member of the clergy died, or if there was a vacancy for other reasons. *Coloni* too were forbidden to leave their estates; landlords harbouring such runaways must give them up, and if those whose *coloni* had left succeeded in recovering them, they were allowed to keep them in chains as if they were actually slaves (*CTh.*V.17.1, AD 332).

Even in the religious sphere, Constantine was following good precedent in claiming to be under special divine protection; it is very possible that he initially saw the Christian God in the same light as Apollo and Sol Invictus, as a protector who would grant favours in return for his own attachment. At any rate, he continued to put Sol on his coins until as late as AD 320–1, although in his letter of AD 313 exempting Christian clergy from curial responsibilities he clearly identifies the maintenance of Christianity with the good of the empire, saying that by being so relieved of fiscal demands, they will

> be completely free to serve their own law [i.e. Christianity] at all times. In thus rendering service to the deity, it is evident that they will be making an immense contribution to the welfare of the community. (Euseb., *Church History* X.7)

Though Lactantius says that before the Battle of the Milvian Bridge Constantine had a dream in which he was ordered to place the chi-rho sign on his soldiers' shields (*DMP* 44), Eusebius's *Church History* (IX.9) does not mention any such vision, and is content to liken the victory, and in particular the engulfment of Maxentius's troops in the River Tiber, to the fate of Pharaoh's chariots at the crossing of the Red Sea. The Latin panegyric of AD 313, our earliest account of the battle, gives it a clearly pagan interpretation, which is reiterated, and further embroidered with a story of heavenly troops sent by Constantius to help Constantine, in a later panegyric delivered in Rome by Nazarius in AD 321. When Eusebius came to write the *Life of Constantine*, he included a more elaborate and significantly different version of Lactantius's story, in which Constantine saw a cross of light in the sky, some weeks before the battle rather than on the previous night (I.27f.). Some degree of mythologizing has evidently taken place. But whatever it was that happened to Constantine before the battle, there is no doubt of his commitment to supporting the Church from AD 312 onwards; in the following winter he was already legislating in favour of clergy, and he did not hesitate to take sides in internal disputes between Donatist and Catholic clergy in North Africa (see below), becoming increasingly irritated when the Donatists failed to toe the line. By AD 315 he was threatening to go to North Africa and sort them all out personally; only the coming battle against Licinius prevented him from doing so, and the stubborn persistence of the Donatists eventually caused him to give up the attempt.

Eusebius has a memorable account of his later habit of preaching to his assembled court, on whom he also imposed a strict prayer regime. The emperor would drop his voice, point upwards to heaven and threaten his hearers with divine judgement, telling them that he and they had been put in their high places only by God. Another of his sermons survives in a Greek version, the so-called *Oration to the Saints*, and shows Constantine putting forward a Christian interpretation of Virgil's fourth *Eclogue*. But even the loyal Eusebius had to admit that though his courtiers clapped the emperor loudly, they did not take much notice of what he said (*VC* IV.29). The fact that Constantine was not baptized until his death was near does not imply doubt, for baptism was taken very seriously and it was common to defer it as late as possible so that there was less chance of committing mortal sin subsequently. The step was a serious one for the believer, and Eusebius tells us how, after his baptism, Constantine refused to wear the imperial purple, dressing only in white (*VC* IV.62–3).

It has often been argued that Constantine supported the Christians only for reasons of self-interest. This seems *prima facie* unlikely, since the percentage of Christians in the empire as a whole was still tiny; yet the subject seems to have been politically charged in tetrarchic circles, and support for Christianity may have helped him in his propaganda war. Both Maxentius and Licinius seem to have been sympathetic towards Christianity, and Constantine's publicists later had to work hard to blacken them both as pagan persecutors. Having once committed himself, Constantine never deviated from his decision. This does not of course mean that every trace of paganism disappeared at once, as Eusebius would like us to believe. Only a very few temples were closed, and Constantine allowed the erection of a new one in Italy to be dedicated to the imperial family late in his reign (*ILS* 705, Lewis and Reinhold, no. 180); sacrifice, however, was not to be allowed, the Eucharist having replaced the need for animal sacrifice in Christian eyes. Nor did Constantine at once become a saintly character: in AD 326 he seems to have had his own son Crispus executed, and this was closely followed by the death of his wife Fausta. Both perished amid such mysterious circumstances that Eusebius omits to mention the affair altogether, while later sources are in doubt as to the reasons. Pagan writers later claimed that Constantine became a

Christian only in order to gain forgiveness for this deed, and the Emperor Julian in his satirical *Caesares* represents him as running round in heaven unsuccessfully looking for a god who would help him; only Jesus offered forgiveness. The Christian historian Sozomen took the trouble to refute the story of his late conversion, which clearly sprang from pagan hostility.

It might be supposed that Constantine's Christianity would show itself in his social legislation, but there are difficulties here too. If what is implied is a softening of penalties and a more charitable attitude, both are conspicuously lacking. Constantine's legislation on sexual matters is marked by an extreme harshness, and recourse to barbaric or arcane punishments. Women are allowed to divorce their husbands and retain their dowries only if the husband is a murderer, a sorcerer or a destroyer of tombs; otherwise the woman is to lose her dowry and be relegated to an island for her presumption (*CTh.* III.16.1). If a slave nurse assisted in the abduction of a girl with a view to marriage, she was to have molten lead poured down her throat (*CTh.* IX.24.1). But slaves were not to be branded on the forehead, since they too were made in the image of God. And in a law discussed in some detail by Eusebius (*VC* IV.26, cf. *CTh.* VIII.16.1, *CJ* VI.23.15), Constantine removed the penalties laid on celibacy since the time of Augustus. Eusebius had no doubt that this was meant to recognize and legalize Christian celibacy and virginity, and whatever the actual motivation for the measure, which was probably part of much wider legislation on marriage and the family, it certainly did have the important effect of allowing and encouraging the Christian choice of an ascetic life style, either individually or in monastic communities; this is turn had profound implications on the distribution of wealth between the upper classes and the church.

Simply having a Christian emperor on the throne did not bring about mass conversion, and the Christianization of society in general took place only very slowly. But the persecution of Christians was now ended, and the Christian church favoured. Constantine liked to refer to himself as 'the bishop of those outside the church', or even as 'the thirteenth apostle', an idea underlined by the plan of his mausoleum in Constantinople, where his own tomb lay surrounded by sarcophagi representing each of the twelve apostles. His main contribution to the development of the church lay however in the attitude which he adopted towards it as an institution; unwittingly, he set a momentous precedent for future relations between emperor and church and for the development often misleadingly referred to as 'Caesaropapism'. This relationship shows itself most clearly in his unhesitating interventions in ecclesiastical disputes and his calling of church councils, especially the first so-called 'ecumenical' council, held at Nicaea in AD 325, and in his dealings with bishops. The latter were the politicians of the church, and thus in his eyes no doubt the natural associates of the emperor. Though he made an elaborate show of deferring to their judgement, professing to consider it equivalent to the judgement of Christ himself, he often took the initiative, and is even credited with contributing the crucial one-word definition (*homoousios*, 'of one substance') which was accepted at Nicaea.

Constantine found himself drawn into internal disputes as soon as he legislated in favour of Christian clergy, when it became apparent that there were two competing parties at Carthage, the orthodox, or Catholics, being challenged by the Donatists, followers of a certain Donatus, who took a rigorist line about readmitting clergy who had 'lapsed', that is handed over the Scriptures in the recent persecution. The latter appealed to the emperor on the pattern of appeals in civil cases, and Constantine in turn referred the matter to a meeting of bishops in Rome, and then, when the Donatists failed to accept its judgement, to a more representative council at Arles, instructing local governors to provide free transport for the bishops who attended. Constantine did not succeed in settling the Donatist schism, which was still a major difficulty in North Africa in Augustine's day, but his dealings set a very important precedent for the future.

The Council of Nicaea in AD 325 was a bigger affair altogether, and subsequently ranked as the first of the seven recognized Ecumenical Councils of the church (the seventh and last was also held at Nicaea in AD 787). It dealt not with a local schism but with a fundamental issue of doctrine, the definition of the relation of God the Son to God the Father. Many bishops, including Eusebius of Caesarea, agreed with Arius, a priest of Alexandria, that the Son must be secondary to the Father, but the question was hotly disputed, as was that of the correct date for the celebration of Easter, on which the churches of Antioch and Alexandria were at variance. By now Constantine had realized that church unity was an essential prerequisite for the Christian empire that his panegyrist Eusebius extols as an ideal in the *Tricennalian Oration* and the *Life of Constantine*; his later years were occupied with trying to achieve it. In practice the issues were far too complicated to be susceptible to speedy resolution. The seemingly triumphant conclusion to the Council of Nicaea, at which Eusebius of Caesarea had swallowed his principles and signed the document, while others, including Arius, who still refused to do so were sent into exile, produced a creed which has been substantially retained by the church ever since; before long, however, Arius had been restored and the leading supporters of Nicaea themselves came under threat. Chief among them was Athanasius, who had become bishop of Alexandria only in AD 328, but had as deacon been present at Nicaea. Exiled in AD 335, he was to suffer the same fate repeatedly over the next generation as the most active opponent of Arianism, Constantine's own sons being Arian sympathizers; Athanasius's polemical writings are a main, though difficult, source for the controversy.

Since there are no surviving official records of the Council of Nicaea, we have to rely for an eyewitness account on Eusebius's description (*VC* III.7–14). This is disingenuous in the extreme, minimizing the extent of actual disagreement and placing all its emphasis on the spectacle of Constantine's impressive appearance at the council, which was largely attended by easterners. Its conclusion coincided with the twentieth anniversary of Constantine's accession, and Eusebius tells how all the bishops were invited to dinner with the emperor,

> the circumstances of which were splendid beyond description. Detachments of the bodyguard and other troops surrounded the entrance of the palace with drawn swords, and through the midst of these the men of God proceeded without fear into the innermost of the imperial apartments, in which some were the emperor's own companions at table, while others reclined on couches arranged on either side. One might have thought that a picture of Christ's kingdom was thus shadowed forth, and a dream rather than reality. (III.15)

Eusebius had reason to pull the wool over his readers' eyes about the actual business of the council, both because Constantine himself had changed his tune by the end of his life, and because of his own compromised position at the time of Nicaea; but his is a revealing account in its own right as a record of the surprise and excitement felt by the bishops as most of them experienced for the first time the sight of an emperor deferring to them and placing matters of Christian doctrine at the very top of the imperial agenda. As Eusebius himself must also have recognized, bishops like himself were now offered an unparalleled opportunity for influence at court, and even with the emperor himself. Bishop Ossius of Cordoba is credited with having had such an influence with Constantine, and Eusebius himself delivered orations at the dedication of the Church of the Holy Sepulchre in Jerusalem in AD 335 and on Constantine's own thirtieth anniversary, and spent some time in Constantinople during the year AD 335–6.

The precedent which Constantine had set in his dealings with the church was followed by all his successors, with the single exception of Julian (AD 361–3), the only emperor thenceforth to be a pagan. Constantine also embarked on a church building programme that made his religious priorities clear for all to see. This began very soon after his defeat of Maxentius with a series of churches at Rome, all built in the period from AD 312 to 325. In deference to existing patterns of Christian worship there, most were erected outside the city walls on sites associated with the veneration of apostles or martyrs. The mausoleum of Constantine's mother, Helena, still exists, as does that built after Constantine's death for his daughter Constantia (S. Costanza). The large Lateran Basilica (no longer standing) could exceptionally be built in the heart of the city by using a site which belonged to the imperial family. The greatest of Constantine's churches was St Peter's, built with immense difficulty into the side of the Vatican hill, on the site of an ancient cult centre of St Peter. The church was built over an existing necropolis containing both pagan mausolea and Christian tombs. Recent excavation shows that the builders were extremely careful to maintain access to this cemetery, which can still be seen below the present church; it is the site of a very ancient shrine, where bones supposedly of St Peter himself have been found. Like Constantine's other foundations, the Roman churches were endowed with their own generous income from specified estates, to provide for their upkeep and for the needs of the clergy and the services which would be held there. Important churches were also built elsewhere, for example at Antioch, but the most important group belongs to Jerusalem and the Holy Land and was not begun until after AD 326.

Eusebius gives a detailed account of the building of the church of the Holy Sepulchre, which linked the sites of Calvary and the Garden of Gethsemane (*VC* III.25–40). Since the second Jewish War (AD 135), Jerusalem had been the site of a Roman colony with the name Aelia Capitolina, and a pagan temple stood on the site of Christ's tomb. Eusebius tells how a cave was miraculously revealed to the diggers, none other than the site of the Resurrection. Constantine built an elaborate ecclesiastical complex on the spot, instructing the local bishop and governor as to the provision of gold for the roof and about other materials and workmen, and the church was dedicated with great solemnity in AD 335. No mention is made by Eusebius of the later tradition, first definitely attested in a sermon by St Ambrose, and ubiquitous thereafter, which associated the Church of the Holy Sepulchre with Constantine's mother, Helena, and claimed that during the building process she found the True Cross. Helena did now go to the Holy Land and was the founder of other churches there, at Bethlehem and on the Mount of Olives, the site of the ascension; both were richly endowed by Constantine, thus establishing Jerusalem and the Holy Land as centres of Christian pilgrimage and paving the way for considerable local prosperity which soon came as a result of the pilgrim traffic. The known Constantinian churches are located in central places of considerable political and religious importance, and though there is no evidence that Constantine himself founded others in less notable cities, they set a symbolic pattern of how things were to be henceforth, as well as providing architectural models for imitation.

The basilica was the main type, with its semi-circular apse joined to a rectangular building, often with side aisles; this was taken directly from the style of Roman assembly hall in current public use. The other type was round, hexagonal or octagonal, associated with a shrine or martyrium, and this was the pattern which Constantine adopted for his own mausoleum in Constantinople, to which the great church of the Holy Apostles was later attached (*VC* IV. 58–60). Imperial building was of course entirely traditional, even if churches were not, and like other emperors before him Constantine wished to establish a city named after himself. This was Constantinople, founded to commemorate his victory over Licinius on the site of the classical city of Byzantium, which had suffered badly in the civil wars of the late second century and had been restored by Septimius Severus.

It is commonly, but wrongly, stated that in founding Constantinople, Constantine intended to move the capital to the east, and indeed, Constantinople did later become the capital of the Byzantine empire. But though it still kept its prestige, Rome had already begun to be superseded as an imperial residence by such centres as Trier and Milan, and Constantine's foundation, with its palace and adjoining hippodrome, had all the hallmarks of another tetrarchic city like the rest. It was not until much later in the fourth century that Constantinople really began to develop into the city of half a million inhabitants that it was to become by the sixth century. Certainly Constantine pulled out the stops, adorning it with such famous statuary as the Olympian Zeus, the serpent column from Delphi and the statue of Athena Promachos; there was also a grand main street (the Mese) and an oval forum with a statue of himself on top of a porphyry column. He gave it special honours, such as the title 'New Rome' and a senate of its own, even though the senators were only to be called *clari*, instead of the normal title of *clarissimi* (*Anon. Vales.*, 6.30). Hostile critics like Zosimus accused him of jerry-building, and of squandering all the wealth of the empire on the new city. Eusebius in turn claims that not a breath of paganism was allowed within it, but it was not quite the Christian city that he claims or that modern authors often suppose. Its chief Christian monument was Constantine's own mausoleum. The first church of St Sophia may have been begun by Constantine, as later tradition held, but Eusebius does not say so, and there is surprisingly little clear evidence for Constantinian church building in the city – Zosimus even claims that two new temples were built to Rhea and Fortuna. But although the tendentiousness of the early sources, and the confused tangle of later traditions about Constantinople make the whole subject of Constantine's foundation extremely difficult to sort out, there is no doubt about its importance in the longer term, or about Constantine's own attachment to it; he spent most of his time there after its dedication on 11 May, AD 330, until his death in AD 337. Rome was not downgraded – as we have seen, Roman senators are to be found holding high office in these years, and are clearly eager to associate themselves with the regime, Christian though it may be – but it was no longer where the emperor and his court resided, and this was to affect its development in the fourth century very profoundly.

Throughout his reign, Constantine was acutely aware of his public image. His portraits evolve over time from the deliberately youthful Augustan model adopted on his early coins and the monumental head now in the Palazzo dei Conservatori in Rome, to the Alexander-like idealized portrait, diademed and gazing up to heaven, on his later coins. Eusebius naïvely or disingenuously interpreted the upward gaze as showing Christian piety (*VC* IV.15), though it was actually a type of ruler-portrait with a long classical history. Eusebius has certainly over-interpreted his hero. Wishing to assert the continuity of Constantine's influence through the reign of his sons, Eusebius rejects a comparison of the emperor to the legendary phoenix, symbol of rebirth and renewal, only to compare him with Christ (*VC* IV.72), and emphasizes the splendour of his Christian burial (IV.70–1). But matters were more ambiguous than this would suggest, and Eusebius also describes the coinage that was struck in memory of Constantine, which drew on the traditional imagery used for the *consecratio* of a pagan Roman emperor (IV.73).

It is unfortunate that we do not have the Constantinian section of Ammianus's history, for, as a partisan of Julian, who had suffered personally at the hands of Constantine's sons, Ammianus had particular reasons for showing hostility towards Constantine. The pagan Eunapius, who wrote his history, like Ammianus, after the disastrous Roman defeat at Adrianople in AD 378, blamed Constantine for the decline of Roman fortunes, a view also borrowed from him by Zosimus. It is less easy to discern pagan reactions to Constantine during his lifetime, for contemporary sources are represented mainly by the highly partisan Eusebius.

However, there seems to have been no great outcry from the pagan population, and Constantine's actions may have been more ambiguous than Eusebius allows. There was no such ambiguity about the affiliation of his sons, in particular Constantius II, of whom Ammianus writes:

> the plain and simple religion of the Christians was bedevilled by Constantius with old wives' fancies . . . public transport hurried throngs of bishops hither and thither to attend what they call synods, and by his attempts to impose conformity Constantius only succeeded in hamstringing the post service. (XXI.16)

Seeing the first stages of this development, and watching the new imperial churches under construction, many pagan subjects of Constantine himself must have shared Ammianus's exasperation.

V

Church and State

THE LEGACY OF CONSTANTINE

WHETHER CONSTANTINE foresaw the long-term consequences of the steps he took in relation to the Christian church during the winter months of AD 312–13 is doubtful. Exemption of clergy from curial duties would have seemed quite in keeping with the tradition of imperial privileges to favoured groups, including pagan priests; Constantine was not to know that the Christians themselves were divided about the legitimacy of certain of their clergy, or that the followers of Donatus would be so stubborn in their resistance to his clearly expressed opinions. His correspondence about the Donatist controversy over the space of nearly a decade shows him moving from initial surprise and anxiety through indignation and disbelief to pained resignation; the last letter from him in Optatus's collection dates from AD 330, and contains an elaborate and unconvincing attempt to persuade disappointed Catholics in North Africa that they must be patient, not expect an imperial solution, and leave the matter to God's judgement. The Donatist schism in North Africa continued throughout the fourth century and still constituted a major split in the African church in Augustine's day, when severe repressive measures were enforced by the Council of Carthage in AD 411. Constantine's tactic of mingling diplomacy with threats had achieved nothing, and he had received a sharp taste of the difficulties which his successors were to experience in trying to deal with Christian divisions.

Constantine's dealings with the Donatists are of particular importance in that they show the emperor adopting a procedural stance towards the church already familiar in imperial transactions with disgruntled provincials, or in individual disputes.

The Donatists for their part appealed to the emperor, according to the standard procedure in secular matters, and Constantine had no hesitation in becoming officially involved. It was also in the course of this episode that he set the enormous precedent of trying to solve the matter by calling a council of bishops. The first such meeting in AD 313, under the auspices of the bishop of Rome, could easily be challenged as being in no way representative. The Council of Arles, which followed in AD 314, was much more highly organized, and great efforts were made to get the highest possible attendance by making the imperial post system (the road system with regular staging posts used for government business) available to the bishops through orders sent out to provincial governors; the letter to the vicar of Africa on this subject still survives. Whether Constantine himself attended the council is not directly attested, but has been deduced from the official letter of the emperor to the bishops attending the council (a practice followed even when the emperor had been present in person). This council also rejected the Donatist arguments, whereupon the Donatist party immediately appealed against its judgement. The Council of Arles was a western council, called to deal with a matter arising in Constantine's dominions alone; thus it does not rank as one of the so-called 'ecumenical' councils, held to be binding on the whole church. It was to be followed, as it had been preceded, by many other local councils or 'synods', to use the Greek term, but it was distinct from most, for example the Council held at Elvira in Spain in AD 305, in having been summoned at the order of the emperor; it therefore marks the entry of the emperor into church matters in a more or less official capacity.

Crucial though it was to be, this relationship is not easy to define. The term 'Caesaropapism' is often used to denote imperial control of the church, which is sometimes traced in modern books to Constantine. In fact matters were far less clear: the situation depended on the personality of the emperor in question, as well as on the identity of church leaders at any given moment. The emperor did not control the church in any legal or constitutional way, nor was he its head. Even in the Byzantine period the emperor did not normally appoint the patriarch of Constantinople, and Byzantine emperors who took an unpopular line on specific issues were apt to find themselves strongly opposed by the church hierarchy. In the fourth century, moreover, while Rome's claim to seniority was recognized, the church was divided between sees which were traditional rivals. The papacy as we later know it was a creation only of the early Middle Ages, particularly the time of Gregory the Great (AD 590–604), while in the east the bishoprics of Constantinople and Jerusalem came to rival Antioch and Alexandria only as a result of Constantine's patronage of both cities. Indeed, the superiority of the bishops of Jerusalem was not immediately welcome to Caesarea, the existing metropolitan see in Palestine, and their rivalry is very evident during the tenure of the powerful bishop Cyril of Jerusalem (c. 349–86).

The Council of Nicaea in AD 325 was a real watershed. For the first time an attempt was made to muster all the bishops together, and it was made clear that the results of the council were to be considered universally binding. Constantine's role was ambiguous: he attended all the sessions, and his imperial appearance very naturally impressed most of the bishops greatly, but he was careful to defer to their judgement. Though he made it clear what formula he favoured, he evidently wanted the final decision to be reached by majority, and preferably unanimously. This he did not quite achieve: the few who still held out were exiled, an imperial rather than an ecclesiastical sentence. But the stance which Constantine adopted laid him open, as it did his successors, to pressure from influential bishops – how was the emperor to pick his way through the tangle? Moreover, while there is no doubt about Constantine's own sense of mission, we owe much of our picture of him to Eusebius of Caesarea, who was himself extremely keen to promote the idea of close relations between emperor and church. In his *Tricennalian Oration* (AD 336) he sets out the foundation of much subsequent Christian political theory by giving a Christian interpretation to existing Hellenistic and Roman conceptions of the relation between the earthly ruler and God. According to Eusebius, the Christian emperor was God's representative on earth, and the earthly kingdom a microcosm, or imitation, of the heavenly one. Such views were enormously influential and formed the basis of political theory throughout the Byzantine period; but they also suggested that God's kingdom had already been realized, so that one could hope for unbroken felicity ever after – an obviously mistaken idea which Augustine later had to explain away. They further carried the dangerous implication that since the emperor's prime duty was defined as 'piety', he must try to establish it in his kingdom by any means possible, a potential justification of religious persecution which Augustine also took up and actually defended. Pagans were not as yet made the objects of actual persecution – after all, they were the great majority of the population – but those Christians whose religious views were judged to be at odds with the official line (always defined as 'orthodoxy') were soon to be subjected to harsh measures.

At least Donatism was geographically limited, and theoretically containable. This was by no means true of Arianism, a term which masks a far more complex and difficult phenomenon, destined to cause major problems over a much longer period. Unlike Donatism, which is properly a 'schism', involving division but not doctrinal difference, 'Arianism' ranked as a 'heresy', wrong belief. Paradoxically, the Council of Nicaea, by which Constantine attempted to resolve what he may have seen as minor differences, in practice opened up a process of attempted definition of correct belief which was to cause infinite problems, and to preoccupy church and state for centuries. The Greek word *hairesis* ('choice') had originally been entirely neutral, simply meaning a set of beliefs or practices. Now, however, 'heresies', deviant beliefs, were catalogued and demonologized, as the church took on an increasingly authoritarian role in defining what was to be regarded as correct. Caught in all of this themselves, the emperors had the task of trying to reconcile the warring individuals and parties.

It is essential to realize the central role which these disputes played in fourth-century history. When in about AD 375, Bishop Epiphanius of Salamis in Cyprus composed a work known as the *Panarion* (*Medicine-Chest*), a repository of arguments (i.e. antidotes) against eighty different *haireseis*, he included such 'sects' as Stoics, Jews and 'Hellenes' (pagans), as well as 'heresies' in the strict sense, such as Melitians, Semi-Arians and Marcellians. The fourth and fifth-century controversies were mainly Christological in character, that is, they centred on the attempt to define the exact nature of Christ in relation to God on the one hand and mankind on the other. 'Arianism', a much wider phenomenon that its association with the name of the Alexandrian Arius would suggest, loosely embraced the beliefs of a very wide range of Christians who were not at all sure that the three 'persons' of the Trinity – Father, Son and Spirit – were exactly equal. The term *homoousios* ('consubstantial') adopted in the Nicene Creed (statement of faith) was part of one attempt at an agreed formula by which this relationship could be expressed, much like the drafting of the final statement from a modern committee, and it did achieve majority assent. But while the Nicene Creed itself was never withdrawn, matters proved not to be nearly so simple.

Constantine had misjudged the extent of disagreement and mistaken temporary agreement for lasting union. Within a few years Arius and the other exiles had returned; Constantine himself was baptized in AD 337 by the Arian bishop Eusebius of Nicomedia. His son, Constantius II, whose brothers Constantine II and Constans were killed in 340 and 350 respectively, and who was sole emperor from 350 to 361, was himself sympathetic to Arianism. The defence of Nicaea and opposition to Arianism was led in the east above all by Athanasius (d. 373), bishop of Alexandria from AD 328 and author among many other works of the *De Incarnatione*, one of the greatest works of Trinitarian theology. Athanasius spent several periods in exile or flight, first in AD 335

Inscription from Aphrodisias in Caria, commemorating a dedication made in honour of Constantius II and his Caesar (unnamed) by one Eros Monaxius, governor of Caria, probably in the 350s.

after the the Council of Tyre, then again in 339, 346, 362 (under the pagan Emperor Julian), and finally 365. Obviously a difficult and quarrelsome person, he was nevertheless not afraid to challenge the state in the person of the emperor; a typical story from his early career tells how he stood in front of Constantine's horse and demanded an audience. His *Festal Letters* (written to his clergy in Egypt), which survive in Syriac, are also a major source for the chronology of the early Arian controversy. A comparable figure from the Latin west was Bishop Hilarius of Poitiers (d. 367), also exiled for four years by Constantius II in 356, and author of a long anti-Arian work *De Trinitate* and another on synods. As a result of the energies of these two bishops in particular, the Nicene 'party' developed its theological armoury and its political influence, and a council called by Theodosius I and attended by over two hundred eastern bishops at Constantinople in AD 381 formally condemned Arianism. However, this by no means implied that people would now change their views, or that Arianism ceased to be a problem – it was a major issue in Constantinople in the early fifth century, while the fact that the various barbarian invaders, as they became Christian, converted to Arianism and not to orthodox Christianity implied a long-term problem for the Roman population in the western provinces. But even though not fully representative, the Council of Constantinople was recognized as ecumenical, and the real possibility that Arianism might become the official and permanent version of Christianity under imperial support was finally averted.

One of the striking features of the middle and late fourth century is the rise to public prominence of bishops. Constantine found a church already organized into an episcopal hierarchy, and with its own powerful network of communications. With imperial sponsorship of the church and the deferential tone adopted towards bishops by Constantine and his successors – at least towards those of whom they approved – the bishops in turn acquired the entrée to public and sometimes also to political life. This trend was further aided by the growing wealth of the church, which by a law of Constantine had been officially enabled to inherit property. A local bishop thus might find himself in control of considerable church wealth, and cast in the role of urban patron. By the end of the fourth and the beginning of the fifth century, bishops like Ambrose at Milan or Paulinus at Nola were building their own local ecclesiastical complexes, and had taken on a central position in the local community. One did not even need to be a bishop in order to acquire such a position of influence: one of the best known examples is provided by John Chrysostom ('of the golden mouth'), whose preaching as presbyter at Antioch in the 380s acted as a magnet for the Christian population. As the pagan rhetor Libanius was teaching and practising oratory in the city at the same period, one can in some cases compare their respective orations on the same event, as is the case with the famous affair of the statues in AD 387, when imperial statues were overthrown by an excited crowd, incensed by increased taxation and fear at the barbarian threat, and the aged Bishop Flavian hastened to Constantinople to try to soften the expected anger of the Emperor Theodosius. Chrysostom became bishop of Constantinople in AD 397, and enthralled his congregations there too, until in 403 he fell foul of the Empress Eudoxia and was sent into exile; after a brief return he was again deposed, partly again at the instigation of the empress, whom he had unwisely denounced in a sermon as Jezebel.

Bishops such as these were men of learning and most had had a thorough secular education. Their sermons, delivered on such great public occasions as the funeral of an emperor, were models of classical oratory. Ambrose of Milan was a star performer in Latin, as was Gregory of Nazianzus in Greek, while Augustine had been trained in Latin rhetoric at Carthage and employed as a teacher in Rome before his conversion in Milan in AD 386. This skill in a traditional public field certainly contributed to the standing of such men, and could give them a substantial following. Ambrose was the son of a praetorian prefect and had himself been a provincial governor in north Italy before he was appointed to the bishopric of Milan by public demand in AD 374, at which stage he was not merely still a lay person, but not yet even baptized. Such sudden elevations were not uncommon: Augustine too was ordained in the town of Hippo in North Africa by popular demand in AD 391 and made bishop in 395, and it was sometimes wise for a prominent Christian to keep away from certain congregations if he was unwilling to be co-opted in this way. Ambrose's earlier career had involved him in all the ramifications of late Roman patronage, and a series of letters of reference survives, written to him by the prominent pagan senator Symmachus, asking for favours for various friends. As bishop, his dealings with colleagues were not dissimilar to those he had had in his secular life. His authority extended to other bishops and clergy in northern Italy, whom he influenced in their relations with pagan and Christian communities, and he was also able to exercise considerable influence over the Emperors Gratian and Theodosius I and to put pressure on them to adopt a more aggressively Christian policy in their dealings with the Roman Senate. When in AD 382, under Ambrose's influence, Gratian ordered the removal of the altar of victory from the senate house, the same Symmachus went in a delegation of protest to the emperor, and in AD 384 sent his famous *Relationes*, effectively a petition for its restoration, to the new young Emperor Valentinian II. Alarmed, Ambrose in a letter reminded Valentinian of his duty:

> since, then, most Christian emperor, you should bear witness of your faith to the true God, along with enthusiasm for that faith, care and devotion, I am surprised that certain people have come to harbour expectations that by imperial edict you might restore their altars to the pagan gods and also provide funds for the celebration of pagan sacrifices. (Ambrose, *Ep.* XVII.3)

The public role of bishops was crucial in fostering the acceptance of Christianity in the upper echelons of society. It did not however impede them from taking a full part in the more technical theological controversies of the day or in writing on more narrowly doctrinal subjects. But the divisions were not always drawn along religious lines: the pagan philosopher and rhetor Themistius, for instance, served a succession of Christian emperors as panegyrist from Constantius II onwards, and was – surprisingly perhaps – out of favour precisely during the reign of the pagan Julian. It would seem that personal loyalties could still be more important than religious affiliations. Ammianus Marcellinus, a pagan, was another who seems to have been relatively unconcerned about religious matters, capable of being equally scathing about pagans and Christians alike. His one criticism of the Emperor Julian is directed against the latter's attempt to exclude Christians from teaching, and thus from influencing the young, a law which Ammianus considered harsh and oppressive (XXV.4), and the pagan aristocrat Petronius Probus is at the receiving end of one of his most biting attacks (XXVII.11); similarly, the Christian Emperor Valentinian I (d. 375), accused by Ammianus of every imaginable sort of greed, cruelty and jealousy, is nevertheless praised for his religious tolerance (XXX.8–9).

All fourth-century emperors supported Christianity, with the sole exception of Julian, who tried to bolster up a pagan alternative (AD 361–3, see Chapter VI), and their patronage was undoubtedly a main factor in the growth in importance of the church. Contrary to what might be imagined, attempts to outlaw or persecute paganism were the exception rather than the rule. Constantine himself is said by Eusebius to have made a law forbidding sacrifice, and while the law itself does not survive, a similar law of Constantius alludes to it:

> let superstition cease. Let the madness of sacrifices be exterminated, for if anyone should dare to celebrate sacrifices in violation of the law of our father, the deified Emperor, and of this decree of Our Clemency, let an appropriate punishment and sentence immediately be inflicted on him. (*CTh.* XVI.10.2, AD 341)

Yet pagan worship was explicitly allowed to continue – a new temple was built in honour of the imperial family at Hispellum in Italy at the end of Constantine's reign. Sacrifice itself did not stop, and a law promulgated by Theodosius, Arcadius and Honorius was still attempting to forbid it in AD 392 (*CTh.* XVI.10.12). Except for a very few cases where there were cult practices objectionable to Christians, pagan temples remained open for most of the time. It seems doubtful whether Constantine stripped them of their treasures to the extent claimed by Eusebius, and Libanius's complaints about their dilapidated state in his speech *On the Temples* (*Pro Templis*) of the late 380s, belong to a period when pagans were on the defensive. After an attempted usurpation by a pagan sympathizer, Magnentius, Constantius II brought in a series of anti-pagan measures late in AD 353 and in 354, and had the altar of victory removed from the senate house during his famous visit to Rome in AD 357 (it was probably restored in the reign of Julian). Yet, as often, laws that sounded savage might have little effect in practice. The legislation stirred up fear and animosity, but it did not put an end to paganism. Even in the early sixth century, upper-class families at Aphrodisias in Caria were still pagan, and pagans are attested among the educated classes at Heliopolis in Syria at the end of the sixth century. In the countryside, of course, pagan cults everywhere continued, either in isolation from Christianity or alongside it. The failure of Julian's attempts at a pagan restoration (Chapter VI) does not mean that paganism itself was dead by any means; it was rather Julian's own ideas which were out of touch with general practice.

But the later fourth century saw a much more determined Christian attack, which provoked violent scenes, for instance at Alexandria, where in AD 392 the local bishop organized the siege and destruction of the famous Serapaeum, the temple of the Egyptian god Serapis. Not long before, in AD 386, Bishop Marcellus had used soldiers to carry out the destruction of the great temple of Zeus at Apamea in Syria. Both these episodes have to be set in the context of the violently anti-pagan attitudes of Cynegius, praetorian prefect of the east at the time, and of the Emperor Theodosius I himself (379–95). The former closed temples in Egypt in AD 384 and the latter, after a period of restraint, passed two edicts against pagan sacrifice and pagan cult in February and July, AD 391 (*CTh*. XVI.10.10–11). His apparent change of policy may have had something to do with his recent humiliation at the hands of Ambrose, who had denied him communion after the emperor had ordered a massacre of the assembled population in the circus at Thessalonica after a riot, and only readmitted him in time for Christmas, AD 390. Whatever the reason, the legislation, and especially the destruction of the great Serapaeum, described by Ammianus as 'next to the Capitol . . . the most magnificent building in the whole world' (XXII.16), provoked high feelings. In the following year, a rebellion was raised against Theodosius under an obscure teacher of rhetoric called Eugenius, and though the latter was himself a Christian, it naturally attracted prominent pagans, in particular Virius Nicomachus Flavianus, who was, with Symmachus, one of the leading members of the pagan aristocracy of Rome. Also in AD 392, in November, Theodosius brought in a long decree which attempted to go further in forbidding pagan cult (*CTh*.XVI.10.12). Even now the ban was neither complete nor universally applied; however, the pagan cause was definitely discredited when Eugenius was defeated and Flavianus committed suicide in AD 394. Christian historians understandably interpreted the final battle at the River Frigidus (modern Wippach), between Sirmium and Aquileia, as a divine judgement on the pagans:

> It may perhaps be hard for the pagans to believe what happened; for it was discovered that, after the prayer that the Emperor poured out to God, such a fierce wind arose as to turn the weapons of the enemy back on those who hurled them. When the wind persisted with great force and every missile launched by the enemy was foiled, their spirit gave way, or rather it was shattered by the divine power. (Rufinus, *HE* XI.33)

Subsidies to pagan priests and cult were withdrawn and the following years saw the destruction of temples and violent clashes between pagans and Christians in a number of different provinces. Some Christian bishops, among them John Chrysostom and Augustine, took full advantage of the situation to urge on, or at least commend, violence at the hands of Christians; the eastern emperor, Arcadius, who with his brother Honorius succeeded their father Theodosius in AD 395, is found trying to restrain these examples of mob action. Bands of monks (see Chapter VIII) were often prominent among the Christians who attacked temples or pagan statues, and the hostility shown towards them by a number of pagan authors, including Libanius and Eunapius, is hardly surprising.

In the same period we can also see signs of increasing Christian hostility towards Jews, expressed not only in Christian preaching, notably by John Chrysostom, but also in legislation. Judaism was not forbidden as such; indeed, the Christian emperors legislated to restrain local Christians from attacking synagogues (*CTh.* XVI.8.9 AD 393; XVI.8.2, AD 423). But Christians who converted to Judaism lost their property, while Jews themselves were banned from the imperial service, from practising as advocates and, in AD 438, from all *honores* and *dignitates*. The large Jewish community in Judaea itself, based in Galilee, was led by the Jewish Patriarch, and a considerable correspondence survives between Libanius and the holder of that office in his day. Prosperous and substantial Jewish

Stone sarcophagus with scenes from the life of Jonah, a favourite theme in early Christian art.

communities also existed in many cities throughout the empire, of which Antioch and Apamea in Syria are good examples. Measures such as those prescribed in the late-fourth century legislation did not amount to full-scale persecution. John Chrysostom's homilies against the Jews indeed reveal a situation in which many Christians in fact seem to have been attracted by Jewish worship. But the sermons themselves, together with other references in Christian literature, also testify to the increasing intolerance of the church and its desire to put a stop to such mixing between the communities.

During the fourth century, the process of Christianization was much slower and more uneven than is sometimes imagined. Whether Christianity would have become the dominant religion without imperial support is hard to say, but must be extremely doubtful. The imperial hand brought several direct effects, ending persecution, giving certain legal and economic privileges to the church which greatly altered its position within the empire, and allowing it to develop into a powerful and wealthy institution. In addition, imperial favour gave Christians, especially Christian bishops, a public presence and a role in political and public affairs. Depending on the personality of the emperor of the day, individual Christians might find themselves promoted to high office, as was the obscure Cretan Ablabius under Constantine, though this probably happened rather less than one might imagine. By the early fifth century, and certainly under Theodosius II (eastern emperor, AD 408–50), the court itself was not merely Christian, but very much open to the influence of monks, ascetics and bishops. The emperor's older sister Pulcheria, who became Augusta at the age of sixteen and for a time acted as regent for her brother, was herself extremely pious and had so earnestly dedicated herself to the religious life that the court is said to have resembled a convent. Nevertheless, though the Christian emperors repeatedly ruled against pagan cult, and though some temples were pulled down or transformed into churches, especially from the early fifth century onwards, imperial decrees alone had only a limited effect. Christianization among the general populace proceeded for a variety of causes, among which imperial influence provided only the framework. More immediate were the effects of active conversion techniques, well documented in the writings of Augustine and Ambrose, the power of example, individual experience and the practical impact of church building and Christian charity on local communities. Not surprisingly, all this took time to show large-scale effects; the Christianization of the Roman aristocracy as a whole belongs to the early fifth century, and only by then can one see church building on a large scale, or begin to speak of a Christian society (see Chapters VIII and IX).

Part of the explanation for the tensions between Christians and pagans at the end of the fourth century lies in social and cultural factors. For the upper classes, and especially for the senatorial aristocracy in Rome, conversion to Christianity presented itself as a rejection of their classical cultural heritage. Jerome, for example, was afraid of being thought more a Ciceronian than a Christian. The conversion of the celebrated pagan rhetor Marius Victorinus in the 350s, when he was over seventy, caused a sensation which Augustine describes in his *Confessions*. It was customary in Rome for converts to say the creed publicly in the presence of the Christian congregation; out of respect for his age and eminence, Victorinus was offered the chance to go through the ceremony in private, but refused. Augustine describes the reaction in the church:

When he mounted the steps to affirm the confession of faith, there was a rumour of delighted talk as all the people who knew him spoke his name to one another. And who there did not know him? A suppressed sound came from the lips of all as they rejoiced, 'Victorinus, Victorinus!' (*Conf.* VIII.2.5, tr. Chadwick)

Victorinus had translated Neoplatonic works into Latin, composed treatises on grammar and rhetoric and tutored many sons of senatorial families. His conversion had a symbolic value, especially when he later resigned his post in order to comply with the Emperor Julian's edict of AD 362 forbidding Christians to teach. The leading pagans in Rome in the late fourth century, men such as Vettius Agorius Praetextatus, Q. Aurelius Symmachus and V. Nicomachus Flavianus, followed long tradition in holding priesthoods as well as public offices such as those of Prefect of the City. Conversion to Christianity for men of such families implied not only religious faith, but also difficult choices relating to social position and traditional obligations. The lives of Praetextatus (d. AD 384) and his wife Fabia Aconia Paulina are attested in several surviving inscriptions, one of which, their funeral monument, begins:

To the Divine Shades. Vettius Agorius Praetextatus, augur, priest of Vesta, priest of the Sun, quindecemvir, curial of Hercules, consecrated to Liber and the Eleusinian mysteries, high priest, temple overseer, initiate of the taurobolium, Father of the Fathers.

Paulina is associated with him on the same stone, with the description:

Aconia Fabia Paulina c(larissima) f(emina) [i.e. a woman of the senatorial class], consecrated to Ceres and the Eleusinian mysteries, consecrated at Aegina to Hecate, initiate of the taurobolium, high priestess. (*ILS* 1259, Croke and Harries, 67)

One of the results of the Christianization of the court and the patronage of Christianity by the emperors was therefore to separate the latter from the Roman senatorial class, which had been revived and enlarged under Constantine. Indeed, it was precisely the fact that the court was now established at Milan (incidentally also the seat of Ambrose), rather than in Rome, that enabled the still pagan members of the Roman Senate to live the lives of luxury that Ammianus describes, and to indulge themselves in being more pagan than their ancestors. We have seen that Flavianus, for one,

S. Maria Maggiore (Rome, fifth century), a well-preserved extant example of a
typical Christian basilica (the canopy, or *baldachino*, is modern).

took this further, supported the usurpation of Eugenius and
committed suicide when it failed. Symmachus on the other hand
famously argued for religious pluralism, though the argument is
less an appeal for tolerance in general than a plea for the restoration
of the Altar of Victory and for the imperial support of pagan
priesthoods. A Christian poet, Prudentius, represents the Emperor
Theodosius as claiming that the Roman Senate was 'hastening to
the pure sanctuaries of the Nazarenes' (*Contra Symmachum* I.
551). The older view that late fourth-century Rome was dominated
by a sharp 'conflict' between pagans and Christians has been
shown to rest on some false assumptions about the evidence on
which it was based (see Chapter X); all the same, for these
traditionally educated members of the upper class, as for their
Greek-speaking counterparts in the eastern empire, conversion did
present a strong break with what they saw as their ancestral
culture.

On the intellectual level, as we shall see in the next chapter, the
most serious alternative to Christianity was Neoplatonism. This

more spiritualized late antique version of Platonic philosophy was associated in particular with the third-century philosopher Plotinus and his follower Porphyry (author of an attack on Christianity which was officially destroyed), and was a system to which Augustine was deeply attracted. Like the Manichaeans, followers of the third-century teacher, Mani, Neoplatonists were ascetics; they cited Pythagoras, the Greek philosopher of the sixth century BC, who taught that wisdom is attained through abstinence.

But many Christians went much further in advocating and practising extreme forms of self-denial and asceticism, dressing in sackcloth, giving up all comforts and boasting that they had never washed. While the emperor in Milan may have hoped to influence the conversion of the Senate, its wives and daughters were being won over by magnetic Christian ascetics, in particular Jerome, who was active in upper-class Roman society in the very year when Symmachus sent his petition, and counted among his female friends and protégées the senatorial widows Marcella and Paula and the latter's daughters Blesilla and Eustochium. Conversion of a young girl of such background to Christian asceticism had serious consequences for her family: under Jerome's persuasion, she was liable to decide to devote herself to a life of virginity, or if already married, to adopt the pattern of celibacy thereafter. These renunciations implied at best difficulties and at worst cessation of the line of inheritance, and were accompanied in some famous cases by the actual sale and disposal of vast family property, with the poor, or rather more often the church, as direct beneficiary. The young Roman matron known as Melania the Younger (to distinguish her from her grandmother of the same name) persuaded her husband Pinianus to join her in the disposal of their huge estates in the early fifth century, and, like Paula, founded a monastery in the Holy Land. Even though it now appears that most such sales included provision for existing family and were thus somewhat less extreme than might appear, there were good reasons why the families that still remained pagan should feel endangered, the more so as some young women adopted a type of personal asceticism so severe as to result in actual death. A sensation was caused when Paula's daughter Blesilla, previously a lively and attractive girl interested in clothes and her appearance, died in this way in AD 384, after she had turned to asceticism under

Jerome's influence. Her mother was devastated; however, Jerome, far from sympathizing with her, instead lectured her on the sin of excessive grief and told her that she should be glad (*Ep.* 39).

Paula and Jerome settled in twin monasteries for men and women at Bethlehem; when Paula died in AD 404 her foundation had fifty nuns, and was taken over by Eustochium, another of her daughters, and the recipient of Jerome's famous letter on virginity (*Ep.*22). Monasticism had been growing as an institution since the late third century, and is associated particularly with Pachomius (d. AD 346) and with Antony the Egyptian hermit (d. AD 356), whose Greek *Life*, attributed to Athanasius (see Chapter II), was translated into Latin and popularized in upper-class circles in Rome by Jerome. The Greek word *monachos* simply means 'one who is alone', and many individual ascetics settled in caves and remote spots in the desert. Egypt, especially the centres of Skete (Wadi Natrun), Nitria and Kellia, was the first home of the organized monastic movement, and there were very many monks living in the desert by the end of the fourth century. Though some were hermits, most gathered at least once a week for a common meal and for the liturgy, a style of monasticism copied in many later foundations known as 'lavras'. Many tales later circulated about these desert fathers, and two historical accounts of the monks of Egypt were written in the early fifth century – the *Historia Monachorum*, a Greek work of *c.* 400, and Palladius's *Lausiac History* of *c.* 420 (Rufinus also wrote an account in Latin). Among the desert fathers, two of the most important were Macarius the Great (d. *c.* 350) and the ascetic writer Evagrius Ponticus (retired to Kellia *c.* 385); the case of the latter, who was highly educated, incidentally shows that the desert fathers were by no mean all illiterate Coptic villagers, as is sometimes thought. They were also frequently visited by important people, sometimes retreating further into the desert so as to be more alone. In Upper Egypt, Pachomius founded a large coinobitic (communal) monastery at Tabennisi in the Thebaid, where the monks lived under a common rule, and which soon became the model for others. Basil of Caesarea in Cappadocia (*c.* 330–79) also founded a monastic rule which was to be extremely influential for future generations. By the fifth century, the model of Egyptian monasticism had spread to Syria and especially to the desert of

Judaea, where there were some large and important foundations, and where over sixty monasteries have been identified by archaeologists.

There were many varieties of ascetic life at this period. Many Christian ascetics, especially those of the upper class, simply lived a religious life together in ordinary houses, as did Jerome's circle of ascetic ladies at Rome, without either the organization or the rules that developed in early medieval monasticism. Macrina, the sister of Gregory of Nyssa and Basil of Caesarea, lived in a religious community at home on the family estate in Pontos with her mother, based on their own household, and the monasteries in the Holy Land founded and headed by ladies such as Paula, Melania and Olympias were also in effect aristocratic households.

By the late fourth century, monks and nuns were enough of a regular feature of life even in major cities as to be mentioned in passing by historians such as Ammianus (XVIII.10.4, nuns near Amida); they might even be highly activist, and quite often took the lead in the mob attacks on temples at the end of the century, when they could be just as aggressive as the pagan crowds, or even more so. It is difficult to quantify the numbers of monks and nuns in this period, but it seems significant that already at the end of the 330s Eusebius was sure that Constantine's removal of the Augustan penalties for celibacy was intended to make Christian asceticism legally allowable from the point of view of inheritance. Whether in the desert or in the towns, monks must certainly be numbered in thousands by the end of the fourth century. A number of the great Christian writers and bishops (though not all – Gregory of Nyssa, for instance, was married) were themselves celibates, and what we might call monks. Augustine assumed that conversion would imply continence, and himself lived henceforth in a religious community (*Conf.* VIII.11.26–7). This part of the *Confessions* also makes it clear that there were other ascetic communities and groups of like-minded friends as well as Christian ones, and Augustine himself passed from one to the other during this period of his life.

Augustine's other masterpiece, the *City of God*, written at the end of his life, between the sack of Rome by Alaric the Visigoth in AD 410 and his death in AD 430, constitutes a sustained discussion of the relation between religious and secular matters, and in particular between church and state. It is no accident that the first half of the long work is a discussion of the thought of certain classical Latin authors, especially Sallust and Cicero. They were after all the writers on whose works Augustine had himself been trained as a teacher of rhetoric, and it was essential to Augustine's personal programme to be able to demonstrate the inadequacy of their thought in comparison with Christian teaching. What was lacking, in his view, in previous Roman history, and especially in the Republic, for all its military success, was justice, which entailed the proper recognition of the divine; instead, the Roman state was based only on the search for *gloria* (*Civ. Dei* XIX.21–4). Contemporary pagans might argue that the sack of Rome demonstrated that the Christian God was not after all protecting his kingdom, as the Christians claimed; yet, he argued, their own history had been hardly more than a series of disasters, while the Christian kingdom was not yet to be equated with the kingdom of heaven, and still had its own times of trial. This was a less optimistic view than that of Eusebius of Caesarea, with his enthusiasm for Constantine; it gains an added poignancy from the fact that Augustine composed his great work on the eve of the invasion and successful conquest of his own province of North Africa by the Arian Vandals. There, the time of trial for Catholics like himself was to last for a century, and to be followed, when reconquest came from Constantinople in AD 533–4, by further doctrinal division, this time imposed by an eastern emperor in the name of church unity.

VI

The Reign of Julian

JULIAN (AD 361–3) was the younger son of Julius Constantius, one of the half-brothers of Constantine murdered by the army in favour of Constantine's sons in the months after his death in May, AD 337. Julian and his older brother Gallus alone escaped the massacre and were allowed to live; at the time Julian was only about six years old. Of the three sons of Constantine who partitioned the empire between them when they became Augusti on 9 September, 337, Constantine II was killed in 340 while trying to invade his brother Constans's territory in northern Italy, and Constans himself, left in charge of the west, was killed by a palace coup in 350. This left Constantius II as sole emperor, and without an heir. When he set off to avenge his brother's murder against Magnentius, the army officer who had been responsible for the death of Constans, and who was now refusing to make terms, Constantius made Gallus a Caesar and left him in charge of the east. Magnentius was finally defeated in Gaul in AD 353, leaving Constantius sole and unchallenged emperor.

It is with the following winter, AD 353–4, that the surviving portion of Ammianus's *Res Gestae* begins. From now on until AD 378, the year of the Battle of Adrianople, we have a Latin narrative history of almost unmatched vigour, fullness and information, on the same level as the histories of Herodotus and Thucydides in Greek, or Tacitus for the earlier Roman empire. Though Ammianus tells us that he had begun his history with the year AD 96 (XXXI.16.7), the earlier part is lost, and Book XIV, the first book we have, opens *in medias res*, in a style totally typical of Ammianus's frequent sharp criticism of personalities, with an attack on the alleged cruelty of the new Caesar Gallus:

Gallus in his early manhood had risen at a bound from what
seemed a hopeless depth of misery to the height of power, and,
going beyond the limits of the authority granted to him, was
causing universal mischief by his excessive harshness. (XIV.1)

Gallus's wife, a daughter of Constantine previously married to
Constantine's nephew Hannibalianus, another victim of the
murders in 337, was goading him on:

she was a Fury in mortal form, incessantly adding fuel to her
husband's rage, and as thirsty for human blood as he.

Ammianus's characteristics and strengths as a historian, and in
particular his admiration for Julian, in whose army he served as an
officer, inevitably colour our perceptions of the entire narrative
that follows, but fortunately, while he is by far the most important
single writer, he is not the only source, and can sometimes be
supplemented by different viewpoints. We have for instance
Julian's own writings, which show a side of the emperor not
emphasized by Ammianus, and the Christian writers who, though
biased against Julian, are especially important. Though a pagan,
Ammianus did not consider that religion should occupy the central
role in his work, and put his priorities elsewhere. His more
traditional focus on political and military events means, incidentally, that his history gives us by far the best picture of the late
Roman army in action. His later books are rather different; unlike
the earlier narrative they concentrate on Rome and are of great
importance for understanding the late Roman senatorial class (see
Chapter X). Finally, his history is full of informative digressions
on all kinds of topics, which besides providing some curious
details, some picked up on Ammianus's extensive travels, also
allow us to see something of the workings of his own mind.
Ammianus was with Julian's army on the fatal expedition to
Persia (see below) which ended with Julian's own mysterious death
in AD 363; after that he seems to have travelled and collected
information for a long period, but he was in Rome in AD 384, when
a food shortage gave rise to the expulsion of foreigners from
the city, and he seems to have been finishing his history in
the years around 390, apparently before the destruction of the

Serapaeum at Alexandria in 391 (cf. XXII.16) and before the usurpation of Eugenius in AD 392. A letter written to him late in AD 392 by Libanius, the pagan rhetor from Antioch, refers to readings from the then newly published work (*Ep.* 1063). However, the exact date of composition of the later books, or even of individual passages in them (for he probably went over them and revised them at different times) depends on difficult questions of comparison with other contemporary writers, among them Jerome and the author of the *Historia Augusta*; the date has been hotly disputed.

Both Julian and Ammianus harboured grudges against Constantius II. By comparison with the material available for his father Constantine, or for his cousin Julian, the first part of Constantius's reign is ill-documented for secular matters, and we have to rely on the brief Latin chronicles of Eutropius and Aurelius Victor, or the unsatisfactory later Greek history of Zosimus. When Ammianus' narrative starts, it gives a gloomy picture of suspicion and political and military crisis: Constantius's rule after the suppression of the revolt of Magnentius is described as arbitrary and cruel – in Ammianus's words, 'it is difficult to call to mind anyone who was acquitted in Constantius' reign, once so much as a whisper had set the machinery of punishment in motion' (XIV.5). Constantius's court is depicted as a place of suspicion, slander and denunciation (XIV.8) and as the home of treason trials (XIV.12); in a manner which recalls Tacitus, Ammianus regrets the death of the emperor's first wife Eusebia and the loss of her good influence (XXI.6), and typically gives far more space to his bad qualities than to his good ones in his final summing up of Constantius's character and rule (XXI.16) . One of the most famous passages in the history describes Constantius's formal entry into Rome in AD 357, one of the rare visits made to the city by a fourth-century emperor after Constantine. There was no real reason for the visit, Ammianus suggests: the emperor had not won a victory and was not deserving of a triumphal procession, but simply wanted to display himself and his magnificence to the unsuspecting citizens. The description that follows gives an extraordinarily vivid impression both of Rome itself in the fourth century and of the appearance of the military escort that made up the procession, utterly different from the traditional Roman legions:

the emperor's person was surrounded by purple banners woven in the form of dragons and attached to the tops of gilded and jewelled spears; the breeze blew through their gaping jaws so that they seemed to be hissing with rage, and their voluminous tails streamed behind them on the wind. On each side marched a file of men-at-arms with shields and plumed helmets, whose shining breastplates cast a dazzling light. At intervals were mailed cavalrymen, the so-called Ironclads, wearing masks and equipped with cuirasses and belts of steel; they seemed more like statues polished by the hand of Praxiteles than living men. (XVI.10)

Most striking, however, is the impassive demeanour adopted by the emperor himself:

he was like a dummy, gazing straight before him as if his head were in a vice and turning neither to right nor left. When a wheel jolted he did not nod, and at no point was he seen to spit or rub his face or nose or to move his hand.

But Ammianus was fair-minded, and admired Constantius for his self-control, one of the qualities the historian most valued:

All this was no doubt affectation, but he gave other evidence too in his personal life of an unusual degree of self-control, which one was given to believe belonged to him alone.

Julian's grievances against Constantius were deeper and more personal. After the murders of AD 337 he and his brother had at first been sent to their grandmother's home in Bithynia, and their Christian upbringing was put into the hands of Bishop Eusebius of Nicomedia; this was a happy time, despite the lack of both parents, but in AD 342, when Julian was twelve years old, Constantius effectively exiled the brothers to Macellum in Cappadocia, where they were kept under close watch at all times. This situation lasted until 348, when Julian was allowed to return to Constantinople before being sent to the supposedly less sensitive Nicomedia, and in 351 Gallus was made Caesar and sent to the west. It is the standard scenario of the suspicious childless ruler who needs, yet fears, potential heirs. What is striking to modern eyes is the fact that while Constantius at first took pains to make sure that the brothers were brought up as Christians, he does not seem to have taken seriously the possibility that once released and exposed to worldly influences, Julian might actually embrace paganism. It was of course dangerous to do so openly, and when Constantius died in 361 Julian led the funeral procession to the Church of the Holy Apostles. But Julian himself, the pagan writer Eunapius, and Libanius, under whose influence he came while at Nicomedia, describe his conversion, or in Christian terms, his 'apostasy'; the latter writers ascribe it to the influence of Maximus of Ephesus, an extreme Neoplatonist given to miracles and calling up the gods, whom Julian sought out contrary to more prudent advice in 351 after he had encountered the circle of the Neoplatonist Aedesius of Pergamum. Thus Julian's enthusiasm for paganism, a predictable enough form of student rebellion, took the form from the beginning of a fascination with the more exotic forms of Neoplatonic mysticism. As long as Constantius lived, Julian kept the outward show of Christianity, and was even allowed to continue his studies at Athens, the very home of pagan Neoplatonism, after the fall and execution of his brother Gallus in 354. Both Ammianus (XV.2, 8) and Julian himself suggest that he was protected from similar dangers by the influence of the Empress Eusebia, though others evidently did try to undermine his position. As Caesar, he wrote two panegyrics on Constantius from Gaul in 356 and 358 which show a keen sense of the diplomatic needs of his position in relation to the aggressively Christian emperor; it was only on Constantius's sudden death, when Julian had already decided to come out publicly against him, that he could openly thank the gods and exult in his paganism, and even now Ammianus claims that he concealed it until he was safely in Constantinople himself (XXII.5).

The rise of Julian to Augustus, though predictable, was thus fraught with danger, and has something about it of the manoeuvrings of Constantine between AD 306 and 312. After the death of Gallus, late in 354, Constantius badly needed another colleague to deal with barbarian incursions in Gaul and Germany while he himself concentrated on Persia, but was held back by his suspicious nature until persuaded by his wife, who according to Zosimus was 'extremely well educated and wiser than women usually are', to appoint Julian, convinced by her that,

> he is a young man of a simple character, who has spent his whole life as a student, and his complete lack of experience in worldly matters will make him more suitable than anyone else, for either he will be lucky and his successes will be ascribed to the emperor, or he will make a mistake and get killed and Constantius will be free of any imperial successors. (Zosimus, III.1)

Neither prophecy came true, and, though totally inexperienced, Julian proved to be extremely successful as a general in Gaul. Most of our evidence admittedly comes from sources favourable to Julian, who go out of their way to discredit Constantius and to glorify Julian by emphasizing the limitations imposed on him by the latter, and the surviving letter which Julian wrote to the Athenians late in 361 gives a very tendentious account of this period. On the other hand, knowledge of the fates of others, including that of his brother Gallus, led Julian to watch his position very carefully. In 357 he succeeded in defeating an army of thirty thousand Alamanni and killing six thousand of them at the Battle of Strasbourg on the left bank of the Rhine, a victory which he followed with considerable further success against the Franks and the establishment of several garrisons along the Rhine. When in 360 Constantius suddenly demanded the immediate recall of a substantial proportion of his troops to the east, Julian's armies proclaimed him Augustus at Paris, for the first time raising the new emperor on a shield in the German manner and placing a soldier's torque on his head (Ammianus, XX.4). It may well be that they had been strongly encouraged to do so, but it suited Julian to claim reluctance; he sent a carefully worded letter to Constantius explaining what had happened (XX.8), and though Constantius angrily ordered him to remain with the rank of Caesar, his orders were ignored. Soon coins were issued in Gaul in the names of the two Augusti (XX.9, XXI.1). From the summer of 361 onwards, Julian orchestrated his advance on Constantius; he was successful in winning over Sirmium, but Aquileia presented more of a problem, and when he encountered delays at Naissus (Nis) he occupied himself in writing justificatory letters to many individual cities and to the Roman Senate; of these that to the Athenians survives. Meanwhile Constantius was on his way back from Persia in order to meet the threat, and quite unexpectedly died in Cilicia while en route, Julian still being at Nis (XXI.15). This lucky chance allowed Julian to claim that the gods were on his side and that Constantius's death had been predicted by divine omens, to announce his paganism openly and to make a convenient show of piety and deference in the conduct of Constantius's elaborate funeral, which took place in Constantinople in December, 361; it was even claimed that Constantius had proclaimed him his successor on his deathbed. It would have been hard for Julian to conceal his overwhelming pleasure and relief at this reversal, which he took as confirmation that he was right to put his trust in the gods, and his own writings make clear just how he felt. The wheel had come full circle since the elation felt by Eusebius and other Christians after Constantine's victory over Maxentius at the Battle of the Milvian Bridge.

Hardly more than eighteen months later, on 26 June, 363, Julian was dead; he was succeeded by an obscure army officer called Jovian, described as 'a passable candidate' by Ammianus (XXV.5), who was also a devout Christian. Few if any emperors aroused such partisanship or such hatred as Julian, and none in so short a period. Nor was it only a matter of Julian's paganism. What had gone wrong?

Even Ammianus, one of Julian's most ardent supporters, recognized that he sometimes suffered from flawed judgement which at times amounted to naïvety. On becoming emperor he did not merely declare his paganism, but summoned Christian bishops to the palace in Constantinople and suggested that they forget their differences and practise religious toleration. His intentions were no doubt good, but, as Ammianus remarks, he was modelling himself on an anecdote told of Marcus Aurelius whose context was in fact totally different (XXII.5). Having made Antioch the imperial headquarters while en route for Persia in the summer of AD 362, he succeeded in annoying not only the Christians of the city but also its educated pagans, who were his natural allies. His expectations of them were quite unrealistic; he was incensed, for example, at the lack of preparation by the city when he decided to worship at the shrine of Apollo at Daphne, and at the unwillingness of the local pagans to share his enthusiasm – an unwillingness that had much to do with his recent poor handling of a corn shortage in the city, and his keenness for animal sacrifice on a big scale, now considered by many to be in somewhat poor taste. Instead of attempting to put things right, Julian did not hesitate to berate the Antiochenes and make matters worse. This attitude made him the butt of jokes and satire, hardly a desirable result for a pagan emperor in the city of Libanius, where he might have expected solid support, or for one on his way to conduct a major military campaign. Again he responded to their criticisms early in 363 in a sharply ironic but over-intellectual lampoon of his own, called the *Misopogon*, or 'Beard-Hater', which he had posted up in the city centre. He also dreamed up the idea of restoring the Jewish Temple in Jerusalem, which would proclaim the symbolic defeat of Christianity, but this ill-fated scheme came to nothing (see below).

Though Julian had conducted his campaigns in Gaul and Germany with great success, the Persian campaign was marked by strange errors of judgement, and preceded and accompanied by a series of bad omens and warnings which suggest at the very least a lack of confidence in his leadership (Ammianus, XXIII.1). Having advanced far east, and opened a forgotten canal allowing the passage of ships to the Tigris, which gave him a critical advantage over the Persian capital of Ctesiphon (XXIV.6), he was within reach of successfully besieging the city when he suddenly gave up the idea and then just as suddenly ordered all his ships to be burnt. This act of folly was probably, as the Christian sources suggest, a response to a Persian offer of guidance overland, which proved in fact to be a trick (Ephrem, *Hymns against Julian* 3.15, pp. 120–1 Lieu; cf. Ammianus XXIV.7). Whatever the explanation, it meant an ignominious and difficult retreat for the army, in the course of which Julian himself was mysteriously killed. His successor Jovian was placed in the invidious position of having to negotiate peace terms which included ceding the important border fortress of Nisibis to Persia, the shame and loss of which were never forgotten by the Christian population of the border regions of Syria and Mesopotamia.

Julian was an idealist with views and aspirations many shared, and about which many besides himself felt passionately. He also seems to have had a magnetic personality which drew some to him even while it repelled others. Had he had the political sense as emperor to match the confidence of his career as Caesar, things would have looked very different. Ammianus's character sketch of the emperor after his death (XXV.4) is high in praise and sparing in criticism; he even exonerates Julian of military blame by putting the responsibility for renewing war against Persia on to Constantine. But this interpretation conflicts with the testimony of his own detailed narrative, and Ammianus's criticism of Julian's superstition and his passion for sacrifice, though damning enough, gloss over the undeniable fact that he alienated his own side. Moreover, Ammianus's restraint where religious matters are concerned totally obscures the violence of the Christian reaction against Julian, expressed by contemporaries such as John Chrysostom, Gregory of Nazianzus and Ephrem Syrus, all of whom had every reason to fear during his reign that his policies would succeed, and corresponding cause for unseemly gloating when they did not. Few contemporaries could afford to be neutral about Julian. This is why the sources available about him are both disproportionately ample, given the shortness of his reign, and in most cases extremely tendentious, a situation which has in itself fostered the growth of romantic modern views.

One cause to which Julian attached himself was the renewal of cities and city administration. In this, his interest was shared by a line of conservative writers culminating with Procopius of Caesarea in the sixth century, all of whom regarded what they saw as the growing demands of the central government as a threat to the independence of local urban elites. In Julian's own day, these opinions were shared by Ammianus, Libanius and Themistius; all of them were pagans, and might therefore seem liable to see the interventions of Christian emperors in urban affairs as unwelcome. However, generosity to cities, for example by tax concessions, had long been a traditional attribute of a 'good' emperor, and was a regular theme in imperial panegyric. Support for the cause of cities had more to do with the traditional values of upper-class secular education than with religious affiliation. It was therefore logical for Julian, who prided himself on an old-fashioned sense of *civilitas*, to strengthen and reform the Senate of Constantinople, by now the

major seat of imperial government (*CTh.* IX.2.1; XI.23.2; see
Mamertinus, *Panegyric* 24, p. 33 Lieu). He also legislated to
reinforce councils in other cities by removing restrictions on
membership, made voluntary the customary gift of *aurum
coronarium*, gold wreaths donated by cities on an imperial
accession whose value had become an object of undesirable rivalry
between cities (*CTh.* XII.13.1) and reduced the burden of the
cursus publicus, the system of public post (see Chapter IV; *CTh.*
VIII.5.12). He also removed the tax exemptions given to clergy by
Constantine and some Christian land doubtless changed hands as a
result of his measure allowing the restoration of city property
(*CTh.* X.3.1). Taxes were remitted where necessary and subjected
to new controls (*CTh.* XI.16.10). Overall, Julian attempted to
shore up the apparatus of city administration, as much for the
benefit of the government as a whole as for ideological reasons, but
his measures had limited impact in view of the shortness of his
reign. They testify to the mixture of the traditional and the
innovatory that is typical of most late Roman legislation, and
illustrate the contradictory pressures under which the government
usually found itself.

The only measure directly aimed at Christians, apart from the
removal of the tax privileges of the clergy, was Julian's famous
edict of AD 362 which forbade them to teach rhetoric or grammar, a
measure which is singled out for criticism in two places by
Ammianus as harsh and oppressive (Ammianus, XXII.10,
XXV.4). This measure effectively debarred Christians from
teaching altogether, since rhetoric and grammar constituted
most of the educational syllabus. However, though it caused
Marius Victorinus to resign his position after his conversion to
Christianity, however, its import was more symbolic than
practical; Christians still regularly went to pagan teachers for their
formal education, as did for instance Julian's contemporaries Basil
of Caesarea and Gregory of Nazianzus. The pagan Libanius had
many Christians among his students, and Christian and pagan
students still mingled together even in sixth-century Alexandria.
Julian was making a gesture designed to curb potential conversion
of pagan students by Christian teachers; it would not have stopped
pagan students being converted in other ways, but he was
doubtless well aware of his own experience when he came as a

supposed Christian under the influence of Libanius and Aedesius. All the same, thoughtful and educated Christians such as Gregory of Nazianzus (*Or.* 4) protested loudly at their separation from the cultural heritage which they too claimed, and Julian combined this with other religious measures, advocating a policy of positive discrimination towards pagans, and nurturing ambitions of forming a kind of organized pagan church on the Christian model. In all of this he seems remarkably modern, in that he realized the importance of education, especially in the adolescent years, the need to have pagans in key positions and the advantage which the high level of organization that Christianity possessed gave it over the pluralism and dispersion of pagan cults. But he misjudged the situation, and underestimated the negative impact of his own highly idiosyncratic religious practice.

The majority of pagans in the empire were to be found among the rural and urban lower classes; with these, Julian had nothing in common. He was himself not only highly intellectual, but also attracted to the more abstruse and semi-religious forms of contemporary Neoplatonism – the attraction of the supernatural played a large role, as a result of the influence of men such as Iamblichus of Apamea in Syria and Maximus of Ephesus. His various writings on religious subjects, including his work against the 'Galilaeans', as he called Christians, display a sharp but often rather off-beat intellect. He was not afraid to write a satire called the *Caesares*, in which he makes fun of Constantine, whom he depicts making the rounds of the gods in heaven, unable to find a protector, until he turns to Jesus out of the need for Christian forgiveness (of the characteristic features of Christianity, Julian himself most disliked humility, thinking that it took away proper pride). Once openly pagan, Julian took delight in experimenting with any and every cult, and especially in blood sacrifices, which Christians particularly condemned. Even Ammianus remarks on his excess, saying that he sacrificed so many animals that 'it was reckoned that if he had returned from Parthia there would have been a shortage of cattle' (XXV.4). Apparently he did not realize that the enthusiasm with which he revived and took part in such holocausts was itself a factor which alienated educated pagans at Antioch. Naturally his attempt to revive the cult of Apollo at nearby Daphne also antagonized Christians, for his brother

The head of Socrates, detail from a mosaic of Socrates and six sages, from Apamea, Syria, centre of a Neoplatonic philosophical school in the fourth century, especially famous for the philosopher Iamblichus (c.AD 250–c.325)

Gallus, a Christian himself, had transfer   there the bones of a local saint called Babylas, and Julian had ordered these remains to be ritually removed and the shrine cleansed. The local Christians escorted the martyr's remains with great pomp to another site, whereupon they were themselves subjected to cruel reprisals. When a fire destroyed the roof of Apollo's temple and the god's statue, Julian took it as Christian arson, and ordered the Great Church at Antioch to be closed and its property seized. The priest of Apollo also suffered torture for his supposed negligence. The Christians in contrast inevitably took the fire to be divine punishment, while Julian made yet another attempt to impose his wishes by having sacrificial meat thrown into the spring at Daphne and ordering all food in the market to be sprinkled with water used in the sacrificial ceremonies by pagan priests, both of which were extreme acts of provocation to the Christian community. John Chrysostom, who was in his teens when this happened, later wrote an emotional and heightened account of these events in his homily on St Babylas. At the least, Julian was guilty of wilful provocation, even though John and other Christian writers may have exaggerated or even distorted what actually happened.

Another episode which attracted intense emotion was Julian's attempt to rebuild the Temple at Jerusalem. Ammianus tells the story with apparent detachment: Julian wanted 'to leave a great monument to perpetuate the memory of his reign' and so decided to restore the 'once magnificent temple at Jerusalem' (XXIII.1). The work ceased because of persistent fireballs erupting near the foundations; the Jews are not even mentioned. The fact was that restoration of the Temple implied the greatest possible affront to Christianity that anyone could think of. Constantine's Church of the Holy Sepulchre and the growth of Jerusalem since AD 335 as a Christian holy site and pilgrimage centre symbolized the Christian recovery of the city, which had been a Roman colony since AD 135. Now Julian proposed not merely to undo Constantine's work, but (in Christian eyes) to associate his own rule with the traditional enemies of Christianity and to disprove the saying of Jesus, much quoted by Christians, that no stone of the Temple would be left upon another (Matt.24:2; cf. 15). The fact that the destruction of the Jewish Temple was already a central theme in Christian apologetic, not least in Jerusalem itself, where Bishop Cyril had recently preached a sermon on the subject, made the matter all the more sensitive. Restoration of the Temple would also make possible the resumption of sacrifice on the Temple Mount, something welcome to Julian but anathema to Christians. Christians were very alarmed when they heard the news, and exultant when the plan proved abortive, and supernatural explanations including appearances of the Cross in the sky were easily found for the fire which had caused the work to cease. Ephrem the Syrian and a letter surviving in Syriac, attributed to Cyril of Jerusalem, describe the events in graphic and emotional terms, and here and in the later accounts by the ecclesiastical historians the story acquires an unmistakable eschatological significance.

As for Julian's Persian expedition, we must remember that while Ammianus' account is written by an eyewitness, it is also composed with hindsight and from the standpoint of one who regarded its failure and the death of Julian as a tragedy. It depicts Julian as wilfully ignoring not only divine omens but also the explicit advice of his friends; yet, says Ammianus, it would have been impossible to avert what fate had already decreed (XXIII.5). Julian therefore ignored all the many adverse signs and in a theatrical gesture had the boats burnt behind them when the army had crossed the Khabur river; Ammianus tells us here that the warnings of the soothsayers were overcome by the counterarguments of Julian's entourage of 'philosophers' who travelled with the expedition. As for the death of Julian, this too is surrounded in mystery and rumour. Having failed to wear his breastplate, he was struck by a spear from a cavalryman about whose identification even contemporaries disagreed. Christian sources including Ephrem suggest that Julian had wilfully exposed himself and therefore effectively committed suicide. Early versions attributed the shot to a 'Saracen' (an Arab fighting in the Persian or Roman army), a Persian, an unknown camp-follower or even a Roman, Christian or pagan. Typically, the Christian writers want to claim Julian's death as divine vengeance, while Libanius on the other hand wishes to imply that the pagan emperor had been killed by a Christian. Ammianus by contrast states simply that the source of the shot was unknown (XXV.3), but then adds his own kind of enhancement by having the dying Julian discourse on the nature of the soul with his philosopher companions.

The myth of Julian had begun to form itself even while the emperor was still alive, and his short reign left an indelible impression on both pagans and Christians. Its drama is heightened for us far above its intrinsic interest and importance by the passions that it inspired in contemporary and later writers, and by the quantity of writing that they produced. As the inspiration of Ammianus and the subject of the major and most dramatic section of his surviving history, Julian also acquires a stature larger than life. In one of those historical might-have-beens, the question is often asked whether he might have succeeded in restoring paganism had he lived longer. The irony is that it was not so much the causes which he espoused in themselves, nor the contemporary historical situation which caused the difficulties, but rather Julian's own character, and, in particular, his unforgettable and infuriating combination of high-mindedness and arrogance.

VII

The Late Roman State

CONSTANTIUS TO THEODOSIUS

ALTHOUGH AT VARIOUS times there were several Augusti reigning simultaneously, the empire itself was not formally divided during the period from the death of Constantine in 337 until that of Theodosius I in 395. When the latter did die, his two young sons Honorius and Arcadius took the west and the east respectively. Again, there was no constitutional division, and the tetrarchic period provided precedents for such an arrangement. The difference now was mainly that the division was maintained continuously from AD 395 until what is regarded conventionally as the end of the western empire in AD 476.

With the death of Julian the rule of the house of Constantine came to an end. Jovian, his successor, was both obscure and short-lived as emperor; his main action was to conclude a humiliating peace with Persia, by which he ceded Nisibis and Singara. Ammianus claims that this was the sole instance in Roman history since the foundation of the Republic when such concessions had been made (XXV.9). Shortly afterwards, Jovian died in Asia Minor on his way back to Constantinople, aged only thirty-two; such was the legacy of Julian's Persian expedition. Like Jovian, the Pannonian Valentinian was also chosen as the next emperor by the high army commanders together with the high civil officials, while still en route for Constantinople from the east. The transfer of power was always liable to be unpredictable. Taking care to avoid an unpropitious day, Valentinian was acclaimed Augustus at Nicaea and shortly afterwards he in turn proclaimed his brother Valens co-emperor in Constantinople. Ammianus's account of their arrangements (XXV.5) illustrates the practicalities of power-sharing: they made an agreement at Naissus, by which Valens took charge of the east, and which included division of army commanders, troops and court officials. They sealed it by each taking the consulship on 1 January, AD 365, as was customary at the beginning of a new reign.

Like Jovian, and like the late third-century emperors and the tetrarchs before him, the brothers shared a military background, and, again like Jovian, Valentinian allegedly came to the fore because of the reputation of his father, who had been commander in Britain, but who was of humble origin (Ammianus, XXX.7, cf. XXV.5). Constantine had succeeded in breaking the pattern only temporarily, and Julian's sudden death, and indeed his personal conduct, had ensured a return to earlier practice. Only three years after his own elevation Valentinian fell seriously ill; movements were made to find a successor, and in order to forestall this, on his recovery he appointed his son Gratian, a child of only eight years old, as co-emperor, presenting him to the troops with an emotional speech before crowning him and investing him with the imperial robes. Ammianus comments:

> In this matter Valentinian went beyond the long-established custom, in that his generosity led him to promote both his brother and his son to the rank of Augustus instead of Caesar. No one before had taken a colleague with power equal to his own except the emperor Marcus [Marcus Aurelius, 161–80], who made his adopted brother Verus his partner without any inferiority of status as an emperor. (XXVII.6)

The child-emperor Gratian set a trend which was to continue. When Valentinian I died in AD 375, though Gratian and Valens, the latter destined to die on the field at Adrianople in AD 378, were both Augusti, another son, born of his second wife Justina and even younger than Gratian had been in 367, was proclaimed by the army as Valentinian II without consulting Gratian (Ammianus, XXX.10). But this dynastic loyalty did not in the longer term survive the weakness of the boy-emperors; in August, AD 383, four years after proclaiming Theodosius Augustus after the defeat at Adrianople, a rival, Magnus Maximus, set himself up in Britain and Gratian himself was murdered by his troops.

To complete the catalogue of emperors in this period: Theodosius I was another whose father had proved himself able as *magister militum*, also in Britain, like Constantius Chlorus and the father of Valentinian I, though he had subsequently fallen from favour and been executed at Carthage and the son had prudently retired for a while to his native Spain. Ammianus praises the elder Theodosius extravagantly (XXVII.8, XXVIII.3), but his son was on the throne when Ammianus wrote, and the historian prudently does not mention his father's fall.

Neither the interlude of Diocletian's tetrarchy nor Constantine's sole reign had succeeded in bringing about long-term changes in the appointment of emperors. Essentially what mattered was the backing of the right group of army officers; after that what counted was success. The Senate no longer had an active role to play, and the people, if they feature at all, do so merely as spectators whose support might be solicited. Ammianus' contemptuous account of the attempted usurpation of Procopius after the elevation of Valens describes a failed coup. According to him, Procopius, who traded on his family relationship to Constantius II and Julian, found a group of venal soldiers to proclaim him in Constantinople, and was invested with whatever came to hand:

> no purple robe was available, and he was dressed in a gold-spangled tunic like a court official, though from the waist downwards he looked like a page. He wore purple shoes and carried a spear, with a shred of purple cloth in his hand. Altogether he was a grotesque object such as might suddenly appear on the stage in a satirical farce. (XXVI.6)

He was allegedly even supported by a hired audience, paid to acclaim him. But as the narrative goes on to make clear, Procopius was able to win considerable support, drive Valens from his attempted siege of Nicaea and take Cyzicus; however, while engaging Valens in battle at Nacolia in Phrygia he was deserted by his own officers, caught and handed over to be beheaded (XXVI.9). Ammianus casts Procopius in the role of a series of failed rebels and usurpers – Perperna, put to death by Pompey, Didius Julianus and Pescennius Niger from more recent imperial history (XXVI.6,8,9); he was not a lawful emperor in his eyes, yet the difference lay largely in the fact that his challenge to Valens was unsuccessful.

During this period, therefore, the Roman state was not for the most part held together by the policies or personality of a single ruler; indeed, plurality of emperors was the rule rather than the exception. Access to imperial power was both unpredictable and unstable; not even dynastic loyalty guaranteed survival. The accession of child-emperors, moreover, carried the danger of placing power in the hands of others, such as Justina the mother of Valentinian II, or, later, powerful ministers such as Rufinus or the eunuch Eutropius, both advisers of Arcadius, the son of Theodosius I, whose influence is savagely attacked by the western court poet Claudian. The young emperor Gratian was put under the tutelage of Ausonius, a rhetor and poet from Bordeaux and Valentinian's quaestor, who after this appointment reached the heights of the consulate and the praetorian prefecture. Rhetorical skill such as his was highly valued, and could lead to rapid advancement, but Valentinian and Valens also promoted Pannonians like themselves who were for the most part men of little education, and were resented as such in more conservative and cultured circles. Individual emperors might also come under the influence of a forceful bishop, as was the case between Gratian, Theodosius and Ambrose. Finally, this period is characterized both by the increasing pressure of barbarian invasion and by the growing use of barbarians even in the higher echelons of the Roman army (see Chapter IX); from the end of the fourth century onwards generals of barbarian origin, of whom one of the first was the Vandal Stilicho, *magister militum* under Theodosius I and prospective regent to his two sons, came to play a critical role in imperial politics, eventually in the western half of the empire exceeding that of the emperors themselves. The fact that the east in the fifth century largely managed to avoid a similar situation, and that the eastern emperors relied on civilian officials rather than generals, is an important factor in explaining the survival of the eastern empire after AD 476.

By whatever means they had been elevated, emperors were judged by harsh standards by traditionally minded con-temporaries, and perhaps the more so since access to the purple was itself so comparatively open. They were expected to strike the difficult balance between dignity and affability, between justice and severity, and to please the different sections of society without showing undue favour. On the other hand they themselves were treated by their subjects with the deference and fawning due to an autocrat, received with lights and flowers and greeted with shouts of acclamation, even by the Senate itself. The image of emperor and subject was the dominant image of the period, and appears as a metaphor in all kinds of literature, including works by Christians. In the same way, when Christian artists needed a repertoire to quarry for their new public commissions, it was natural for them to turn to imperial art. In two of the earliest surviving Christian mosaics in Rome, Christ is depicted with his apostles at S. Pudenziana (late fourth century) in the style of emperor and Senate, while the Virgin inappropriately appears in the church of S. Maria Maggiore (fifth century) in the dress and attributes of a Roman empress. One of Julian's problems in the eyes of contemporaries, which is also what makes him interesting to us, had been precisely that he had failed to live up to the dignity expected of his position.

Late Roman society was a society in which gradations of dignity were ordained by law, highly prized and jealously preserved. Ranks and titles underwent an inflation: everyone wanted the rank of an *honoratus* (a member of the higher *ordines* into which Roman society had been divided since the early Republic). By the middle of the fourth century, large-scale imperial grants caused the equestrian order to grow to such an extent that it began to lose its attraction. Of the highest equestrian ranks, the *perfectissimi* and *eminentissimi*, the former grade became so overcrowded that it had to be divided into three sub-categories. The senatorial order grew too, as a result of a process begun by Constantine and already criticized by Eusebius (*VC* IV.1). Far more posts were designated as senatorial than before, new senators were created on a large scale, especially in Constantinople, and honorary membership of the order was bestowed so widely that it was no longer enough to be a mere *vir clarissimus*, the traditional rank of a senator. While birth could still admit one to senatorial status, by the end of the fourth century rank depended on office; thus the highest rank, that of *illustris*, was reserved for consuls, patricians and holders of the top ministries; below them came the *spectabiles*, a group which

City *tyche* (representation of Fortune), from the Esquiline treasure, Rome. A decoration for the arm of a carrying-chair for an important person, probably an official such as the Prefect of the City.

included the higher provincial governors and certain eunuch officers of the emperor's bedchamber, and only lastly the *clarissimi* – all other senators. Inevitably the overgrown equestrian class began to shrink as many of its members acquired senatorial rank. Constantine had also created a third order, the *comitiva*, carrying the rank of *comes* (divided in turn into differing grades) and bestowed by imperial gift or by appointment to the emperor's *comitatus* (see Chapter III), and which gave enhanced rank if combined with equestrian or senatorial status. Like the equestrian order, this grade also greatly increased in numbers at first, but was then overtaken by the expansion of the senatorial class. The fourth century thus witnessed the transformation of the old 'orders', still closely linked to birth and wealth, into a service aristocracy, in which rank depended on office. Now the son of a senator still had senatorial status, but only as a *clarissimus*; he had to hold office in order to improve his rank.

The inflation of rank illustrates again the tension apparent between the needs of the state and contemporary social expectations and attitudes. The emperors bestowed equestrian and senatorial rank carrying exemption from curial obligations even as they tried to increase their fiscal pressure on the cities to which the same men belonged. Rank and titles also conferred privileges such as protection in the courts; thus the upward drift simultaneously undermined the government's efforts to enforce the law, stimulating from the emperors ever greater flights of legislative rhetoric, and constantly spiralling penalties for trifling offences. There was one law for the rich and powerful, another for the lowly. All the same, evasion of responsibilities by the *potentiores* sometimes elicited imperial legislation: 'Men of high rank (*potentiores*) must appear in court when a criminal charge, formally registered, requires their presence' (*CTh.* IX.1.17, AD 390).

Entry into the imperial service was extremely attractive for men of middling status from the municipal class, since these positions now carried military ranks and entitlement to provisions (*annona*), and, still more important, the opportunity in most cases for substantial fees (*sportulae*) on the side. Emperors therefore legislated to stem the flow of recruits from the cities, where they were needed in order to perform their municipal responsibilities: 'all those who have aspired to imperial service (*militia*) which is not their due are to be released from that service and returned to their own orders and offices' (*CTh.* XII.1.120, AD 389). The trend was already apparent in Constantine's day. However, the general approach of the emperors was pragmatic: success was rewarded or at least recognized, and if a man had managed to stay away from his city for long enough the situation was *de facto* accepted.

The government responded in the same way to the fact that many people were prepared to pay large amounts in order to secure themselves such advantageous positions: by the fifth century, payment for office had become the norm, and so in AD 444 Theodosius II regularized it by law (*CJ* XII.xix.7). Some sections of the imperial service were far more desirable than others. The corps of imperial couriers (*agentes in rebus*) were for instance in a position to exact substantial fees for their services; these posts were accordingly so desirable by the end of the fourth century that the right of nomination to appointment had to be controlled by legislation (*CTh.* VI.27.8). The eunuchs of the bedchamber (*sacrum cubiculum*, whence *cubicularii*) also had great opportunities for enrichment by receiving bribes and exploiting inside information, and by the early fifth century the highest of them had acquired top senatorial rank. Court eunuchs were of course in a special category; in general, access to office was obtained by a combination of influence, recommendation, and the expenditure of cash, practices which the lucky candidate then continued in other spheres or practised in reverse once he was appointed.

An army of officials – the late Roman system looks at first sight like corruption run riot. Everything was for sale, including government. The rhetoric of the law codes, and the vivid stories in the literary sources, not least Ammianus, cast a lurid light over the period, which is to many modern historians still merely the prelude to the decline and fall of the western empire. But the North African prince Jugurtha had made similar criticisms of Roman society in the second century BC, and on closer inspection some doubts emerge as to whether things were really quite as bad as they seem. Much of the apparatus of a modern state was simply non-existent: there was for instance no police force to seek out criminals or enforce the law and no organized system of legal advice or representation (though there were innumerable laws to be obeyed). There was no banking system as such, and health was a matter for whichever agencies were available, from doctors for the few to sorcerers and holy men for the many; though education received more attention from the state, the benefits were reserved for an elite. There were many state employees in the later Roman empire, but when compared with the proportion of citizens directly employed by the state in modern developed societies their number pales into insignificance. A large majority of the population was not directly 'employed' (working for wages) at all, but belonged either to the class of patrons, especially as wealthy landowners, or dependants (slaves, tenants, *coloni*); the latter class also included the urban poor, sustained by public grants and religious charity. The Roman empire differed little except in scale from other pre-modern societies, and people resorted to the same mechanisms, chiefly forms of patronage and dependence, in order to get round the sheer practical difficulties of living. This was recognized in practice by all parties, but some practices upset the established pattern and drew down imperial condemnation. Libanius's speech *On Protection Systems*, probably dating from AD 391–2, asks the Emperor Theodosius to enforce imperial legislation against army officers who are extracting protection money or payment in kind from the *coloni* of large villages who then use the military protection they have bought in order to terrorize and exploit their neighbours. In Libanius's view, protection between landlord and tenant was to be expected, but this intervention by the army upset the status quo to an unacceptable extent. In societies like the later Roman empire the state is seen as distant and threatening and its agents are only too likely to use protection rackets in order to supplement their own income. But viewed from the other perspective, we can also see in the later empire a competition among the powerful for patronage of the poor. Either because resources were shrinking, or because the apparatus of government was not working well, the need for protection, dependency and patronage seems to have increased, and the opportunities for patrons increased with it.

Several reasons may be suggested for this development, if we look at the problem in terms of the structure of government. First, there were certainly increases of scale in the number of state officials, and therefore also in the potential for abuse in a system where there was little chance of control in the modern sense. Jones, followed by MacMullen, estimates the late Roman civil service at something between thirty and thirty-five thousand strong, as against a few hundred at the end of the second century. Thanks to the nature of the evidence now available, above all in the law codes, we know a great deal about the structure and size of the major departments. One such, that of the *largitionales*, was divided into eighteen sub-groups, graded in seven classes in order of rank and pay. The sixth-century writer John the Lydian also tells us a great deal about the working of the praetorian prefecture, where he had spent his career. The law codes are full of regulations adjusting and fine-tuning these grades, down to the smallest details, yet the rules and the gradations of status do not sound wholly unfamiliar to anyone who has worked in a large modern office. Second, however, these officials were concentrated in certain areas of government, while others, equally necessary for the running of the state, were completely neglected, thus leaving a vacuum to be filled only by patronage. Third, the opportunities open to the state either for enforcing the law or for efficient government in general were extremely limited. The empire was enormous, and though there was much more travel than one might expect, it was very slow and uncertain, if not actually dangerous; almost all forms of modern communications were simply lacking. Thus the emperors issued ever more strident laws, and imposed ever more ferocious penalties, without any guarantee that either would have any effect.

When even modern states have great difficulties in finding systems of government that really work, it would be anachronistic to imagine that late Roman emperors or their ministers were able to conceptualize their problems and absurd to suppose that they had the capacity for initiating change on the scale that such conceptualization would imply. The late Roman government was attempting to run a vast empire, under difficult economic and military conditions, without any of the necessary apparatus. The emperors had a religious, moral and symbolic role, they devoted much attention to military security, and they attempted to maintain order, for all of which purposes they needed to collect revenue. This was as much as could be expected, and it was often more than could actually be achieved. Given the previous habits of the ancient world, the increasing complexity of the problems which faced late Roman emperors, and the continued deficiency of government machinery, the growth of patronage and the many references to forms of corruption which we find in our sources were inevitable developments, but they are not absent even from supposedly developed modern states. It has also been argued that economic decline caused patronage to increase as the powerful competed for resources and influence, and the poor had greater need of protection. But that is again to beg the question of 'decline'. Because historians know with hindsight that 'decline' was round the corner, they tend to focus on the negative evidence. But 'decline' can have several different meanings; the sheer problems of organization faced by the late Roman government were enormous, and anyone reading the pages of Ammianus will sense both the contemporary social extremes and the awareness of rapid change. But while there may have been some economic contraction (see Chapter VIII), no one could really imagine on the basis of Ammianus that this was a society in serious decline.

The question of whether or not the later Roman empire was a 'totalitarian state' with a rigid caste system in which everyone's position was strictly controlled must also be answered in the light of the argument presented above. The evidence of the law codes has encouraged such a view, which is indeed still commonly held: numerous laws in the Theodosian Code from the time of Constantine onwards restrict freedom of movement in a variety of ways (see also Chapters III and IV above). Many attempt to compel the sons of tradesmen and artisans to remain in their fathers' professions; *navicularii* (shippers) and bakers, for instance, were forbidden to change their professions, and had to ensure their continuance after their own death. As time went on, such men were forbidden to escape by entering the civil service, the army or the church. A law of Valentinian, Valens and Gratian (AD 369) states that 'no member of the guild of ragmen shall be able to withdraw stealthily to a municipal council'. The guild is made responsible for information about such cases: 'a penalty is established for the aforesaid guild unless they immediately lodge a complaint about such withdrawals' (*CTh.* XIV.8.2). Another large category of legislation attempted to keep decurions – members of town councils – in their place of fiscal registration (*origo*) and to prevent them from seeking a more lucrative and less burdensome way of life elsewhere; they too were evidently escaping in the same directions, especially into the imperial service. Since it was they who were responsible for the organization and collection of the all-important tax revenue, and who even had to guarantee it out of their own pockets, the government's interest was to keep them where they were, but keeping the balance was far from easy, as a whole plethora of laws shows. It was not only the emperors and their ministers who found themselves in a contradictory situation: while Libanius for example, might uphold the cause of duty to one's *curia* (town council) in his public orations, he also spent much of his time writing letters of recommendation for individual decurions who were trying to escape their situation, many of whom succeeded. Many certainly did manage to escape into more attractive lifestyles, and rhetoric and the practice of letters as a teacher or even as a freelance orator or poet was one route to social advancement followed by some with conspicuous success. We must always set the evidence of these 'ones that got away' against the prescriptive material offered by the law codes.

The largest proportion of laws restricting freedom of movement relate however to the class known as *coloni* (tenant farmers), which might also include small-holders who also leased plots of land from others. It was on the rural poor that the major tax burden, and the weight of the whole agrarian-based economy in practice rested. The collection of the poll tax (*capitatio*) imposed by Diocletian in theory necessitated regular censuses which would have been difficult to carry out with reliability; movement of the labour force made them still more so. Regulations restricting movement thus followed from the tax reforms of Diocletian. Before AD 332, the tenant or his landlord were held responsible for tax arrears; after AD 332, landlords harbouring the *coloni* of others must not only give them back but also pay their poll tax for the period while they had been with them; further,

> it will be proper also for tenants who meditate flight to be bound with chains and reduced to a servile condition, so that by virtue of a servile condemnation they shall be compelled to fulfil the duties that befit free men. (*CTh*.V.17.1)

This law suggests, first, that *coloni* opted to flee in order to evade the poll tax, an evasion in which they were abetted by landlords in search of labour, or cheaper labour, and second, that *coloni*, though still technically free, could be treated as if they were slaves. But while Constantine's law illustrates the gulf between rich and poor, the contempt for the poor and the actual weakness of the late Roman government, the modern conception of the so-called 'tied colonate' (Chapter III) tends both to obscure the great variety of forms of free and unfree labour which actually existed and to exaggerate the degree of change which took place in the late empire as a result of imperial pronouncements.

The state resorted to these legal mechanisms not for ideological reasons, but out of a desire for regularization and in the attempt to guarantee the essential tax revenues. In AD 320, Constantine proclaimed that taxpayers should not fear the law, but the same decree represents paying taxes as a matter of moral obligation and 'human feeling', and provides that the defaulter's property be confiscated and redistributed to others, to whom his tax obligations are also to be transferred (*CTh.* XI.7.3, Lewis and Reinhold, no. 132). Such laws represent attempts at economic control which, while they are by modern standards crude and inadequate in the extreme (see Chapter VIII), aimed at holding the overall balance. The provisions tended to be taken over and repeated by subsequent emperors, even when the need for them had changed; thus when the *capitatio* was abolished in Thrace, it was firmly stated that *coloni* were nevertheless still to be tied, and that 'the landowner shall enjoy his right over them with the care of a patron and the power of a master' (*CJ* XI.52.1, AD 393). There were certainly substantial regional differences; laws of the 370s and 380s, for instance, seemingly tie *coloni* to the land for the first time in Illyricum and Palestine, the latter for the explicit benefit of landlords (*CJ* XI.53.1, 51.1). The legal distinction between *coloni* and slaves had been blurred long before, and it is a matter of discussion how far we are simply dealing with matters of nomenclature; *coloni* were strictly free, yet they could be termed 'slaves of the soil' (*servi terrae*, *CJ* XI.52.1,1). In the east in particular, other rights, such as the right to own property, were restricted in the case of *adscripticii* (*coloni* 'bound to the soil' by virtue of *adscriptio glebae*) as if they were indeed slaves. On the other hand *coloni* were not serfs in the later sense of the term and had no obligation to military service. Inevitably, however, their legal position came closer and closer to that of the many slaves left on the great estates (see Chapter VIII); moreover, the confused situation was further complicated by frequent mixed unions of *coloni* and slaves. Finally, one could be both a slave and a *colonus*. Though it has been argued that a virtual 'enserfment' of the free agricultural population took place, and is to be accounted for by a decline in the use and availability of slave labour during the imperial period, both the concept of enserfment and the extent of the supposed decline in actual slavery seem questionable. Recent studies have indeed reopened the whole issue of the nature of the agricultural labour force in the late empire.

At first sight the laws restricting freedom of movement present a gloomy picture in terms of human liberty. Again, however, one may wonder whether things were really much different in practice from what they had been like earlier in the empire. Concern for such modern ideas as human rights would be completely anachronistic. Nor is anything remotely approaching democracy any longer on the agenda. G. E. M. de Ste Croix is entirely right to see the history of the Roman empire in terms of increasing authoritarianism. On the other hand, the very confusions and ineptitude of late Roman government and legislation left many loopholes, and the ample non-legal sources do not suggest that the laws made much difference in practice. The problem may therefore lie more in interpreting late Roman legislation than with actual practice. As also with questions of marriage, dowry and inheritance law (see Chapter VIII), knowing how to assess the practical effects and relevance to real situations of this mass of often conflicting and certainly often varying legislative material is one of the hardest problems faced by historians of this period.

The later fourth-century emperors essentially continued or developed the patterns set under Diocletian and Constantine. The Roman state at the end of the fourth century differed from its predecessor in terms of natural development, or changing external factors, rather than because of any major change of direction. Among the most obvious changes that would however have been noticed by an observer are two that we have already discussed – the growth of the church as an institution, and the rise in importance of bishops both centrally and in their own communities. Others include the development of Rome in the fourth century and the rise of Constantinople as a capital city and particularly the growing impact of barbarian invasion and the difficulties experienced in dealing with it, which many perceived in terms of the weakness of Roman defences, or of the Roman army generally. These will be discussed in subsequent chapters. The next however will address some of the issues of interpretation raised here, by asking how we should assess the late Roman economy overall, and by focusing on specific aspects of economy and society in the fourth century.

VIII

Late Roman Economy and Society

INFLATION CONTINUED to rise precipitously during the reign of Constantine, irrespective of Diocletian's attempts to control prices and to reform the coinage. The main base of the economy still lay in agriculture, and while Constantine imposed new taxes on senators and traders, little could be done to bring about a general turn-round. Neither general considerations nor such indicators as there are would suggest that the actual shrinkage of the economic base which probably took place during the mid-third century had been significantly reversed. Even if we are sceptical about the very large figures for the size of the late Roman army in the literary sources (see Chapters III and IX), the state would still be hard pressed to finance it. It seems unlikely, moreover, that the level of taxation could really have been raised on a significant scale, simply because most of those paying taxes had no effective way of increasing their surplus. Nor – though the reverse is often claimed – could seizure of temple treasures by Constantine really have accounted for wide-scale economic recovery. Finally, while as part of his fiscal policy, Diocletian introduced 'state factories' (*fabricae*), mentioned in the *Notitia Dignitatum*, of which those at Carnuntum and Ticinum specialized in shields and bows respectively, it can be seen that they were set up to meet military needs rather than for wider economic reasons. Thus, if economic improvement took place in the first part of the fourth century, much of the credit must go to improved methods of tax collection, combined with the return to relative stability.

In some areas indeed it is possible to point to actual reductions of scale. Mining, for example, ceased to be organized in centrally controlled large-scale enterprises, and was more dispersed. Archaeological evidence suggests that mining for gold, silver and tin continued, for example, in Spain during the fourth century. The Theodosian Code also refers to gold mining in the Balkans, Pontos and Asia Minor, and archaeological evidence provides signs that it continued elsewhere too. However, it may have been on a reduced scale in comparison with earlier periods. A second example may be found in the size of late Roman legionary fortresses, as computed from archaeological evidence (see Chapter III) and from the fact that soldiers in the late empire are typically dispersed and barracked in or near cities rather than in large concentrations in the frontier zones. However, a variety of factors was at work in both cases, including the fragmentation of political control in far-flung areas like north-west Spain and the fact that since the *annona*, the army supplies, was now organized and distributed substantially in kind, the distance between supplier and recipient needed to be as short as possible; finally, the need to use the troops for internal security made it sensible to disperse them into smaller units. In the case of mining, though the state was certainly interested in the supply of gold, the process of change actually reversed the pattern of greater state control which many historians have emphasized in the past: in the later empire state-owned mines coexisted with privately owned ones, and increasingly allowed private individuals to lease mining rights.

Though it is notoriously hard to demonstrate that there had been a population fall in the third century, this still seems probable in general terms for the western provinces. In contrast, there is evidence to suggest a considerable population rise in the east from the end of the fourth century and especially in the fifth. However, by the fifth century, political conditions in the west were very different, and did not conduce to a similar rise.

There are many complaints in late Roman sources about the impoverishment of *curiales*, and about rapacious tax-collectors. Motivated by political advantage or traditional expectations, emperors still resorted to *en bloc* remission of tax arrears, as Constantine did in Gaul (*Pan. Lat.*V.5 ff., Lewis and Reinhold, II, no.133); whatever the actual reason, this indicates a system not under full control. Yet to set against these negative indicators there are also contrary signs. The first stages of a return to collection and delivery in gold of the main taxes, the poll-tax and the *iugatio*, can be seen in the late fourth century, though it took several generations to complete the process. Many landowners, especially the senatorial class in the west, amassed enormous quantities of wealth and land. According to Ammianus, they

> hold forth unasked on the immense extent of their family property, multiplying in imagination the annual produce of their fertile lands, which extend, they boastfully declare, from farthest east to farthest west. (XIV.6.10)

The church also became wealthy from a variety of sources, which now included inheritance. Many Christians gave large sums to the church and a good deal of expenditure went on church building and works of Christian charity, while the growing fashion for pilgrimage to the Holy Land stimulated local trade and settlement (see Chapter XI). Some sectors of society were very rich, and Ammianus's many scathing remarks about the contemporary love of display and extravagance are not wholly confined to the senatorial class. These and other developments, which run counter to the theory of decline and impoverishment, require further explanation.

The effect of the third-century debasement of the silver coinage, and of the various fiscal measures of Diocletian and Constantine, was to leave the empire in the fourth century with a coinage consisting mainly of gold on the one hand (*solidi*) and copper on the other. Silver continued to be struck, but was gradually ousted by the *solidus* as the main unit of account. Unlike the silver *denarii* of earlier days, the *solidus* was never debased, and continued in use until well into the Byzantine period. It depended however on the availability of a regular supply of gold, which was in the first stages assisted by a combination of particular circumstances and new measures, including Constantine's acquisition of the treasuries of his defeated rivals, the confiscation of gold and silver treasure from pagan temples and the exaction of new taxes payable in gold and enforced purchase of gold from the rich. As yet the monetary system was far from stable: for instance, a papyrus of AD 300 set a price of 60,000 *denarii* per pound of gold, but shortly afterwards it rose to 100,000 and had reached 275,000 by the end of

Constantine's reign. Yet this apparently impossible situation was in practice highly artificial and did not represent the real state of affairs in economic terms. The problem was that there were far too many base-metal coins – *nummi* or *folles* – in circulation (*denarii* now being purely a notional unit); furthermore, it was actually the government that was mainly responsible, since it regularly minted copper but then failed to recover it again through taxation. The government also put still more into circulation by buying gold from money-changers in return for copper. It is hard for us to imagine a system in which coins of different denominations were not strictly interchangeable, but the late Roman government was still interested in the currency largely for its own purposes – for collection of revenues, for some payments, for reserves, and for prestige. The gold and the base-metal coinages were not part of a unified system, and unless matters got quite out of hand, the government was not too worried about it. In any case, its options were limited: Valentinian resorted to the standard expedient of legislating about it (*CJ* XI.11.1, AD 371), but that was not the same as putting control into practice.

The *annona* (military rations) was still paid partly in kind, though the new gold coins, struck at seventy-two to the pound, were used for donatives. The level of understanding about monetary systems has often been questioned: the anonymous writer of *De Rebus Bellicis* complains in the late 360s about the use of gold, as though merely to use it represented an extravagance in itself (c.2). A further implication of the discrepancy between gold and copper was the large role which must have been played by money-changers in every sort of transaction, from ordinary purchases to the payment of taxes in money. Indeed, money-changers (Gk. *trapezitai*, whence the modern Greek term for 'bank', Latin *collectarii*) and silversmiths (Gk. *argyropratai*, Latin *argentarii*) came to take on elementary banking functions. At the other end of the scale, gold bullion was regularly transported as part of the baggage-train which accompanied the emperor, even while on campaign. Thus it was a stroke of luck that when the Emperor Valens was defeated and killed by the Visigoths at the Battle of Adrianople in AD 378, he had left his treasuries inside the city, though most of the rest of the baggage-train was captured (Ammianus, XXXI.12). A very important development which

begins at the end of our period was the repeated payment of large
sums in gold as annual subsidies or one-off payments to barbarian
tribes, simply in effect to buy them off; this apparently disastrous
policy was continued over a long period and in fact became a
cornerstone of early Byzantine diplomacy. To a modern eye, the
whole monetary system in the late empire seems incredibly
unsatisfactory; moreover, we are extraordinarily ill informed
about most of the practicalities of its working. But the state did its
best to keep things under some sort of control in our period, with
measures against counterfeiting and parallel control of weights and
measures. As for the peasants, many still managed for the most
part without having to use money, as a law of AD 366 relating to
Africa suggests (CJ XI.48.5). All in all, the shortcomings of the
system from a modern point of view cannot but have had a
depressive effect on the level of economic activity at least in some
areas, but they did not spell economic collapse.

One striking feature of the fourth century is the tendency of
landowners to amass estates and wealth on an enormous scale. This
manifests itself particularly in relation to senatorial estates in the
late fourth and early fifth centuries, on which we are well
informed. Most impressive is the wealth of the younger Melania
and her husband Pinianus, whose estates were spread throughout
the western provinces, from Italy to Britain, Gaul and North
Africa. No one in Rome could afford to buy their palace on the
Caelian when they put it up for sale, and they were able to send
45,000 pieces of gold to the poor at one time, 100,000 coins at
another, and to distribute funds to Mesopotamia, Syria, Palestine
and Egypt. Even so, their wealth may not have put them in the
richest category, although their property at Thagaste in North
Africa had silver and bronze workshops, was larger than the town
itself and included two bishoprics. The fifth-century Greek
historian Olympiodorus says that the richest senators had annual
incomes of 4,000 pounds of gold, and middling ones 1,000 to 1,500
pounds (fr.44). Petronius Probus (cos. AD 371) was another
wealthy senator with estates all over the Roman world (Ammianus,
XXVII.11), and Symmachus, though not one of the richest by any
means, had nineteen houses and estates scattered through Italy,
Sicily and North Africa, and spent 2,000 pounds of gold on the

games given during his son's praetorship. Though by no means all senators were as rich as these, the general phenomenon of large estates had both economic and political implications. It revealed a dangerous concentration of wealth in the west in private hands, especially in the fifth century, while the government itself became increasingly weak. In the east, by contrast, senatorial fortunes were smaller, partly in view of the very recent development of the Senate of Constantinople and the prominence in it of men of much more ordinary origins (see Libanius, *Or.* 42).

How and when did their owners acquire these large estates? One answer must be that they did so in the troubled conditions in the western provinces in the later third century and after. The families of the late Roman senatorial aristocracy were not all as old as they liked to pretend, and much land was either deserted or ravaged by warfare, making it easy and cheap to acquire. Another question involves the impact of such conglomerations on neighbouring settlement, their use of local labour and their effects on the local economy. Finally, the question of how they were themselves managed affects our understanding of late Roman trade and commerce generally, as well as that of slavery *vis-à-vis* free labour in the late empire.

Slavery as an institution (we are here talking mainly about the use of slaves in agricultural production) has assumed a major place in all discussions of the late Roman economy. In particular, the role of slavery in the economic systems of the ancient world has been a major theme of Marxist historiography, which has always seen a connection between the existence of classical slavery and the fact that classical antiquity eventually came to an end. Recent discussion has moved the issue onto a more sophisticated level. Thus the notion of a typical 'slave mode of production' has come under heavy criticism, and it has been pointed out that chattel slavery on large estates was never the norm outside Italy, and even there only for a short period and in limited ways. At the same time, it is now clear that contrary to what had been claimed, slaves were not replaced by free labour in the late empire but continued to exist in large numbers. But since there has also been a persistent assumption among historians (despite comparative evidence from other historical periods) that slave-run estates must inevitably have been more productive, it is necessary to ask not just whether slaves were still used on the large estates, but also how they were used and how their condition differed from that of free men.

Late Roman agricultural slavery does not seem to have been organized along the lines familiar from the American Deep South. Nevertheless, the younger Melania had many slaves on her estates; while she freed eight thousand of them, this was perhaps more as part of the process of liquidation of property than from Christian conviction, and many were also sold with the land. Melania had the problems of a landowner as well as the convictions of an ascetic, and she was worried when the slaves on certain estates rebelled as to whether the unrest would spread; moreover, freeing eight thousand slaves would have created considerable local problems in itself. Slaves could themselves be tenants, but how often they occupied this role is unfortunately very difficult to establish; we must allow for a good deal of variation, both between estates and between regions. Rural slavery had never in fact been a general phenomenon in the empire, and while it is attested in late Roman Italy, Spain and Asia Minor, and the islands, it does not appear in the Egyptian papyri. We very rarely have direct information about individual estates, still less generalizations or of course figures for larger areas, and Palladius, the author of a fourth-century manual on agriculture, makes no mention of slave labour in the fields. However, his descriptions of a typical complex and diversified estate, with villa, vineyards, gardens, cattle and fields, suggest central organization of the work rather than a simple parcelling out of the land into tenant-farmed plots; so do the mosaics depicting the busy life of North African villas like that of a certain Julius from Carthage, now in the Bardo Museum at Tunis. This does not however in itself imply the use of slaves. One of many such villas in the west was at Mungersdorf near Cologne, while in Britain, where there was considerable expenditure on villas in the fourth century, there was also local variation in their economy, combined with interdependence on local towns, as is also attested for villas in the area round Trier in Germany. By the end of the fourth century, however, in Britain as in Gaul, there is evidence of a degree of destruction and decline which must be connected with the barbarian invasions, even if this is not certain in an individual case.

In any case, the degree to which ancient agricultural writers are a

Villa mosaic from Tabarka, North Africa. Other examples show workers engaged in various tasks.

reliable guide to real economic activity at any period is itself problematic. Symmachus writes as though slaves are the norm, and Augustine describes the practice of slave-traders who kidnapped unsuspecting villagers to sell; poor parents often sold the children they could not rear. But hired labour had been used alongside slaves for centuries, especially at peak times like harvest, and even the Italian *latifundia* in the main period of so-called slave production seem to have been engaged in mixed farming rather than specialization for cash crops.

Much remains obscure about slaves in the late empire, and their importance should neither be overestimated nor minimized. We need to remember that they now became plentiful at certain times through conquest (though barbarian prisoners of war could also be treated as *coloni*), and that following Roman precedent, slavery continued as a well-established institution in the medieval west. Yet, as we have seen (Chapter VII), the status of agricultural slaves and free *coloni* gradually came closer and closer together. As for estate management in the late empire, it no doubt varied greatly. While we should not think in lurid terms of slave chain gangs, we should also not give up the idea that central management ('domanial farming') continued to exist.

It is nevertheless risky to attempt to argue from the presence or absence of slavery to the level of production. But another feature of the existence of large estates had a more direct impact on the general economy. This is the fact that many dealings will have taken place between one estate and another of the same landowner, or through arrangements with his friends and relations, and so will have by-passed the open market altogether. The nobles needed money and reckoned their income in gold; but much of their production went to maintain their estates and their labour forces, while other goods were given as gifts, in accordance with the social expectations of their class. Rich landowners did not need to pay others for transport either – they owned their own ships, just as when they needed anything, they called upon all kinds of skilled craftsmen from their own estates. The evidence for market exchange as such, as it affected this class, is elusive: there was much arranging to be done by *negotiatores*, and we hear something about that in the sources, but the *negotiatores* themselves might be middle men rather than traders in their own right. Furthermore, as the lands of the great landowners increased in number and extent, the place left for markets in general will have been correspondingly reduced. As the church acquired estates it inevitably took over the same system and the same habits – after all, most bishops came from exactly this class of rich landowners themselves. We see the Alexandrian church engaging in trading ventures, just as we read of landowners profiteering from agricultural sales. Finally, the pattern of non-market exchange was also built into the state system of supply and distribution in kind. The state had even taken the initiative in setting up its own means of manufacturing necessary items such as arms, and even if these were far from being factories in any modern sense, but rather conglomerations of craftsmen, they nevertheless circumvented the very limited processes of market exchange which did exist.

Patronage, dependence, 'tied labour', all these are characteristic of the late Roman economic system, and all are factors which tell against growth on any real scale. A further deep-rooted feature of late Roman exchange and distribution which points in the same direction needs to be noted, namely the provision of free food supplies to the population of Rome and on the same model to Constantinople. This was a long-established practice which entailed that much of the grain production of North Africa and Egypt was in practice commandeered for the purpose as part of the land tax. In Rome, the distribution went back to the late Republic. In the fourth century AD, as before, the ration was given out on the strength of tickets, by now both hereditary and saleable. Following precedent, Constantine extended the distribution to Constantinople, with eighty thousand destined recipients, and by the later fourth century these tickets too (*annonae populares*) had become hereditary and saleable; thus it is by no means clear that those properly entitled to the ration actually received it. However, those who built houses in Constantinople were automatically entitled to be among the recipients. Not just corn, or bread, but also oil and pork were distributed free in Rome, the latter being levied from other towns in Italy. A similar system operated in Alexandria in the third century, and may have been taken over later by the church.

Not surprisingly, there were all sorts of practical difficulties involved in making the necessary arrangements, of which we hear a great deal in the *Code*, and by the mid-fifth century, rather than receiving pigs of unspecified weight and quality from the supplying towns, the *suarii* (pork butchers) of Rome received money with which to select and buy their supplies. Wine was also provided, not free but at a discount price, and for this too the government exacted a levy in kind from nearby parts of Italy. The origins of these provisions were political, to ensure the support of the population of the capital; they remained in practice over several centuries and despite the practical complications and the opportunities for abuse to which they gave rise, their extension to Constantinople was an entirely logical step. At the same time they were an expression on the part of the state of the impulse towards euergetism (benefaction) which had been so deep-rooted among civic notables earlier in the empire. But they had obvious economic implications too, encouraging the growth of a dependent urban lower class, impeding what development there might have been towards wage-labour activities in the capitals and finally monopolizing the grain production of North Africa and Egypt. In practice, the distribution in Rome was something of an anachronism during the fourth century, when Rome was no longer the capital or the seat of imperial authority; however, the natural inertia of late Roman government and the power of tradition made the idea of its abolition out of the question.

Many factors therefore combined to depress the level of large-scale market exchange, in addition to general considerations based on the agrarian society of the Roman empire and the nature of ancient towns. Trade has recently been receiving more attention from economic historians of the ancient world, as is clear for instance from the second edition of Finley's *The Ancient Economy*, published in 1985; this allows a larger place to trade than was the case in the very influential first edition. At the end of our period, the evidence of late Roman pottery, a relatively recent subject of serious study for archaeologists, seems to suggest that long-distance exchange, for example between Vandal Africa, Italy and Constantinople in the fifth century, took place on a greater scale than had been previously imagined on the basis of the literary evidence. This is extremely important in relation to the highly contentious issue of the decline of the west and the transition to the medieval world, though it is not at all clear for instance how much of that exchange was accounted for by trade as such; furthermore, the debate has focused mainly on the period after the substantial barbarian settlements in Gaul and the Vandal conquest of North Africa in AD 430. But it is now clear that the cities of North Africa were in a surprisingly flourishing condition in the fourth century, while the later fourth century in Palestine and Syria represented a time of clear population growth and increasing prosperity. Local conditions were extremely important here as elsewhere: the limestone *massif* of northern Syria was particularly suited to olive cultivation on a large scale, and was exploited in this way, though not apparently as exclusively as formerly argued, while in the desert of the Negev in southern Palestine irrigation systems which had been in existence since the Nabataean period, permitting mixed farming and working monasteries with market gardens, contributed to support a larger population than at any time until the present day. At Antioch, one of the few cities for which we have detailed information from the sources, it is clear that the population included many different sorts of craftsmen and traders, though on what scale or for whom they worked is less clear.

Scholarship is moving fast in this area, and generalizations about the late Roman economy are as yet necessarily crude; nevertheless, we can at least now begin to set real archaeological evidence with more confidence against the copious and potentially misleading evidence of the law codes, and thus to reach a more rounded picture than was possible only a generation or so ago.

The spread of Christianity also brought with it various forms of redistribution of wealth. One, already mentioned, was through inheritance; permitted to inherit by a law of Constantine, the church itself, or in practice individual sees, in this way became a substantial landowner. Bishops thus found themselves taking on the same responsibility of managing estates with slaves and *coloni* as lay landlords, and the permanent upkeep of new churches was frequently also guaranteed by endowing them with the revenue of certain estates; we know a good deal about the arrangements for Constantine's Roman churches, for example, from the medieval *Liber Pontificum* (*Book of the Popes*). Another important way in which wealth was redistributed through Christianity was by the deliberate renunciation and disposal of their property by wealthy Christians. Here the younger Melania provides a striking example. Another about whose renunciation we know a great deal from his own letters and other sources is Paulinus of Nola, a correspondent of Ambrose, Augustine and Sulpicius Severus, who sold his property and set up an elaborate ecclesiastical complex at Nola in Campania, while Sulpicius Severus (d. 420) did the same at Primuliacum, probably a villa-site, in southern Gaul. Both these men were interested in developing a cult-centre which would also be the centre for their own activities. Others built monasteries in the Holy Land, and contributed directly or indirectly to the pilgrim-traffic that had been growing there since the visit of Constantine's mother Helena in 326. Christian travel had economic implications in itself. The best-known traveller is the Spanish nun Egeria, who visited the Holy Land in AD 384 and has left a vivid diary of her experiences. No doubt like other well-connected travellers, she was helped at every stage, often by bishops, but also by local officials who put accommodation at the disposal of her party and facilitated their travel to the next stage: in the more dangerous areas from Clysma (Suez) to the Delta of Egypt she was accompanied by the regular military escorts who were garrisoned along the road; elsewhere it was monks, or the local bishop, who assisted her. When Jerome's friend Paula went to Jerusalem, the governor of Palestine made rooms available for her in the official residence. The pilgrims also needed transport, travelling by ship, and while on land, usually on horseback.

Even the monks in the Egyptian desert were constantly receiving visitors (Chapter V), including rich ladies who did not always get a pleasant reception. Arsenius, a monk who had been tutor to Arcadius and Honorius and who went further than most in his rejection of the world, was visited against his will by a rich young woman of senatorial class who insisted on coming to see him at Canopus and who had been aided in her pilgrimage by the Patriarch Theophilus of Alexandria. She threw herself at his feet, and,

> outraged, he lifted her up again, and said, looking steadily at her, 'If you must see my face, here it is, look.' She was covered with shame and did not look at his face. Then the old man said to her, 'Have you not heard tell of my way of life? It ought to be respected. How dare you make such a journey? Do you not realize that you are a woman and cannot go anywhere? Or is it so that on returning to Rome you can say to other women: I have seen Arsenius? Then they will turn the sea into a thoroughfare with women coming to see me.' (trans. Ward, 13–14)

The journey itself could be very dangerous, and pilgrims of all classes had all the needs of travellers today. They also bought souvenirs – lamps, bottles (*ampullae*) of Jordan water, seals, pictures or other mementoes of the local saint. One of the important shrines outside the Holy Land was that of Thecla at Seleucia in Isauria, visited by Gregory of Nazianzus in the 370s and by Egeria, and already the site of a three-aisled basilica. Accommodation for travellers was provided at many pilgrimage sites, but they also stayed in local inns: John Chrysostom warns pilgrims to stay away from the taverns at Daphne near Antioch. Finally, the feast-day of the saint was usually celebrated by a fair, which was a major occasion for local trade.

It is very difficult to assess the economic impact of church building or Christian patronage of visual art in this period.

Certainly imperial building might divert resources directly, and emperors might instruct provincial governors to make materials and workmen available, as they did the public post. The scale of some major churches was impressive, as with Ambrose's Basilica Ambrosiana in Milan, to which he transferred the opportunely discovered relics of the two local martyrs Gervasius and Protasius in AD 386 in the presence of a large crowd (Ambrose, *Ep*.22). A cruciform basilica dedicated to the Holy Apostles was attached to the mausoleum of Constantine in Constantinople by the middle of the fourth century. Every bishop wanted to build a worthy monument; thus Gregory of Nazianzus describes that built by his father, who was also his predecessor, and Gregory of Nyssa his own martyrium at Nyssa. In Rome, Pope Damasus built a basilica on the Via Ardeatina where he was buried with his mother and sister (*Lib. Pont*. I.212–13). Individuals also made donations for this purpose: thus Serena, the wife of Stilicho, had the floor of the church of S. Nazaro in Milan paved as a vow for the safe return of her husband (*CIL* V.6250). Besides churches, and despite widespread Christian disapproval of bathing, clerical bathing establishments are also attested in Italy under episcopal patronage. Though Christian art as such developed rather slowly in the fourth century, church building and the development of pilgrim shrines and holy places led the way; both involved the diversion of funds, and, just as importantly, precedents were set and examples provided for the great development in such building that can be seen later, and especially in the fifth-century east.

Just as bishops inherited a civic role as the patrons of urban building in our period, so also Christian charity began to take the place of civic euergetism. Already in the third century the church of Rome maintained some eighteen hundred widows, orphans and poor by its charity; in fourth-century Antioch, three thousand widows and virgins were registered, quite apart from needy men. Bishop Porphyry of Gaza also provided for regular distributions of money to those in need, which were continued after his death according to arrangements made in his will (Mark the Deacon, *Vita Porph*., pp.72–3). The idea of giving to the poor was an important part of the Christian ethic, and such charity might also take the form of individual renunciation, as with Melania or Olympias. Wealthy Christians sold up their estates on a vast scale, giving the proceeds to local churches, making provision for feeding the poor on a regular basis, or giving them direct distributions of money. Charity was also formalized in the provision of charitable establishments such as the hospices, and homes for the old and for orphans which were frequently attached to church buildings; while there is far more evidence from the fifth and sixth centuries for these, they too found their prototypes in the earlier period. Between these and the charitable foundations of the early empire the fundamental difference lay in their purpose and in the identification of the beneficiaries, specifically designated as the poor and needy in contrast to those of the early imperial foundations, which were often restricted to those of higher social class. On the other hand, the benefits to the donor of such giving sometimes came close to those derived from civic euergetism; Paulinus of Nola and Sulpicius Severus acted as patrons just as surely as the civic dignitaries of the early empire. Viewed in these terms, it does not seem that the supposed contrast between earlier euergetism and Christian charity was always as great as has been proposed. In practice the most spectacular renunciations of property by members of the upper class in the west came in the first decade of the fifth century, at precisely the time when the state was most threatened by barbarian invasion. In one sense they reflect a kind of withdrawal, a survival option for the privileged upper class, who could thereby perpetuate their status as patrons in a different form while dissociating themselves from direct involvement in the political crisis.

Some women gained economic independence through Christianization, rejecting the traditional demands of marriage and family and living as they chose, either as ascetics at home or travelling and founding their own monasteries. These however were limited to the upper class, and the extent to which they exchanged one sort of confinement for another is also of course debatable. Nevertheless, their own enthusiasm is evident. Paula had pored over the Scriptures and knew Hebrew better than Jerome, and Melania the Elder had read 'seven or eight times' three million lines of Origen, two hundred and fifty thousand lines of Gregory, Stephen, Pierius, Basil and others (Palladius, *Lausiac History*, trans. Butler, 149). Fabiola, another female friend of Jerome, founded a hospital in Rome in which according to Jerome she shared in the nursing herself, while Marcella, another Roman convert to asceticism, defied the victorious Visigoths who sacked Rome in AD 410 when they entered her house and accused her of having buried her riches (Jerome, *Ep.* 127). In the east, John Chrysostom's friend the widow Olympias is said to have supported with her wealth and her advice Nectarius the patriarch of Constantinople, Gregory of Nyssa, Amphilochius of Iconium, Epiphanius of Constantia in Cyprus and 'many others of the saints and fathers who lived in the capital city'; other recipients of her aid included the bishops Antiochus of Ptolemais, Acacius of Beroea and Severian of Gabala (*Life of Olympias*, 14).

The upper classes were legally permitted to remain single by Constantine's law of AD 320 (*CTh.* VIII.16.1) which removed the existing penalties under the Augustan marriage legislation. Women however were still strictly treated under the law. In AD 331 Constantine legislated on divorce, declaring that women were not allowed to get away with seeking divorce out of 'depraved desire', for reasons such as adultery, gambling or excessive drinking by their husbands, but could only get back their dowry if the husband was a proven 'murderer, sorcerer or destroyer of tombs' (*CTh.* III.16.1); in contrast, adultery by the woman immediately justified divorce by the husband. Augustine gives a bleak picture of human relations in the typical Roman household; the husband was still the stern *paterfamilias*, and the wife might expect the same discipline as the children. His own mother Monica and his relationship with her are unforgettably depicted in the *Confessions*, but the father, Patricius, a less sympathetic figure, is constantly in the background as one whose sudden anger must be carefully anticipated and whose wants must be supplied:

> many wives married to gentler husbands bore the marks of blows and suffered disfigurement to their faces. (*Conf.* IX.9.19)

On the other hand, many texts indicate relationships of affection and intimacy, and Christian writers (still overwhelmingly male themselves) are much more ready to give space and attention in their works to women; as a result, we know far more about individual women in the later empire than in earlier periods.

One difference in legal attitudes seems to be a progressive sense of women as weak and in need of protection. Though the evidence is quantitatively speaking limited, inscriptions do not suggest that Christians differed significantly in terms of family size or age at marriage from pagan ones; in good society, marriages were arranged and girls married at twelve or fourteen and betrothed before puberty; Augustine was betrothed at about thirty to a girl of ten. Imperial legislation by Theodosius I and Justinian forbade close-kin marriage, in contrast with the practice common on the eastern borders of the empire; however, the legislation was not new – a precedent had been set by Diocletian – and it is clear that Theodosius's law was not a success. Nevertheless, Roman society in the west did not secure its inheritance by marriage of kin (endogamy) but rather by exploiting networks of friendship and social interest. In relation to children, Christian emperors condemned exposure of infants (*CJ* VIII.51 (52).2), but typically also recognized that parents did *de facto* sell children by forbidding them to take them back once given up (*CTh.* V.9.1). The greater attention given to women in the Christian sources does not extend to children, who remain largely ignored in the literature as feeling subjects; Augustine, with his interest in child development, is an exception, but his picture of babies and young children is unforgettably negative:

> I have personally watched and studied a jealous baby. He could not speak, and, pale with jealousy and bitterness, glared at his brother sharing his mother's milk. Who is unaware of this fact of experience? Mothers and nurses claim to charm it away by their own private remedies. But it can hardly be innocence, when the source of milk is flowing richly and abundantly, not to endure a share going to one's blood-brother, who is in profound need, dependent for life exclusively on that one food. (*Conf.* I.7.11, trans. Chadwick)

The Church Fathers also mostly took a poor view of women, however much they might cultivate rich ladies as individuals; women were seen as sources of temptation for men, and many Christian writers took the view that not just sex but even marriage itself was sinful. A lively debate at the end of the fourth century concerned the question of whether Adam and Eve had been sexual beings in the Garden of Eden; many argued that they had not, and that human sexuality was the result of the Fall. The exact details of the birth of Christ were also hotly disputed, many maintaining that Mary retained her virginal status during and after giving birth. Trivial or absurd as they may perhaps seem, these were critical issues in contemporary theological understanding of the Incarnation, and thus occupied a major part in Christological controversy, and the status of the Virgin Mary was the central issue debated at the Council of Ephesus in AD 431. But while it is true that celibacy and virginity were enjoined on men as much as on women, one cannot escape the fact that it was usually women who were cast in the roles of seductresses and blamed, like Eve, for the sexual weaknesses of men – not least because the authors of the many treatises on virginity and marriage were invariably men. It is much more difficult to assess how much effect if any all this preaching and moralizing had on the sexual mores of individuals and couples, and it seems very unlikely that these severe views were put into practice as yet by more than a tiny minority; but even if we discount a good deal, the prevailing views of a highly vocal elite do, as we know from modern experience, eventually have an impact on the ideas and practice of individuals themselves.

It is hard to give a picture of daily life in the late empire, when the area is so vast and the sources so disparate, and when so much of the statistical and documentary evidence available for later periods is simply lacking. In such circumstances, even the best we can do will inevitably remain impressionistic. The evidence itself is however extremely ample, in comparison with earlier periods of ancient history. To take one example of the change of emphasis in the sources, the poor are certainly more visible, thanks to the Christian evidence, though they usually feature as a group rather than as individuals. It is noticeable that in terms of communication, unlike classical orators, Christian preachers were conscious of the need to address the uneducated as well as the upper classes, and Augustine wrote a special treatise on the subject. We do begin to hear more about ordinary people, especially through the development of hagiographic literature (saints' lives), though this genre was still only in its infancy in the fourth century. From the latter part of the period however come the first stages of eastern monastic literature, sayings and

anecdotes about the desert fathers of Egypt, and here we find an
interesting social mixture of illiterate country people and members
of the upper class like Arsenius. From the late fourth and fifth
centuries onwards Christians begin to be buried in churches, and
to record their burials in simple funerary epitaphs; these usually
tell us little about the person commemorated except for his or
her name, but their directness contrasts with the much more
elaborate epitaphs that the better-off were still commissioning for
themselves.

While the appearance of cities was slowly beginning to change as
more and more churches were built, people continued to live in the
same kind of houses as in earlier periods. For the rich, the 'peristyle
house', with its rooms built round a central colonnaded court,
continued in use in most cities until the sixth century. Grand
mosaics were installed in many such buildings in the fourth
century. Notable examples are those at Apamea in Syria, home of
the Neoplatonist philosopher Iamblichus, and Paphos in Cyprus,
depicting more or less philosophical subjects such as Socrates,
the Seven Sages, Orpheus and Aion. A connection has been
suggested in the case of Apamea with the pagan revival under
Julian. But house decoration did not necessarily follow the
personal affiliations of the owner, even when he was a Christian,
and classical styles and motifs remained popular for a very long
time. Christians also continued to go to the baths, the games and
the theatre, all habits on which John Chrysostom had strong and
puritanical views. Dress, jewellery and cosmetics were as popular
in the fourth century as at any other time, and dressing in sackcloth
was therefore the first requirement of asceticism. Jerome tells
Eustochium that she had better avoid married women whose
dresses are woven with gold thread, though men with long hair
wearing necklaces and bracelets were in his view just as bad an
influence. Fashion did not extend to swiftly changing styles, as it
does today. The long tunic with some kind of cloak was still
standard. What was valued most was decoration, especially
embroidery and the use of precious stones, colour and material,
especially silk. Ammianus also inveighs against excessive display:

others [he is referring to the senatorial class in Rome] think that
the height of glory is to be found in unusually high carriages and

an ostentatious style of dress; they sweat under the burden of cloaks which they attach to their necks and fasten at the throat. These being of very fine texture are easily blown about, and they contrive by frequent movements, especially of the left hand, to show off their long fringes and display the garments beneath, which are embroidered with animal figures. (XXIV.6)

Modern writers often give the impression that life in the late empire had degenerated into a state of crisis. The following statement, taken from a recent book, is by no means untypical:

In all periods of Roman history, poverty, lack of freedom and oppression were the normal facts of life for broad strata of society. But in the Late Empire the sufferings of the population were worse than ever before in some respects.

The key factors singled out are the increased element of compulsion and the alleged alienation of the mass of the population, which is said, among other things, to have led to mass desertion to the barbarians and the inability of the state to deal with the military problem: 'men preferred to live under barbarian rule as the lesser evil, compared to the system of the Roman state'. The next chapter will discuss the dealings of the late Roman state with the barbarians. As for the general issues, such historical judgements depend not only on one's own perspective, but also on where one looks.

IX

Military Affairs, Barbarians and the Late Roman Army

THE ECONOMIC AND social changes which took place in the fourth century happened against a background of constant military conflict of one kind or another. Even though the reign of Diocletian and the tetrarchy brought a degree of respite from the troubled third century, it is hard to find a time during our period when the empire enjoyed a peace of any duration, and the extravagant claims of the panegyrists tend to represent devout wishes rather than actualities.

Thus in AD 321 the Latin panegyrist Nazarius wrote of the deep peace and prosperity which the empire then supposedly enjoyed, on the eve of renewed hostilities between Constantine and Licinius. While the poet Publilius Optatianus Porfyrius (V.1 ff., XIV.9 ff.) and Eusebius (*VC* IV.7) claimed that all nations acknowledged the might of Constantine, new hostilities were breaking out between Rome and Sasanian Persia in Constantine's last years, leaving to his son Constantius II a legacy of campaigning in Mesopotamia. The first years of Constantine's reign had been spent leading a Roman army against Frankish tribes in Gaul, a period during which he built a bridge over the Rhine at Cologne to increase Roman prestige and deter further invasion (*Anon. Vales.* 8). Civil war was also going on more or less continuously during the years 306–13, and was renewed again by Constantine and Licinius in AD 316 before their final campaign in AD 324. The reign of Constantius continued the pattern: the war between Constantius and Magnentius from 350 to 353, besides distracting Constantius's attention from the east, put the west in danger and weakened Roman defences on the Rhine; Ammianus speaks in his account of Julian's campaigns in Gaul of forts and towns destroyed by barbarians (XVI.11, XVII.9–10), and the Alamanni had also penetrated across the Rhine and far into Gaul itself (XV.4).

A dangerous situation then arose: Silvanus, the general who had been put in charge of defeating the Alamanni and who was himself of Frankish origin, declared himself Augustus at Cologne (XV.5). Ammianus himself was among the officers who accompanied Ursicinus to put down the usurper, and says that he and his companions were so frightened for their own safety that they 'were like condemned criminals thrown before fierce wild beasts'. His account of the whole affair and its aftermath well illustrates the interplay of barbarians and Romans, the divided loyalties and the opportunities to which they gave rise, and the atmosphere of suspicion at court and in the field. Cologne itself was now besieged and taken by barbarians, and the job of remedying the situation in Gaul was given to the inexperienced Julian (XV.8), whose campaigns are described in detail by Ammianus. Julian proved to be a talented general, recovering Cologne and defeating a large Alamannic army in a pitched battle near Strasbourg in AD 357 (Ammianus, XVI.12), after which he crossed the Rhine, and subsequently attacked the Franks, who were occupying Roman territory (XVII.1–2, 8–10).

The campaigns in Gaul, though told by Ammianus in such as way as to enhance Julian's military reputation, are nevertheless instructive for understanding the problems which Rome faced from barbarian tribes in Gaul and Germany. First, Julian did not have an easy time: Roman arms were not automatically superior to those of the barbarians; the Alamanni had penetrated deep into Gaul and were dispersed in a number of areas, so that Roman troops were likely to find themselves surrounded; finally, they could not always rely on being welcomed by local towns, whose citizens had learned to be ready to expect anything. Ammianus's narrative enshrines the view that barbarians were unable to conduct successful sieges (XVI.4); nevertheless, many towns, including Cologne, had evidently been taken and destroyed or damaged. While the Romans might have successes, as at Strasbourg, which broke up a threatening alliance of tribes, the problem was long-term, and already involved an awkward mixture of military action, diplomatic initiatives and concessions.

The shift of Roman attention to the east with the invasions of Mesopotamia by Shapur II in AD 353 and 360, followed by Julian's disastrous Persian expedition of AD 363, on which he took an army of sixty-five thousand, encouraged new incursions across the Rhine. Diplomacy was again required in view of commitments elsewhere, and Ammianus describes Valentinian I's meeting with the Alamannic chieftain Macrianus on the Rhine near Mainz in AD 374:

> on the day appointed for the conference he [sc. Macrianus] stood majestically erect on the very bank of the Rhine, while his countrymen clashed their shields around him. From the other side the emperor, also attended by a host of officers of various ranks amid a display of gleaming standards, embarked in some river-boats and came to a safe distance from the shore. When the frantic gesticulations and chatter of the barbarians at last died down, there was much exchange of talk from both sides, and a pact of friendship was concluded and confirmed by solemn oaths. (XXX.3)

But in AD 378 Gratian was again fighting beyond the Rhine, and with some success (XXXI.10). The Danube was another traditional danger area, as were the Balkans. Constantius II, based at Sirmium, campaigned on the Danube against Sarmatians and Quadi who were threatening Pannonia and Upper Moesia in AD 358; again, he had considerable success, and having forced the Limigantes to leave, and having defeated the Sarmatians, 'he returned to Sirmium like a conqueror' (XXVII.13). Yet the Sarmatians were again petitioning Valentinian in AD 375, and the emperor, a Pannonian himself, made his base at Carnuntum on the Danube and attacked the Quadi from Aquincum (Budapest). Ammianus attributes his death, apparently from apoplexy, to the anger induced in him by the excuses of their envoys (XXX.6). The troops on the spot then proclaimed the child Valentinian II, rather than leave the Danubian front exposed, with the Emperor Gratian far away in Trier, and indeed, Gratian was deserted by his own troops when Magnus Maximus was proclaimed in Britain in AD 383 (Zosimus, IV.35). Valens, too, had campaigned on the Danube against the Goths in AD 367–9, defeating the Gothic leader Athanaric (XXVII.5).

But the greatest Roman disaster of this period in the west, and one which Ammianus viewed as being serious enough for him to use it as the terminus of his history, was the defeat and death of the Emperor Valens at Adrianople in AD 378 (Ammianus, XXXI.12–13), a shock which gave a new complexion to the whole situation and which stemmed from a variety of different factors. First appearing in the 250s, by the time Ammianus's narrative opens in AD 354, the Franks and other west German peoples such as the Alamanni are already a factor to reckon with, and individual Franks have even found their way to high-ranking positions in the Roman army. The westward movement in the fourth century of the Tervingi, the later Visigoths, the Ostrogoths and other eastern Germans was a different matter. This group of peoples had already launched attacks on Roman territory in the third century from bases north of the Black Sea, especially in the 250s, when they crossed the Black Sea itself and raided Pontos, on the Black Sea coast of Turkey (Zosimus, I.27, 31–6) . By the fourth century they evidently controlled large areas of the territory north of the Black Sea between the Danube and the Don (Dacia having been long given up as a Roman province); and they too served in the Roman army, for instance on Julian's Persian expedition (described as 'Scythians'). The Arian bishop Ulfila had spent seven years converting the Goths with the approval of Constantius II, until he was forced to leave their territory in the late 340s, and he is credited with the invention of a Gothic alphabet and the translation of the Bible into Gothic (Philostorgius, *HE* II.5). In simple terms, these Goths were now displaced by the westward and southward movement of a different and nomadic people, the Huns, who came from the steppes of central Asia, and who were so unfamiliar as to be viewed with intense fear and horror by the Romans. This is clear from remarks made by Jerome as well as from Ammianus's famous description, where they appear as barely human, living on roots and raw meat that they have softened up by riding with it between their thighs and the backs of their horses (XXXI.2).

The eastern Goths, whom Ammianus calls the Tervingi, arrived at the Danube as refugees, and as a result of a historic decision by the Emperor Valens were allowed to pass into Roman territory in AD 376, crossing, as Ammianus says, on boats and rafts and canoes made from hollowed tree-trunks. The crowd was such that, though the river is the most dangerous in the world and was then swollen by frequent rains, a large number tried to swim and were drowned in their struggle against the force of the stream. (XXXI.4)

Valens was persuaded by the promise that once admitted, the Goths would serve in the Roman army as auxiliaries, which as Ammianus says, 'seemed matter for rejoicing rather than dread', especially as Roman provinces would apparently pay highly in gold for the privilege of being relieved of their duty to provide recruits. Nevertheless, it proved to be a fateful move. The new recruits were handled badly on the Roman side, and the Goths in Thrace rebelled. Despite Roman efforts to end it, the revolt continued and when Valens eventually led out an army of 15–20,000 men against them, it was severely defeated by Visigoths and Ostrogoths at Adrianople in August, AD 378. Valens himself was killed on the field (XXXI.13; Zosimus, IV.20–4). Recent writers have pointed out that the battle of Adrianople in itself was not such a turning-point or such a catastrophe for Rome as has often been supposed, not least by the writers of the next generations who were keen to draw religious or political lessons. Thus Rufinus in his Latin continuation of Eusebius's *Church History* referred to it as 'the beginning of the calamities at that time and since' (XI.13) and Zosimus attributes it to the work of Fate (IV.24).

The military writer Vegetius claims that the death of Gratian in AD 383 marked the end of the efficiency of the Roman infantry (*De Re Milit*. I.20), and that from then on the traditional armour was given up and Roman troops lost all advantage over barbarians. However, this judgement too fails to do justice to an erosion of the difference in capabilities which had long been developing. The Goths were not sufficiently united to be a threat to the empire as such, and failed to take either Adrianople or Constantinople; Theodosius I, now Augustus, even included many of them in the new army which he raised in the Balkans, and pushed the rest back towards the Danube in AD 379, celebrating a triumph in Constantinople in 380. But the problem itself did not go away, and Gratian recognized a Gothic confederacy in Pannonia in AD 380, while Theodosius concluded a treaty with the Goths on

3 October, AD 382, which apparently assigned them lands in northern Dacia and Thrace, between the Danube and the Balkan mountains, in return for military service as auxiliaries under their own leaders. Under the terms of the treaty they were also to be settled as a group, to be exempt from taxation and to receive a yearly payment – all of which set momentous precedents (see Zosimus, IV.30,33,40,56) . That they were not given *conubium*, the right to intermarry with Roman citizens, further set them apart and stood in the way of assimilation. Furthermore, the frontier along the lower Danube, their own area of settlement, was thus protected by the Visigoths themselves.

The policy of using Gothic auxiliaries, and of rewarding them with land, was not the invention of Theodosius I, though the treaty of AD 382 took it a significant step further and Theodosius has consequently been blamed for its later ill-effects. The award of land has also been challenged, with the suggestion that what was offered was not land itself but tax-revenues from certain lands; however, Pacatus, in his panegyric to Theodosius of AD 389, refers explicitly to admission of Goths into service 'to supply soldiers for your camps and farmers for our lands' (*Pan. Lat.* XII.22). Gifts of money and supplies to barbarian tribes were also a well-established fact of life, whether or not they were referred to by the charged term of 'tribute'. Themistius can claim that earlier tribute had been stopped as a result of Gratian's treaty of AD 369:

No one saw gold coin counted out for the barbarians, countless talents of silver, ships freighted with fabrics, or any of the things we were in the habit of tolerating before . . . paying yearly tribute, which we were not ashamed to do, although we refused to call it by that name. (*Or.* 10. 205/135)

But Themistius's speech is highly tendentious, and if the tribute stopped at all, it was soon resumed.

Theodosius's policy was no more than a stop-gap measure which did little to remove the danger or to address fundamental problems; these problems became more difficult during the years between the emperor's death in 395 and AD 410, with the emergence of Alaric as leader of the Visigoths. There were now separate eastern and western governments, and this made it easier for barbarian leaders to play off one against the other; during these years Alaric consistently demanded annual cash payments and food, and for himself the post of *magister militum*. Stilicho at first attempted to use him and then was forced to meet him in battle in Italy at Pollentia (AD 402). Five years later in AD 407 he made a treaty with him which conceded Alaric's demands in return for his allegiance; such concessions however resulted in Stilicho being declared a public enemy by the east (Zosimus, V.29, Olympiodorus, fr. 5). The eastern government turned against the use of barbarian generals, and the garrison of the Goth Gainas was massacred at Constantinople in AD 400.

Though the politics of these years are extremely complex and hard to follow in detail, the importance of this change for the future of the eastern empire was very great. The west was not so fortunate. When Stilicho's offer to pay four thousand pounds of gold to Alaric was rejected and Stilicho himself fell from power in AD 408, Alaric invaded Italy and blockaded Rome (Zosimus, V.38–43). Soon the terrified Senate had agreed to pay him much more than Stilicho had promised, but Alaric marched on Rome again and this time entered the city and proclaimed a puppet emperor. When he himself began to lose the support of other Goths, his army sacked Rome for three days in late August, AD 410 (Olympiodorus, fr.3), an event which shocked Jerome when he heard of it in his monastic cell in Bethlehem: 'who could believe', he wrote in his commentary on the book of Ezekiel, 'that after being raised up by victories over the whole world Rome should come crashing down, and become at once the mother and the grave of her peoples?' Christian efforts to explain and justify to pagans the fact that the Christian city of Rome had been taken and sacked, and still more the fact that it had been taken and sacked by other Christians, led to the writing of Orosius's apologetic *Historia contra paganos* and ultimately to Augustine's masterpiece, the *City of God* (see Chapter XII).

The same period had seen further major incursions: a rebellion in Britain in AD 406 culminated in the proclamation of the usurper Constantine as Augustus, while a large group of Vandals, Sueves and Alans crossed the frozen Rhine at the end of the same year and had reached Spain by AD 409. Constantine crossed into Gaul, set up a base at Arles and even made for Italy; though the

Emperor Honorius managed to send troops and to have him executed, the Roman army seems to have been withdrawn from Britain after four centuries of Roman occupation, and the British cities were told in a letter of Honorius that they would have to look to their own security henceforth (Zosimus, VI.5).

Hindsight is easy: if only contemporaries had realized, they would have made the best of it and assimilated the barbarians properly rather than trying vainly to keep them out or patch up unsatisfactory alliances. But it was not only inability to foresee the future but also contemporary ideology that kept the Romans from being so prudent. They were not guilty of racism; nevertheless, following Greek precedent, they saw the divide between barbarians and Romans as a gulf between boorishness and civilization. As a Vandal, Stilicho was always suspect because he was of barbarian origin, and there is no clearer indication of typical attitudes than the poems of the fifth-century bishop Sidonius Apollinaris who lived surrounded by barbarians himself in Gaul and who prided himself on maintaining civilized manners amid such boorishness. We must also remember that contemporaries saw the invasions in terms of individual raids rather than as a long-term process – indeed, the reasons for the invasions are still far from clear today. The old notion of barbarian hordes being 'pushed' against the frontiers of the empire has been exploded; first, actual numbers were probably quite small, and second, this model does not explain why the Huns themselves left their home in central Asia. Equally, the 'Hun empire' of Attila (d. AD 453) is a fifth-century phenomenon which postdates the migrations and was not their cause. A different kind of explanation would see the movement of the Ostrogoths in terms of changing economic conditions in the area between the Don and the Dniester, and set the whole phenomenon in the context of the relation between settled and nomadic societies. Contemporaries were more likely themselves to point to an alleged weakening of the Roman frontiers as explanation for the barbarian inroads. In practice the fourth-century emperors up to the time of Theodosius I were able for the most part to deal with the situation, though it took much time and expense; only in the fifth century did the invaders penetrate so deeply into Roman territory as to require settlement and to threaten the unity of the western provinces. Yet once that process began it progressed with astonishing ease and speed, a modest band of eighty thousand Vandals having successfully taken over the whole of Roman North Africa by AD 439. By that time the Roman army in the west was in severe difficulties, a subject to which we must shortly turn.

First, however, these events in the west and north of the empire must be set against the context of what was happening on the eastern frontier with Persia. The wars between Rome and Sasanid Persia were of a different kind; this was a case of two empires in a more or less permanent state of conflict, but one in which a kind of balance of power was maintained until the final stage in the early seventh century. The Sasanians periodically invaded Roman territory and carried back large quantities of tribute, plunder and prisoners to Persia, where the latter were settled on occasion in new cities. This was the case with the citizens of Antioch who were captured when Shapur I took the city in AD 260; on this occasion the Emperor Valerian was taken prisoner, carried off to Persia and subsequently put to death in humiliating circumstances. All these events were recorded on a grandiose trilingual inscription (Parsi, Pahlavi and Greek) set up by Shapur I near Persepolis, known as the *Res gestae divi Saporis*. On one of several similar raids into Mesopotamia and Syria by Chosroes I in the sixth century, Antioch was again taken and sacked by the Persians (AD 540). During the fourth century, Constantius II made his headquarters at Antioch for annual campaigns against the Persians from AD 338 to 346, during which time the Persians under Shapur II several times besieged the border fortress of Nisibis, attacking it once more in AD 350, though again without lasting success. Julian's Persian expedition and the treaty of AD 363 resulted in the ceding of Nisibis to Persia, but this was exceptional, and after this date neither side made significant gains until the seventh century.

Roman investment in the eastern frontier areas, which had been growing steadily since the Severan period when they annexed Northern Mesopotamia, where all the campaigns of Constantius II were also fought, was now extremely heavy. There was no natural frontier: in the fourth century, after Diocletian's reorganization, Roman forces were stationed in forts along the so-called *strata Diocletiana*, a military road running from north-east Arabia and

Damascus to Palmyra and the Euphrates, and along another road from Damascus to Palmyra.

Legionary bases were usually in major towns, for instance Aela (Aqaba, on the Red Sea), Udruh, Bostra, Palmyra, Sura and Circesium on the Euphrates, and in the north legions were based at Singara (before AD 363, when it was ceded to the Persians with Nisibis) and even further north at Melitene, Satala and Trapezus. Though these legions were not large in comparison with those of the early empire, the amount of military building is impressive and considerable attention was evidently paid to good communications and ease of movement. The function of the installations is a matter of dispute. Edward Luttwak's influential book, *The Grand Strategy of the Roman Empire*, supports the common idea of a policy of 'defence-in-depth', whereby the frontier forces were to be reinforced at need by a mobile army, and this conception has been widely followed. However, other studies, especially those by Mann, Graf and Isaac, have shown that it is supported neither by the literary nor by the physical evidence. Soldiers in the east in the later empire were dispersed, there was no clear distinction between frontier troops and the mobile army (see below), and forts had as much to do with internal security as with defence against putative invasion, while the statements in literary sources often cited, including a description of Arabia in Ammianus (XIV.8), are too vague to be of real help. A large part of the problem lies with the identification of the military sites themselves; scholars have been too hasty in concluding that they can only be forts, and that their purpose must therefore be defensive. But as Isaac points out, similar structures existed in Egypt, where there was no comparable question of frontier defence, and some may actually have been guard posts, watering stations or halting places along communication routes, or indeed they may have performed several functions at once. Much of this still remains highly problematic, and is currently the subject of much scholarly activity. A further distinction needs to be made between the northern and southern sectors of the eastern frontier areas; military activity against Persia was concentrated in the north, while in the south, in Palestine, Arabia and southern Syria, though there was less danger from that source, it has been suggested that increased insecurity in the face of threats from nomad tribes may account for the level of military installations. Long-term changes taking place in the balance of local populations in Arabia and southern Palestine perhaps also contributed to instability. But none of this is yet fully clear, and even if it were, it is unlikely that the reasons were conceptualized in these terms by the Romans themselves. On the whole, Roman interest in southern Arabia and Ethiopia seems to have been commercial and diplomatic rather than military.

Whatever the reasons, focusing attention on the eastern frontier regions had cultural as well as military implications; these will be discussed further in Chapter XI. As for Roman military involvement in the east during our period, Isaac points to three noteworthy features. They are, first, an increased focus on the north-east from the late fourth century on; this is connected with the appearance of the Huns, who had penetrated Persian territory already in the mid-fourth century and after 394 invaded Persia, Melitene, Syria and Cilicia. Armenia had already been a centre of operations under Diocletian and in AD 335 it was again invaded by Persia; since it had been Christian since AD 314, as had Iberia in the Caucasus since soon after AD 324, religious factors made these regions an object of dispute between Rome and Persia, and this was still an issue in the sixth century. The Christian population of Persia itself had also featured in the diplomatic relations between the two powers since Constantine, whose letter to Shapur II on the subject is preserved by Eusebius (VC IV.8–13).

The second feature to be noted is the use made by both sides of nomad allies or federates, called 'Saracens' by Ammianus and criticized by him, with typical hostility to 'barbarians' (e.g. XIV.4). This was not dissimilar from the Roman way of dealing with German federates in the west; it continued until the sixth century, when the Romans and the Persians respectively made heavy use of the tribal groups known as Ghassanids and Lakhmids. In the earlier period the Romans relied on the Tanukh west of the Euphrates and later the Salih, in the desert of Syria and Mesopotamia. By these means Roman forces themselves could eventually be heavily reduced, as they apparently were in the east after the peace between Rome and Persia in AD 532. But though it is so conspicuous a feature of the next two centuries in the east, there was certainly nothing very new in using tribes and their chiefs in this way. The famous Namara inscription of AD 328, written in Arabic but in Nabataean letters, celebrates a certain Imru'l-qais, son of 'Amr, a tribal chief, apparently a Lakhmid, who is described as 'king of all the Arabs, crowned with the diadem'; the inscription lists his subjection of other tribes as far afield as central and southern Arabia, and his placing of his sons at their head. Several scholars believe that Imru'l-qais was an ally of the Romans, and he was indeed buried in Roman territory next to a Roman fort, but the inscription presents considerable philological difficulties and the problem is compounded by the existence of a later Imru'l-qais with whom this one can easily be confused. About AD 376, however, we are on somewhat firmer ground with a certain queen Mavia (Mawiya), who took over the leadership ('phylarchate') of the 'Saracen' allies of Rome on the death of her husband and led them in attacks on Roman territory from Phoenicia and Palestine as far as Egypt. This posed considerable danger to Rome, as the church historian Sozomen says: 'this war was by no means a contemptible one, although conducted by a woman' (*HE* VI.38). Mavia agreed to make peace, and an alliance with Rome, only if a certain Christian hermit called Moses from the desert of Sinai (Theodoret, *HE* IV.23), himself an Arab, was consecrated bishop of her people, and when this was done, he is said to have converted many Arabs to Christianity (see especially Sozomen, *HE* VI.38, with Socrates, *HE* IV.36, from Rufinus, *HE* II.6) . The balance between nomads and sedentaries was evidently shifting, especially in southern Palestine, causing Arab raids to become a major problem for Rome. Her initial response was to build up the level of military forts and installations, but alliances with the Arab tribes in southern Palestine and elsewhere were also a feature of fourth-century policy, and a law of the fifth century refers to payment of the *annona* to Arab *foederati* (*CTh.*, *NTh.* 24.2).

Finally, fourth-century military history in the east is characterized by a concentration on Mesopotamia, where hostilities centred on fortified cities such as Singara, Dara, Amida, Zenobia and Sergiopolis. From the fourth century onwards the Persians regularly attacked such cities or demanded substantial payments from their inhabitants, who were often simply left to fend for themselves by the Roman army. By this means pitched battles between Roman and Persian forces could be avoided and after

AD 363 the border itself remained stable for a long time.

Nevertheless, however its aims are assessed, Roman military involvement in the east continued up to the sixth century, and the Emperor Heraclius in the seventh century was even able (though with great difficulty) to reverse the consequences of the recent disastrous Persian invasion led by Chosroes II. This is in great contrast to the situation in the west, where already in the early fifth century the Roman army was beginning to disintegrate. Roman forces were withdrawn from both Britain and most of Spain; the ease of the Vandal conquest of North Africa can only be explained by lack of Roman opposition, and indeed the troops had been shipped to Italy not long before to engage in civil war there. In Gaul, progressive settlement of barbarian groups, starting with the Visigoths in Aquitaine in AD 418, reduced the geographical competence of the Roman army, whose numbers also shrank. The complex situation of these years, for which we have to rely on Gallic and Spanish chronicles, makes it clear that the government in Ravenna was in no position to do much more than to play one set of barbarians against another, and eventually to look on as Gaul gradually fragmented. One feature of these years was the use made of Hun mercenaries; another was the quickly growing importance of powerful generals such as Flavius Aetius, who actually ran the western empire from AD 433 to 454. The Huns also extracted annual tribute from the eastern emperor, and when the Emperor Marcian (AD 450–7) put a stop to this they turned westwards and invaded Italy in AD 452; however, by an extraordinary stroke of luck for Rome, Attila their king died suddenly the following year, whereupon the Hun empire broke up.

With the exception of Ammianus's campaign narratives, judgements about the late Roman army in the literary sources are not very helpful, particularly as later writers invariably looked back for explanations of what they naturally saw as military decline and collapse. Their answer is usually rather simplistic – the frontiers had not been properly defended. Thus the anonymous author of the treatise *De Rebus Bellicis*, written in the late 360s, believes both that too much is being spent on the army and that the frontiers are too weak, and intends to propose remedies for both ills:

I shall describe how, with a reduction of the taxes by one half, the farmer in the provinces may be restored to his traditional prosperity; how also, with the abolition of abuses in the system of taxation, the frontier-dweller may do honour to the lonely stretches of the imperial boundaries in safety, after the erection of fortified defences. (*De Rebus Bellicis*, 1)

The 'vast expenditure on the army' must be cut, he says, since it is distorting the whole tax system (*ibid.* 5); his programme for reform includes a system of quick promotion combined with early retirement, with the frontier territories to be farmed by veterans, who would thus also be taxpayers. Thus the anonymous writer shared the view of some modern historians, including A. H. M. Jones, that the overall tax burden was simply too high; however, there is no indication that anyone took any notice of his ideas, any more than they did of the ingenious machines and inventions which he proposes for military use. The literary sources on the army are also characterized by religious bias; thus the pagan tradition represented by Zosimus (II.34) blames Constantine for weakening the frontier defences and giving the barbarians 'unhindered access to the Roman empire'. According to this scenario, Diocletian was the hero, fortifying the entire frontier and devoting all the army's resources to that end, so that no barbarians could cross, whereas Constantine is alleged to have removed troops from the frontiers and stationed them in cities

which did not need assistance, thus both stripping of protection those being molested by the barbarians and subjecting the cities left alone by them to the outrages of the soldiers, so that henceforth most have become deserted. Moreover, he enervated the troops by allowing them to devote themselves to shows and luxuries. In plain terms, Constantine was the origin and beginning of the present destruction of the empire.

It was of course easy to complain about the behaviour of soldiers billeted in cities, but the fact was that the uses to which the late Roman army was put had also changed. For one thing, requisitioning of the *annona* in kind made for a closer relation, not always a happy one, between taxpayers and soldiers, and soldiers were themselves also employed in collecting taxes, for instance in Egypt, where the papyri reveal the existence of a good deal of local friction as a result. Collection and transportation of the *annona* gave rise to obvious problems and resentments, as well as to corruption, for which those caught risked torture. Other sources of problems were the system of *angareia*, requisition of transport, the subject of Libanius, *Or.* 1, and the compulsory billeting of soldiers, on which the codes register many complaints and testify to many exemptions given out by the emperors in response. Thus if the level and frequency of complaints about soldiers in the sources rises, it is because they inevitably impinge more on the lives of provincials. Yet another burden was that of providing recruits or paying money in lieu; even if recruits were available, it was tempting for the government to ask for money instead, and recruits were not always available. A law of AD 412 justifies the practice:

> The necessities of the exhausted treasury require the payment of commutation money for the purchase of recruits and horses. (*CTh.* XI.18)

As we have already noted, Valens allowed the Goths into Thrace in AD 376 with the welcome thought that the provinces could thus be asked for gold instead of recruits (Ammianus, XXXI.4). According to this short-sighted policy, it seemed easier and more profitable for the state effectively to buy in barbarian mercenaries, avoiding the trouble of conscription in its own provinces and (if it was lucky) exacting payment instead. There were also times when recruits were desperately needed, as in the years immediately after Adrianople, when both the law-codes and the literary sources indicate that both conscription and the recruiting of barbarians took place on a massive scale and in great haste.

We must return to the question of army size (see also Chapter III). There could hardly have been such need to resort to barbarian federates, if Jones was right to take the information on army units given in the early fifth-century *Notitia Dignitatum* as suggesting a regular army of over six hundred thousand. As he himself realized, these calculations may be too high in themselves, but it is also very likely that the total of 645,000 given by Agathias is a paper figure only, not representing the actual numbers in about AD 425.

It is certainly hard to believe in such a total in view of the retreat of the Roman army from the western provinces in the early fifth century noted above. In any event, there was evidently no regular field army as such which could be used against barbarian leaders like Tribigild or Gainas, or there would not have been such a need either to try to turn them against each other or to use Uldin and his Huns. In the west, allied federates effectively replaced a Roman field army altogether during the fifth century, with predictable results.

Was the late Roman army also ineffective as a fighting force? This has often been suspected (and is argued by A. Ferrill as though the argument is a novelty) but is very difficult to establish. The army's decline as a fighting force is assumed on several grounds: first, on the *a priori* argument that barbarian mercenaries must be less effective than a citizen army, especially when used against other barbarians; second, on the grounds that the mass of the population, by definition including the army rank and file, was disaffected and alienated; third, on the grounds that the so-called *limitanei* on the frontiers were part-time peasant-soldiers, who could not be expected to be much use in time of actual war; finally, on the grounds that the late Roman army was often defeated in practice. Most of these arguments are highly subjective, though they come from differing points of view; typical is the statement that the 'inability of the western empire to withstand the pressure of the barbarian peoples in the fifth century . . . was especially the result of the alienation of society from the state' (G. Alföldy). As for the *limitanei*, whether or not they were any good as soldiers, the term itself does not not come into being for frontier troops until the late fourth century, and then not for a 'peasant militia', but simply for 'troops in the frontier zone'. Thus they cannot bear the responsibility for decline which has often been assigned to them.

It is also the case that whereas there is a good deal of suspicion directed at individual barbarian generals such as Stilicho, there is little if any direct evidence either of barbarian mercenaries in the ranks or of federate forces defecting to the opposite side; the argument imposes modern preconceptions on a quite different situation. There was indeed much hostility to barbarian troops as such, which shows itself clearly in relation to Stilicho's barbarian recruits. When a rumour came in AD 408 that the Emperor

Arcadius had died, the situation for Stilicho was extremely difficult, with Alaric and his army on the one hand and the usurper Constantine on the other; he had to face mutiny in his own ranks, and several important officials including the praetorian prefect were murdered by the soldiers. It was not clear whether the Emperor Honorius himself was safe. Should he too turn out to have been killed, it was debated whether to let the barbarian troops loose on the Roman soldiers to take reprisals; this was prevented by Stilicho on the grounds that the Roman soldiers were too numerous and the prospect therefore too risky (Zosimus, V.31–3). Within days, however, Stilicho himself had lost his imperial support and without allowing his barbarian guard to defend him, voluntarily submitted to the party sent to Ravenna to arrest and execute him (V.34). At this point the regular soldiers in the surrounding cities of north Italy fell upon the families of the barbarians recruited by Stilicho, killed them and seized their property, whereupon the barbarian troops themselves, said to be thirty thousand in number, decided to join Alaric (V.35).

These circumstances are however exceptional; it was not just the barbarians but also the regular army that was in disarray. It was rivalry between politicians and generals which provoked dangerous barbarian interventions rather than the divided loyalty of individual soldiers on the field, and the early years of the fifth century marked a crisis point in this regard. In the east, by AD 399 the Goths Tribigild and Gainas had acquired a dangerous position, both having followings of Gothic recruits; by devious means Gainas secured imperial support from Arcadius, brought about the fall of the powerful eunuch Eutropius, apparently secured the submission of Tribigild, and was then able to terrorize both the emperor and Constantinople itself. At this point however (AD 400) things went dramatically wrong for him, and instead of his barbarians taking the city, the citizens themselves rose up and massacred seven thousand Arian Goths by setting fire to the church in which they had taken refuge; Gainas himself (who had left the city earlier) had no choice but to face armed attack, and was in due course killed by a Hunnic force led by a certain Uldin or Uldes (Zosimus, V. 17–22). The version of Zosimus depends on the pagan historian Eunapius, whose work was also used by the ecclesiastical historians Socrates and Sozomen, who however tell a different story which emphasizes the religious factors and presents the fall of Gainas as divinely ordained. Synesius, later bishop of Ptolemais, who was in Constantinople as an ambassador from Cyrene, also wrote of these events in the *De Providentia*, a highly literary and allegorical work in which political personages are disguised as figures in the myth of Isis and Osiris. Finally, John Chrysostom, who was bishop of Constantinople at the time, also played an active, though perhaps somewhat equivocal role. He allowed Gainas and his Goths to use one of the city churches, though he tried to prevent them from holding Arian services in it, and he had acted as an ambassador to Gainas. There is no sermon extant on the burning of the Goths inside the church, but this shocking event touched John closely, since it violated asylum, and he himself had been under criticism for surrendering Eutropius, who had also taken refuge in a church. The essential issues in these events, which are extremely difficult to disentangle in detail, are political rather than military. They concern not only the danger of relying on barbarian generals, but also the position of the emperor *vis-à-vis* his ministers, and reflect the jostling for position which took place in both eastern and western courts after the death of Theodosius I. The difference was, as W. Liebeschuetz has pointed out, that in the east the Gainas affair produced a lasting reluctance to depend on extensive barbarian recruitment; when Uldin invaded Thrace in AD 408 and was defeated, his men were dispersed as settlers rather than enrolled as federates (*CTh.* V.6.3). The contrast with the west could not be greater: the fall of Stilicho in the same year was succeeded by Alaric's march on Rome, and by years more of threats by individual barbarian leaders and their armies. But deeper structural factors, both political and economic, were also responsible for the difference; during the fifth century, while the west fragmented, emperors became weaker and more and more starved of resources, the east became steadily more prosperous, able to buy off barbarians at need. Finally, the less grand but more integrated senatorial class of the east allowed the development of the more stable and essentially civilian government which can be seen during the reign of Theodosius II and later.

X

Culture in the Late Fourth Century

FOR THE SAKE OF of simplicity, this book separates out various ways of looking at late Roman social organization: economic, military, religious, political, without debating the issue of whether such a separation is really the best way of studying history. By 'culture' we mean the conglomerate of ideas and information on which each society depends for its communal identity, and which is passed on through processes of learning and training. This in fact includes much of what has been treated in other chapters: knowledge of how one's society is organized politically, for instance, is learned, not innate, and general agreement as to the political framework binds a society together. Religion certainly belongs to the realm of culture, and presupposes a certain view of how the world is or should be organized. But the term 'culture' is also commonly used in a narrower sense, to indicate the fields of learning, education, habits and taste.

We have become accustomed in the modern world to the idea of a plurality of cultures, and to the view of a multicultural society as a desirable aim; however, the latter ('the terrors of multiplicity', in the words of a recent writer) can be difficult to accommodate both for individuals and groups. In contrast, traditional societies are usually dominated by a single culture. Yet though a traditional society, the late Roman empire was geographically vast, and comprised many different individual cultures. Moreover, late Roman society itself was changing fast in several important ways: barbarians (outsiders) were becoming prominent, serving in the army or settling within the empire; the advance of Christianity brought social as well as religious change; the gap between rich and poor was in some aspects widening. All this led to variety, but also at times to conflict.

One such tension was in the field of education. There was of course no state system of education as such, and schools and especially higher education were for the better-off; nevertheless, the demand for a traditional training based on grammar and rhetoric (the standard type of education available) was high, and grammarians, teachers in the schools, and still more, rhetors, who taught at higher level, enjoyed high status. The workings of the bureaucracy and civic life at local level both demanded rhetorical skills for the many formal speeches delivered on public occasions, and these skills could lead in turn to personal advancement, as was the case with Ausonius of Bordeaux. Nazarius under Constantine, Themistius under Constantius II and later emperors, Pacatus under Theodosius I and countless unnamed others composed imperial panegyrics for formal occasions. The same practice was also extended to important Christian events such as the dedication of a major church. Eusebius's speech at the dedication of the Church of the Holy Sepulchre in Jerusalem in AD 335 was only one of several given on the occasion. Eusebius also composed a Christian panegyric for Constantine's thirtieth anniversary. The Latin poems of Claudian, written for occasions such as imperial consulships, had a similar function; all of these categories of public oratory might also have a strongly political content. A rhetorical education was therefore a saleable commodity, which parents wanted for their sons; we can see this illustrated vividly in Augustine's account of his own training and early career in Carthage and Rome. Most of the well-known bishops of the period, like Basil of Caesarea, who studied in Athens, had had a similar education themselves.

The culture that was handed on in this way was strictly classical in character, still based on the standard authors – in Latin, Cicero, Sallust, Livy, Horace and Virgil. No subjects such as maths, geography or even history were studied as such, and the training had little relevance to everyday life, and was largely confined to an elite. Though there was no state system in a modern sense, teachers were nevertheless granted privileges by the state, and in AD 425 the Emperor Theodosius II founded a 'university' in Constantinople; the subjects taught were 'Latin eloquence', divided into oratory and grammar, and 'Greek *facundia*' (a different word for the same thing), the teaching of which was divided between sophists and grammarians, in addition to one philosopher and two lawyers, for 'the more profound knowledge and learning' (*CTh*. XIV.9.3). These provisions underline the fact that the only alternatives to rhetoric were philosophy or law, each regarded as more specialized.

Julian, who had experienced it himself, was exceptional in recognizing the important influence teachers could exert in social terms (see Chapter VI), and in general the system as such was not questioned. It did not encourage any kind of original thought or experimentation, but concentrated on thorough learning, exposition and imitation of the great writers of the past. Inevitably it had a great effect on the style and content of what those who had experienced it wrote themselves. Thoughtful Christians however who had been through the standard education themselves sometimes found themselves in difficulties. First of all, much classical literature was either directly or indirectly concerned with pagan gods and pagan mythology. Some Christians therefore argued that it should be avoided altogether, while others, like Basil, who wrote a treatise on Greek literature addressed to his nephews, argued that only the useful parts should be read and the rest avoided. The conflict also affected individuals: Jerome felt guilty about his love of Cicero, and Augustine was deeply torn throughout his life between the classical learning which he had imbibed and taught himself, and his later conviction that knowledge could not come from secular learning, but only from God. He discussed the problems directly in two important works, the *De Doctrina Christiana* ('On Christian Learning') and the *De Magistro* ('On the Teacher'). A further source of tension was the fact that Christianity directed itself at men and women of all classes. This was certainly not the case with classical education, and indeed many educated Christian writers, including Jerome, felt uncomfortable about the 'simplicity' of Christian literature, which had supposedly developed from what they called *sermo piscatorius* ('the language of fishermen'). Reaching the uneducated members of the congregation was nevertheless seen as an important duty; bishops such as Ambrose were concerned about the means of bringing about the conversion of the *rustici* (rural population) and Augustine had a keen awareness of how to reach them in a sermon. Yet it has been rightly pointed out that this did not lead to a Christian programme of education as such. Churchmen wanted to convert, but to think of doing so in the context of schools or of improving standards of literacy is a modern idea. Indeed, literacy as a whole did not increase in this period, and with the fragmentation of the west it more probably declined.

By the fifth century, when churches were beginning to be decorated with narrative scenes from Christian mythology, it was recognized that these could also be a way of educating the illiterate. But the relation between Christian and secular learning still produced unease. Some monks and hermits were uneducated themselves and aggressively anti-intellectual, but others had come from comfortable backgrounds. A number of the bishops and theologians of the day, such as Basil of Caesarea and Epiphanius of Salamis in Cyrus, had also spent periods of religious withdrawal in the desert. The ascetic writer Evagrius of Pontos had been part of the circle of Basil and Gregory Nazianzen, had attended the Council at Constantinople in AD 381 and been nursed during an illness in Jerusalem by the Elder Melania before he became a monk at Nitria and Kellia in Egypt. The other monks were uncomfortably conscious of his learning, and after he had discoursed on one occasion, he accepted the implied rebuke when one said to him,

> Abba, we know that if you were living in your own country you would probably be a bishop and a great leader, but at present you sit here as a stranger. (trans. Ward, 64)

While in symbolic terms, the 'city' signified worldliness and temptation, 'the desert' ascetic virtue, in practice there was frequent contact between the two, and 'the desert' was populated by the educated as well as by the rustic. Nevertheless, education in such circumstances came to stand for worldly culture, and its rejection became a *topos* of ascetic literature, like the rejection of marriage. Once in the desert, ascetics tended to adopt a hostile stance towards learning. But in other circles learning directed to Christian ends was enthusiastically pursued, and the ascetic women of Jerome's circle combined an ultra-harsh lifestyle with a zeal for scholarship which extended even to the Hebrew Bible.

Such a situation gave plenty of scope for personal uncertainty, and we can see in many cases that the theme of education itself had taken on a contentious aura. Gregory of Nyssa makes a favourable comparison between his sister Macrina, educated at home on the Psalms, and his brother Basil, fresh from the learned circles of Athens. John Chrysostom's sermons proclaim the triumph of fishermen over philosophers, even while the speaker drew on a solid traditional education himself. They also vehemently attack secular culture in general, especially those aspects to which his Christian audience was evidently addicted, such as the theatre, chariot races, fine clothes and other kinds of adornment, love of money and possessing unnecessary numbers of slaves. Some received a mainly Christian education, but there were still no Christian schools to compare with the traditional grammarian. Thus sermons such as these constituted a form of Christian education, expounding the Scriptures, conveying basic Christian teachings and telling Christians what they must not do. Moreover, though much of John's attack is directed at the rich citizens of Antioch and Constantinople, sermons in general were aimed at all classes. In church, ordinary people and cultivated society alike were at the receiving end of the same precepts.

The ideal upbringing for Christian children, according to John Chrysostom and others, should be carefully regulated by the parents so as to avoid undesirable influences and inculcate Christian principles; however, the various works of instruction which survive, such as John's *Address on Vainglory and the Right Way for Parents to Bring Up Their Children*, suggest that most failed to reach these standards. Augustine's account of his own development in the *Confessions* shows himself and other young men of an older age group swayed by different influences, searching among competing philosophies – Neoplatonism, Manichaeism, Christianity – and trying out different lifestyles. Augustine's circle experimented with communal living and his friends included at different times Firminus, apparently a member of the administration, Romanianus, an old friend from home, Alypius, also from Thagaste, who became a lawyer, Nebridius, a close friend from Carthage and Verecundus, a rhetor at Milan. Limited though the contemporary forms of cultural transmission were in comparison with modern society, the effective influences on them came via reading, personal contacts and anecdotes, much as anyone's experience might be formed today.

Classical culture was high culture, confined to the wealthier classes. Books, like education, were expensive and hard to get, and a high proportion of the poorer classes will have been either illiterate or barely literate. The narrowness of elite culture also powerfully militated against the possibility of assimilation between Romans and barbarians. With Christianity, the poor and the lower classes received more attention. Even so, at this period the cultural tensions between pagans and Christians that are revealed to us in the sources are largely those between different members of the same class. Of these we hear a great deal, while we are badly informed in contrast about the many lower-class Christians in the city congregations, or about the social origins of the bands of monks who caused so much trouble in the 390s. Similarly, the paganism of Julian, for instance, was a very highbrow affair, and while we have a lot of information about such matters as Neoplatonism, we know far less about ordinary pagans on an individual basis.

One place and period from which a large concentration of evidence has survived is late fourth-century Rome, where advancing Christianity threatened the values and the social equilibrium of the senatorial class, and where pagan members of the great families were liable to be confronted with unseemly scuffles between groups of Christians supporting rival candidates for the post of bishop (Ammianus claims that 137 corpses were found in the basilica of Sicininus during the bloody preliminaries to the election of Pope Damasus in AD 366 – XXVII.3). In this milieu, individual conversion and the prospect of a more stringently Christian policy on the part of the emperors presented themselves in sharp social and class terms. Men like Praetextatus and Symmachus, who were emotionally committed to a self-identity which included continued attachment to pagan cult, viewed with dismay the strong influence of Ambrose on imperial policy, and some took their paganism to the lengths of open opposition, like Nicomachus Flavianus, who committed suicide when Eugenius was defeated in AD 394. But Ammianus' denunciation of the *mores* of the Roman senatorial class does not suggest that religion came high on the list of priorities for more than a few. Most were concerned with maintaining their luxurious way of life, with little concern for serious things:

> the few houses which once had the reputation of being centres of serious culture are now given over to the trivial pursuits of passive idleness. (XIV.6, cf. XXVIII.4)

We should not think of a general 'pagan revival' in this period centred round a clearly demarcated 'circle of Symmachus', as formerly proposed, but rather of a range of attitudes existing among the pagan upper class, from commitment to pagan cult and Roman tradition down to a simple fondness for the status quo. It is also necessary to distinguish between literature which preserves or revives classical (and therefore pagan) precedents, and works which are directly anti-Christian in character. Most belong to the former category; several works which have been assumed to be works of 'pagan propaganda', or otherwise anti-Christian in character, have now been shown either to be quite neutral, or to have been wrongly dated. This is the case with the so-called *Saturnalia* of Macrobius, a kind of miscellany in the form of a dialogue in which the principal speakers are Praetextatus and Symmachus, and whose dramatic date is placed on the eve of Praetextatus's death in AD 384. This work is now seen to belong to the following generation, and is not therefore a document of the supposed late fourth-century pagan revival at all; the same goes for Servius's great commentary on Virgil. Ammianus has also been supposed to be the mouthpiece of these pagan senators, but there is no evidence to support such a view, and his violent criticism of this class makes it hard to see him as its protégé. Yet another case in point is provided by the *Historia Augusta*, the compilation of imperial biographies purporting to be the work of six authors writing under Constantine, but actually the work of a single author, probably writing in the early 390s. This strange work, more scandal sheet than history, but unfortunately an essential source, in particular for the badly documented third century, has been the subject of vigorous scholarly controversy, both as to its date and its purpose. Claims that it was meant as pagan propaganda fail however before the simple fact that the alleged propaganda is so well hidden as to be nearly impossible to detect. It is far more likely to have been a product devised to satisfy the taste of the senatorial class for sensational reading, on which Ammianus comments:

> some of them hate learning like poison, but read Juvenal and Marius Maximus [another imperial biographer] with avidity. These are the only volumes that they turn over in their idle moments, but why this should be so is not for a man like me to say. (XXVIII.4)

His disingenuous concluding remark conceals the well-known fact that Juvenal's satires and Marius Maximus' lives alike were notorious for their prurient content.

But despite Ammianus's scorn, a number of these Roman aristocrats did interest themselves in the copying of earlier Latin literature, mainly the standard works by Virgil, Horace, Terence, Livy and Quintilian, but also the less commonly read Silver Latin authors Martial, Juvenal and Persius. The copies which they had made were provided with elaborate *subscriptiones* (a kind of short preface) describing their editorial labours, so that we must certainly think in terms of a literary fashion. However, as Alan Cameron has pointed out, in most cases the authors whose works were re-edited were also read by Christians, who themselves shared in the enthusiasm for copying texts. The phenomenon is interesting and important, but it is not a case of classical literature having been saved for posterity by the pagan intelligensia. The case may seem rather different with Nicomachus Flavianus's Latin translation of Philostratus's *Life of Apollonius of Tyana*, a biography of a famous pagan wonder-worker which some wanted to set against the Christian Gospels; this too, however, was a work read by both Jerome and Augustine, and the translation may not have had the religious import modern scholars have imagined. Again, Christians too were translating Greek works into Latin with impressive industry; thus the works of Origen, Gregory of Nazianzus and Basil of Caesarea were all translated for a Roman patron, Apronianus. Jerome himself played an important role in encouraging such activity and in spreading knowledge of Greek Christian works, notably the *Life of Antony*, and the works translated were read by Christian ladies as well as their male relatives. Generally, then, there was an interest in reading and learning on the part of both Christians and pagans that belies the criticisms of Ammianus about the reading habits (or lack of them) of the Roman senatorial class, and there is some evidence of interaction and mutual borrowing; but we must not assume that every work written by or sponsored by a pagan was automatically meant as anti-Christian polemic.

These rich Roman families were also, naturally, patrons of the arts in other respects. We should not here think of 'works of art', or music, in the modern sense, but rather of luxurious objects which could adorn their grand houses. The late antique period, from the fourth century on, is rich in such works in two particular media, silver and ivory; both were much admired in late fourth-century Rome, and many works were commissioned by the aristocratic families themselves. Certain of these works carry dates, especially some of the ivory 'diptychs', panels carved in relief and given out to mark such occasions as consulships, but many can only be dated on stylistic grounds. Here again the persistence of classical motifs on silver plates or ivory panels has been used as a direct argument for paganism, or at the least for a 'classical revival' on the part of their owners. This is however a dangerous argument to use, and is all too likely to be circular: 'since we know there was a classical/pagan revival in the late fourth century, this or that work must belong to that period'. But Christians did not reject every element in their culture, or throw away the objects they already had, especially when they belonged to the upper class and were accustomed to being surrounded by beautiful objects in traditional style. Christianization was gradual – not every member of great Roman families such as the Anicii and the Aproniani became Christian at the same time. Finally, Christian art did not immediately and wholly reject classical style. A few examples will illustrate the point, starting with the famous ivory diptych whose two halves, showing a woman in classical drapery making an offering at an altar, and which are respectively in the Musée du Cluny, Paris, and the Victoria and Albert Museum, London, are inscribed with the names of the Nicomachi and the Symmachi, the very families so prominent in pagan circles in the period. The argument hinges on the dating of the panel, which has been assigned for obvious reasons to the supposed 'pagan revival'; other undated panels are

Half of an ivory diptych apparently showing a priestess performing religious rites, and with the inscription 'of the Symmachi'. The other half also survives, with the inscription 'of the Nicomachi'. Thus the diptych links two of the leading pagan families in Rome in the late fourth century. However, the date and explanation are both disputed: it has recently been argued that it belongs to the early fifth century.

then given similar dates by comparison with these. Once the dating is accepted, one can go on to imagine Q. Aurelius Symmachus and Nicomachus Flavianus as patrons of classicizing art, in keeping with their role as self-appointed defenders of paganism. But both families flourished into the fifth century and beyond, and the panels may well not date from the key late fourth-century period any more than do Macrobius's *Saturnalia* or Servius's Virgil commentary. Another undated panel is the very unclassical ivory in the British Museum showing a figure ascending to heaven, and below, a quadriga and four elephants. This has a monogram whose interpretation is not agreed but which may also stand for 'Symmachorum'; if so, since the panel clearly depicts a pagan *apotheosis*, at the least it illustrates that classicizing style is no sure indicator of paganism, and that works cannot be dated as though it is. Finally, the great 'Proiecta casket' in silver-gilt (see cover illustration), part of the group of silver objects in the British Museum known as the Esquiline Treasure from the place where it was originally discovered in the late eighteenth century, is a marriage casket covered with mythological, that is classical, figures and motifs, but with a Christian inscription fixed round the top: *Proiecta et Secunde, vivatis in Christo* ('Proiecta and Secundus, may you live in Christ'). A lively debate has centred on the identification of the bride and groom and therefore the date of the casket itself, with Kathleen Shelton arguing for the 350s and Alan Cameron supporting the more common dating to the 380s. In

One portion of an ivory diptych, showing symbolic scenes of a pagan funeral pyre and apotheosis. The subject has been variously identified as the Emperor Julian, or as a Symmachus, the latter on the basis of the monogram at the top of the panel; the date depends on the identification, and the diptych may be fourth or early fifth-century.

either case, we are dealing with a set of silver objects owned and presumably commissioned by members of the late Roman senatorial aristocracy. A Proiecta died at age sixteen in AD 385 and was commemorated in an epigram by Pope Damasus; as for Secundus, the name was commonly held by members of the great family of the Turcii, and 'Turcius' may be the correct reading of one of the monograms on the serving dishes also included with the treasure. But in any case, the addition of the Christian inscription to the classically styled casket demonstrates again that taste did not automatically follow religious conviction. This example also shows, incidentally, some of the difficulties which exist simply in interpreting the surviving evidence, and the danger that lies in too-hasty generalization.

Would the house of a late fourth-century pagan family in Rome have differed much from a Christian household? Jerome's picture of ascetic households where all comfort was rejected will have applied only to a few, if any, but while pagans presumably still had their household shrines, Christian religious items as such were still not common. There were no icons as such at this date, and crosses in the form of crucifixes did not become common until much later. On the other hand, Christians might have seal rings or embroideries with religious images, or possibly lamps and bottles from the Holy Land; glass vessels with engraved medallions of gold-leaf in the bottom were particularly favoured in the fourth century, and there is also a little evidence of religious pictures on their walls. Many of the themes used in the small objects had been taken over from catacomb art and sarcophagi; they include the Good Shepherd, Jonah, the three men in the fiery furnace. Adam and Eve also appear on the gold-glass marriage vessels, as does a youthful unbearded Christ on an example of gold-glass in the British Museum. However, the amount of surviving Christian art that can be dated with certainty to the fourth century is in fact rather limited. The earliest surviving figural mosaics in churches, for example, are from the end of the century; in other cases, we have to rely on literary descriptions. In the case of small objects, pagan and Christian artists worked side by side and frequently drew on the same repertoire, as they had in the early period of Christian art. We have seen that the Christian Proiecta casket simply adopted existing styles. From the end of the period,

Head of Christ (*Cristus*) in gold-glass from the bottom of a dish or bowl. Many such fragments of gold-glass survive from the period. Here, the interest is the representation of Christ, shown as a youth and without a beard, in contrast to the bearded philosopher-type which was to become the norm.

Christian ivories as such begin to appear, in the form of small boxes with Biblical scenes (though most examples are from the sixth century), while a fifth-century diptych shows a scene of the ascension. In contrast, official diptychs sponsored by Christians such as the diptych of Probus (AD 406) simply add Christian symbols such as the chi-rho to the standard representation of late Roman dignitaries.

But even if pagans and Christians were not necessarily in conflict during the late fourth century, this was certainly a tense period in cultural and social relations. During the reigns of Valentinian and Valens the Senate endured a series of trials brought by imperial agents for such offences as magic, adultery and other sexual transgressions, and heard under the law of treason (*maiestas*), which allowed the use of torture. Beginning in the mid-360s, they are associated by Ammianus with two henchmen of Valentinian, Maximin and Leo, while the prefects of the city, who included Praetextatus in AD 367, are carefully distanced from blame; the victims were mainly men and women of senatorial rank. The circumstances of these trials, and Ammianus' narrative itself (XXVIII.1), give rise to several problems; nevertheless, he cannot be far wrong in his description of their impact on contemporaries:

> the tocsin which heralds internal calamities was now ringing, and people were numb with horror at the frightfulness of the situation.

A similar series of trials for magic and divination had been held under Constantius II at Scythopolis in Palestine (XIX.12), and more were held at Antioch under Valens in the early 370s, this time linking divination with conspiracy (XXIX.1). During the latter episode Maximus of Ephesus, the philosopher who had introduced Julian to theurgy, was beheaded; the main trials, which involved stories of seances, and the use of a pendulum to spell out the name of the next emperor after Valens, were followed by a witchhunt to seek out any sign of magic or treason (XXIX.2). Books and papers were at risk for fear of being suspected of harbouring spells and charms; Ammianus no doubt exaggerates when he writes that all over the eastern provinces people simply burnt all their books so as to avoid suspicion, and that at Antioch men crept about 'as if in the shadows of the underworld', but both the executions and the fear were real enough. They show, first, the importance in the ancient world of the grey area between religion and magic, which persisted long after the spread of Christianity; Christian writers fight a losing battle against Christians who still clung to popular superstitious practices and to the belief in sorcery, magic and astrology, and as late as the seventh century the church is as concerned with this problem as it is with the Arab invasions themselves. But even allowing for some exaggeration, these trials also show the degree of suspicion and division among the upper class itself, the tensions between the senatorial class and the emperors and their appointees, and the lack of common ground in social and political matters. They are the outward signs of a nervous atmosphere in which people no longer knew where they were, and which could explode all too easily.

The main intellectual alternative to Christianity was Neoplatonism, which also had a distinctly religious and superstitious tinge, especially through the practice of theurgy, a technique of calling on the gods by magical or occult means; it was associated in particular with the early fourth-century philosopher Iamblichus from Apamea in Syria, and passed to Julian by Maximus of Ephesus. The ultimate aim of theurgy, as of Neoplatonism in general, was the union of the soul with God; everyday magic and miracles were simply a lower rung of the ladder leading the adept to this mystical union, for the skills of the theurgist gave him knowledge and control over the physical world. Eunapius's *Lives of the Sophists*, written *c.* AD 399, describes how Maximus could make statues move, and how Iamblichus could conjure up divinities. The latter wrote a vast commentary on the so-called *Chaldaean Oracles*, a set of supposed oracular revelations in verse about God and the nature of the universe, which he also presented in his work *On the Mysteries* as the ultimate key to understanding Plato's philosophy. Plato's works, indeed, in this way acquired the status of a holy book, a set of philosophical Scriptures. In the fifth and sixth centuries Neoplatonism, especially as taught at the Academy at Athens, became more and more identified with pagan opposition to Christianity, until the Academy was closed in AD 529. In the late fourth century, however, many Christians as well as pagans were deeply influenced by it, especially in the more intellectual form developed in the third century by Plotinus and Porphyry, just as members of the senatorial class of Rome had attended Plotinus's lectures, according to Porphyry's *Life of Plotinus*. Acquaintance with the writings of Plato was part of the mental equipment of many upper-class Romans, among them Augustine, who in Book XII of the *Confessions* seeks to reconcile Christian and Platonic views of Creation. Marius Victorinus translated works by Plotinus and Porphyry into Latin, and Calcidius translated Plato's *Timaeus*; later, Macrobius and Servius both show knowledge of Neoplatonist doctrines. In the east, Gregory of Nazianzus and Gregory of Nyssa were deeply imbued with Platonic ideas, which overlapped or coincided in many respects with Christian ones, for instance on the relation of the soul to the body, the aim of mystical union with the divine, or the ineffability of God. Works of Plato which especially appealed to Christians thus included the *Symposium* and the *Phaedrus*, which deal with the ascent of the soul to God. Neoplatonism also shared with Christianity an emphasis on asceticism and self-restraint; Porphyry wrote a work entitled *De Abstinentia*, and a *Letter to Marcella* (his wife) counselling sexual abstinence. The *De Abstinentia*, like Iamblichus's *On the Pythagorean Life*, advocated vegetarianism, on the model of the teachings of Plato's predecessor Pythagoras.

For those looking for something in which to believe, or for some system to adopt, there was plenty to choose from. For a time Augustine also belonged to the Manichaeans, a rigorist sect which followed the teachings of the third-century Mesopotamian guru Mani, according to which there were two gods, an evil creator god who was responsible for matter, and the good god of spirit. Likewise the Manichaeans themselves were divided into the 'Elect', on whom very strict asceticism was enjoined, including complete abstention from sex, which was regarded as evil, and the 'Hearers', who were regarded as weaker brethren. Manichaeism addressed the real problem which orthodox Christianity has in explaining evil, and drew on the same ascetic tendencies observable in both Christian and Neoplatonic circles. Despite official persecution there were Manichaean groups all over the empire, thanks to Manichaean missionaries, and Manichaeism was to have a long life in the east in countries as far afield as China.

Alongside the highly educated bishops such as Ambrose and John Chrysostom, who took so well to public life, were monks, nuns and hermits who ostentatiously rejected any attachment to secular culture or education and thus directly challenged the values of their surrounding society. Like similar challenges to conventional *mores* in our own day, this pose often had more than a little affectation about it, and the alternative lifestyle adopted had its own conformism. Real lives were beginning to be fashioned according to the pattern set out in the hagiographical literature that was now developing. But early Christianity was also a religion of words, based on sacred writings which were in need of interpretation, and with elaborate doctrines requiring learned exposition. At the same time as they advocated 'simplicity', Christian writers were turning out vast quantities of learned theological literature, from treatises on virginity, the Trinity or Creation, to commentaries on books of the Bible. All the great bishops of the later fourth century wrote technical treatises on theological subjects as well as sermons, letters and speeches; the more disagreement there was, the more they wrote and the more they refined their academic positions. These writings too required a high level of rhetorical skill. They are of importance for cultural history, even if their actual audience was limited, for they show secular learning and philosophical argument being put to the cause of doctrinal issues, and demonstrate the search for a comprehensive system of Christian knowledge suitable for the desired objective of a more unified state. They are also evidence of the direction into which so many of the best minds of the day put their talents. This had important consequences for the future development of the church, and some, like A. H. M. Jones, have seen in it a drain on the limited resources of the empire.

During the heyday of the Roman empire in the second century, elite culture was remarkably homogeneous for so vast a political unit. The ideal of a rhetorical education was shared throughout the provinces; its content naturally differed depending on whether it was obtained in Latin or in Greek, but the overall style and conception differed little from one area to another. By the late fourth century various factors have intervened to introduce a greater degree of cultural diversity, even though the premium placed on rhetoric itself continued. One such factor was Christianity, which on the one hand presented different values and alternative ways of living and on the other gave new opportunities for the exercise of rhetorical training. Another factor which challenged traditional attitudes was the impact of barbarians, both individually and collectively; in the longer term, this would make the old system impossible to maintain. A third factor was the rise of local cultures, which had been a feature of the third-century upheavals.

The growing importance of local cultures in the east is indicated by the development of Syriac as a major literary language, which can effectively be dated from the works of Ephrem the Syrian in the fourth century. Ephrem's career began at Nisibis, where he lived through the repeated sieges of the city by the Persians in the reign of Constantius II, leaving it for Edessa only when it was ceded to the Persians by Jovian in AD 363; Ephrem is indeed traditionally said to have founded the School of Edessa. He is the author of a large quantity of metrical hymns and homilies in Syriac, as well as exegetical, ascetic and polemical works in prose, some of which were quickly translated into Greek. His heavily symbolic and figurative style, and the use of elaborate metres for singing, give his works an unmistakable character, which has usually been seen as essentially Semitic, although its connection with Greek literature has also been emphasized. At any rate, Ephrem is one of the greatest writers in Syriac, and his importance was quickly recognized in Greek circles too (see Sozomen, *HE* III.16). From his day on, a substantial body of Christian literature in Syriac grew up, including homilies, church history, hagiography and chronicles, and an increasing amount of translation between Greek and Syriac and vice versa. This phenomenon in itself mirrors the increase in attention paid to the eastern provinces and their growing importance from the late fourth century onwards. Coptic literature also begins in the third and fourth centuries, though it takes off only in the fifth. A vernacular Christian literature develops in Armenian after the invention of the script around AD 400, and then progresses from translations from Syriac and Greek to its own historical works, and the same kind of development can be seen somewhat later in the case of Georgian. Over the next centuries, translation between these languages becomes a major preoccupation, and evidently took place on a large scale. All these literatures arose to fulfil Christian needs, and as we have seen, the Gothic alphabet was devised for a similar purpose.

After AD 395, the east and the west grew steadily apart, and this too was reflected in the linguistic sphere. Knowledge of Greek in the west had already diminished, as we see from Jerome's translations of Greek patristic texts into Latin, and Augustine's reliance on translations of Plato and the Neoplatonic writers. For some generations yet, Latin writers including Faustus of Riez (Rhegium in Provence), Sidonius Apollinaris of Clermont-Ferrand, Ennodius of Pavia, Caesarius of Arles, Dracontius in Vandal Africa, Cassiodorus in Ostrogothic Italy and, in the late sixth century, Venantius Fortunatus at Poitiers were able to maintain the traditions of Latin rhetoric and to continue to write in classicizing Latin prose or verse. We even have an anthology of Latin verse in classical metres from the last period of Vandal rule in North Africa in the early sixth century. However, the *History of the Franks* by Gregory of Tours, of the later sixth century, shows the extent to which the Latin language itself was now changing.

Considering the degree of social and political change in the west, the determined continuity of Latin culture is remarkable; in the east, of course, where there was continuity of government and administration, and no comparable barbarian settlement, things were easier for the continuation of classicizing writing in Greek, though here too a change in the spoken language is evident by the sixth century.

Even in the fourth century, there was considerable cultural change, extending for instance to the limited increase in prominence attached to women (Chapter 8). This was certainly no renaissance or revolution; no fundamental economic or political movements were taking place in late Roman society to match those which happened in later periods of European history. But the conventional model of decline does not fit what was happening either. It is true that the mass of legislation in the codes seems to suggest that the government, or the emperors, were uneasily aware that things were going on which were out of their control. The rhetorical hyperbole to which they resorted represents their attempts to halt changes of whose underlying causes they could not be aware. But this amounts less to totalitarianism than to an unenviable helplessness. Turning to other texts and other evidence can give a quite different picture of what it was like to be alive in the fourth century AD.

XI

Constantinople and the East

A SURPRISING DEGREE of mystery surrounds the early history of Constantinople, from Constantine's own motives in founding his city to its physical appearance (Chapter IV). Much of this is due to the understandable desire of later inhabitants, who lived in a different world, to write or rewrite the history of their own origins. Since real historical knowledge of the age of Constantine had faded away by the seventh century if not earlier, and Constantine himself had become a figure of myth and legend, their efforts could lead to some bizarre results. Already in the sixth century the battle before which Constantine was said to have had had his vision was thought to have been against 'barbarians'; soon his antagonists became the mythical giants Byzas and Antes, after whom the existing city of Byzantium supposedly derived its name. We can see that part of the motivation which lay behind these stories came from the fact that by the early sixth century Constantinople had taken on the mantle of Rome, now under Ostrogothic rule; its inhabitants needed to believe therefore that it had always been destined for such a role. In the same way, it was believed that the ancient palladium of Rome, which Aeneas had according to tradition carried there from Troy, had also been transferred to Constantinople, where it lay buried under Constantine's porphyry column as a talisman for the city.

This column, set up in the forum of Constantine, with a statue of the emperor on top, acquired a special imaginative significance for later inhabitants, some of whom believed that the statue actually depicted Apollo. The dedication ceremonies of the new city, which took place on 11 May, 330, are said to have included the formal acclamation of this statue, and on each subsequent anniversary until the sixth century a wooden image of Constantine bearing a statuette of the Fortune (*Tyche*) of the city was paraded into the Hippodrome and honoured by the reigning emperor (Malalas, *Chronicle*, trans. Jeffreys, p.175). Despite Eusebius's assurance that not a trace of paganism was left in Constantinople (*VC* III.48), Zosimus claims that two new temples were built there (II.31), and pagans and Christians alike later sought to claim credit for its future greatness. Another sixth-century writer says that the pagan philosopher Sopater and Praetextatus (a memory of the pagan Roman senator of that name who died AD 384 – he would have been too young to participate in AD 326) took part in the foundation rites (John the Lydian, *De Mensibus* IV.2). This story too is probably a later attempt to invest Constantinople with the prestige of Rome.

In these circumstances it is hard to disentangle the truth about Constantine's foundation. The archaeological remains in modern Istanbul are not very helpful either. Little if anything remains of Constantine's palace, buried or destroyed beneath centuries of later imperial building, and the existing church of St Sophia is the one that was built by Justinian in the sixth century. Constantine's mausoleum has long since disappeared, and the great Church of the Holy Apostles which stood next to it, on or near the site of the existing Fatih mosque, is also gone. The Hippodrome can still be seen in outline, together with the serpent column, one of the famous pieces of Greek sculpture brought there by Constantine, and the obelisk and base erected by Theodosius II, the latter one of the major monuments of late antique imperial art. As for the porphyry column and statue of Constantine, the column survives, damaged, under the name 'Burnt Column', but the statue itself is gone. Except in certain areas, excavation has been limited, and much of the physical history of the city can be reconstructed only by recourse to later texts, which are unfortunately often confused and contradictory. Constantinople was not a new foundation but a refurbishment of the small classical city of Byzantium, which had already been rebuilt by Septimius Severus after being severely damaged in the recent civil wars. By the reign of Justinian in the sixth century AD, the population of Constantinople had reached a peak of nearly half a million, but Constantine had set the number of recipients of grain at eighty thousand, and the population in the mid-fourth century may well have even been below that figure. The substantial later growth was made possible by the construction of the aqueduct attributed to Valens, and the present land walls, which enclose a much larger space than the Constantinian city, were constructed under Theodosius II, in the fifth century, when three large cisterns were also built. Though Constantine laid out the general lines of the new city, it can have begun to take real shape only gradually, with the appointment of an urban prefect about AD 360, and with the building of St Sophia and the Holy Apostles. But already in 340 Julian attended lectures there, and Libanius moved from Athens to Constantinople. Even more important was the fact that it so soon became a main imperial residence; Constantine spent part of each year there from AD 330 to 337, and even the pagan Julian set himself up at the court of Constantinople in AD 362, before departing for Antioch and the start of his Persian expedition. Together, however, Constantinople's senate and the city's role as the chief imperial residence in the east soon made it the actual seat of eastern government, and by the time John Chrysostom became bishop in 397 the interaction of emperor, church and population is easily apparent, still more so after the events of AD 400.

As Constantinople grew and developed, so did other great eastern cities. At Ephesus, for example, where two great church councils were held in AD 431 and 449, the late antique period was a time of prosperity and major building programmes. Baths were restored, the great colonnaded street from the reign of Arcadius known as the Arcadiane and the cathedral of the city, dedicated to St Mary the Virgin (it was believed that the Virgin had lived at Ephesus and had been taken up to heaven from there), were constructed. The city had a busy centre, with a market area, fountains and other amenities.

In the 380s, the proconsul of Asia restored a temple at Ephesus dedicated to Hadrian, and placed on it a frieze with reliefs of the Emperor Theodosius I, his father (also Theodosius), his wife and his son Arcadius, surrounding the goddess Artemis – a strange way, it might seem, of commemorating the ultra-Christian emperor, and something that could hardly have been done after Theodosius's edict of AD 392 forbidding pagan cults. Elsewhere in the east, the temple of Zeus at Apamea had been destroyed as early as AD 386 by the city's bishop, aided by government troops (Theodoret, *HE* V.21), and Porphyry of Gaza was licensed to destroy the Marneion there in AD 402 (*Life of Porphyry*, 47 f.,63 ff.). A law addressed to the *comes Orientis* in AD 397 ordered the use of stone from destroyed pagan temples for public works (*CTh.* XV.1.36).

In the case of Antioch, the second great city of the east, we are very well informed by Libanius about its municipal life in the fourth century; he wrote a speech in its praise, the *Antiochikos* (*Or.* 11), which emphasizes the continuity of the Greek civic traditions which Julian valued so greatly. It was also the seat of Roman military organization in the east, and the headquarters of the *comes Orientis*, and not least, the home of Ammianus, who describes its street lighting (XIV.1) and says of it that it was 'a city known throughout the world, incomparable in the resources imported and produced there' (XIV.8). The so-called Great Church at Antioch (which does not survive) was octagonal and had been begun by Constantine. It was dedicated in AD 341 in the presence of ninety bishops, who also took the opportunity to hold a council, and had a Greek verse inscription which read:

For Christ Constantine wrought these beautiful dwellings in all ways like the vaults of heaven, brightly gleaming, with Constantius obeying the commands of the ruler; the *comes* Gorgonios carried out the function of *cubicularius*. (Malalas, trans. Jeffreys, p. 177)

In the early 370s Valens built a new forum at Antioch, and the mosaics excavated at Antioch in the 1930s are among the most famous in the late antique period, especially the fifth-century mosaic with personification of *Megalopsychia* (Greatness of Soul) amid hunting scenes, from a villa at Yakto, part of suburban Daphne. Only one of the Antioch mosaics is definitely Christian; many depict personifications of abstract virtues. In AD 387 came the so-called 'riot of the statues', when imperial statues were overturned and abused. The immediate causes were banal: food shortages and higher taxation after the defeat at Adrianople. But the action taken was swift – the *comes Orientis* brought in troops, seized the rioters and quickly had them executed. The emperor ordered an inquiry, and demoted Antioch from its status as provincial metropolis, making it subject to Laodicea, closing places of entertainment and suspending the free bread ration. Many *curiales*, local councillors, were put on trial amid an atmosphere of mounting tension and fear, in which John Chrysostom says even the hermits came down from the mountains to intercede on behalf of the defendants (*On the Statues*, 17.1–2, one of twenty-one sermons on the subject). But fortunately intercession with the emperor in Constantinople on the part of the old bishop, Flavian, helped to make Theodosius relent, and the *curiales* and the city were let off just in time to celebrate Easter amid great rejoicing. We are extremely well informed about this dramatic episode, which tells us so much about civic life and the interconnection of the cities with the imperial government, thanks to five speeches of Libanius (*Or.* 19–23) which deal with the affair and supplement John Chrysostom's passionate sermons. In addition, the *consularis Syriae*, the governor of the province, also resided at Antioch, and Libanius has many critical remarks to make about the administration from the point of view of the citizens themselves.

Late antique cities were theatrical and dramatic places, in several senses. The era when ordinary citizens participated in decisions about the running of their cities had long gone, a casualty of Roman rule in the early empire. In its place, the task fell on the *curiales*, who found it at first a privilege, then increasingly a burden, because of the financial responsibilities it implied. Though they naturally housed many small craftsmen and traders, late antique cities were not major centres of production, any more than their predecessors had been. In other cities as well as in Rome there was therefore a large (and growing) lower-class population, many of whom were sustained by free food distributions or charitable hand-outs by the church. They were thus extremely vulnerable to temporary food shortages or disasters, and ready to riot if a cause presented itself, as is shown by the affair of the statues at Antioch. This tendency became much more pronounced in the cities of the east in the later fifth and sixth centuries: probably the most serious and the best known of such riots was the so-called Nika revolt in Constantinople in AD 532, when the centre of the city was burnt down and thirty thousand or more citizens are said to have been killed by the soldiers who put down the riot. The same set of circumstances contributed both to the ready availability of audiences at every kind of spectacle from theatre to chariot races, and to the tendency of such events to become the place where the people and the city authorities met, and occasionally, confronted each other.

Such confrontations were not new: Cassius Dio, for example, describes the demonstrations against Macrinus that took place at the races in Rome in AD 217 (78.20.1–4), and the practice of popular demonstrations on such occasions goes right back to the Principate and even before. The theatre, and still more the amphitheatre or circus, were places where there was a large concentration of people, and where the emperor, or in the provinces the governor, or at least the city officials, would be present. In the later empire, and especially in the east, chariot racing was the rage, and the hippodrome the key place for excitement and potential affray, although at Antioch Libanius claimed that the hippodrome was quite innocent in this regard (*Or.* 11.268), while the theatre was one of the glories of the city (*ibid*, 219). Christian preachers, and John Chrysostom above all, railed against all public entertainments, and especially against the enthusiasm shown for them by the populations of Antioch and Constantinople. The Christian rhetor Choricius of Gaza indicates from his disapproval the intense enthusiasm for mimes, chariot-racing, wrestling and athletics in sixth-century Palestine, and a sixth-century Greek inscription from Gaza commemorates a teenage participant in the races. Though not part of the Greek tradition of festivals, gladiatorial combats had become increasingly popular in the cities of the east in the Roman period, but the Christian emperors tried repeatedly to stamp them out, and while their efforts were often unsuccessful in the face of local enthusiasm, the gladiatorial contests did eventually give way to wild beast shows (*venationes*) held on an equally lavish scale. Part of the reason for Christian opposition to such occasions lay in the fact that they were rivals for the attention of the populace; but the church had its festivals too. Choricius describes those held to mark the dedication of two new churches in Gaza, which included public banquets and drinking, stalls with all kinds of things on sale and an elaborate firework display as good as anything one might expect even at Alexandria. Pagan and Christian festivals like these were apparently held regularly throughout the year. Moreover, churches themselves were places of public assembly and even entertainment— crowds were drawn by the activities of larger-than-life preachers and politicians like Chrysostom, and clever Christian orators soon learnt the techniques of crowd manipulation and audience control.

Crowd participation was even organized by paid groups (claques), who led the applause and the rhythmical shouting ('acclamation') which could so easily acquire a political content. The theatre claque at Antioch took a prominent part in stirring up and managing the mob rioting in AD 387; the members also regularly led 'popular' expressions of opinion to the governor when he attended the theatre and effectively presented himself there for popular reaction. It had no regular political aim of its own, any more than did the 'Blues and Greens', the supporters of the teams at the chariot races (contrary to persistent modern assumptions); indeed, the claque could be hired at will. Inscriptions from Aphrodisias in Caria (where there was no hippodrome for chariot-racing) show that the theatre supporters were also divided into Blues and Greens, and this was no doubt also true elsewhere. With or without the intervention of a claque, the importance of popular acclamation of governors was recognized in law: Constantine required in AD 331 that records of acclamations be sent regularly to the emperor, so that they could be taken into account in determining the future careers of the officials in question (*CTh.* I.16.6; VIII.5.32). Again, the practice was taken over by the church, and acclamations and gangs of supporters also feature in ecclesiastical disputes and during the preliminaries to church councils, as at Ephesus in 431 and Chalcedon in 451, where the lead was taken by groups of monks. Perhaps the most striking recorded example of acclamation occurred however when the Theodosian Code was itself officially promulgated. The new code came into force on 1 January, AD 439, and on 23 December the Senate of Rome met to receive it formally. The praetorian prefect announced its promulgation in the names of Theodosius II and Valentinian III, whereupon the senators cried out in unison 'Well spoken'. According to the *gesta senatus* (official proceedings), as the reading proceeded, the Roman senators applauded and shouted their approval in unison, their cries repeated twenty or thirty times after each clause. Public life, church councils and theatrical displays alike had become spectator sports.

The church also intervened in urban life through the various forms of public charity dispensed by bishops and local churches as well as by rich individuals. In the west, the pressure of barbarian incursions was more immediately felt, and helped to dictate the form and development of official charity, with the ransoming of prisoners assuming a major role. In the early fifth century the Visigothic invasions of Italy generated many Roman captives, and prompted corresponding efforts by Christian leaders such as Paulinus of Nola, Maximus of Turin and Ambrose of Milan to redeem them; this religious duty (confirmed in *CTh.* V.7.2, issued in AD 408) became a recognized part of Christian alms, to be combined with distribution of grain and clothes to the needy. The proceeds of some of Melania's sales, which took place in these years, went directly towards ransoming prisoners. In the eastern cities, though the situation was somewhat different in this regard, bishops took on responsibility for regular distributions to the poor, and although most of the evidence centres on the fifth and sixth centuries, such distributions were already taking place on a large scale in fourth-century Antioch (Chapter 5).

The sales of property by eager ascetics sometimes directly enriched individual religious communities and churches to an excessive degree, causing envy in others. In the case of Melania and Pinianus, the church of Hippo tried so hard to get for itself the benefits which Thagaste had acquired as a result of the couple's sales that Pinianus had to flee in order to avoid being forcibly ordained. The official target of such charity was however 'the poor', that same 'mob' which is commonly blamed in the sources for every kind of urban violence, and there are some indications that their number in the cities was increasing. Libanius complains of the influx of people with no homes, no employment, no family ties and nothing to do but make trouble (*Or.* 41.11). Cities, after all, offered the prospect of free grain, and now the possibility of Christian charity, in contrast to the difficulties of rural life and taxation. On the other hand, a closer look at the theory of charitable distribution in the west, where we have the evidence, suggests that priority was sometimes given to specific Christian groups, including specific churches, rather than to the urban poor indiscriminately. Furthermore, the development of a theory of Christian almsgiving, a subject on which much was written during this period, itself focuses attention on the category of 'the poor' and may give a false impression both as to its composition and its numbers. As Jesus said, 'the poor are always with us'; what was really different in this period was that consciousness of the poor changed dramatically. In a sense, the existence of the poor was required by Christian ideology in order to neutralize the fact that the church itself was not only growing rich but also actively courting wealthy patrons. Moreover, there were many subtle ways of interpreting and modifying the scriptural injunction to give up all that one had. Bishops, for instance, came into considerable disposable assets on election, even if they had officially adopted poverty themselves, while even the religious life offered possibilities of accommodation. The urban poor in the east were rather different from the rural poor in either east or west. Finally, while 'the poor', in Christian mentality, stood for all that was wrong in the fallen state of man, this recognition did not give rise to social revolution or to the attempt to remove poverty *tout court* (indeed, Christians argued that the division of society into rich and poor was divinely ordained), but rather to the practice of almsgiving, which offered at one and the same time a convenient palliative and a source of prestige for the givers.

There is now evidence in some areas of the beginnings of the prosperity that became so striking in the east in the course of the fifth century and that continued in the sixth. First, the Holy Land itself benefited during the fourth century from the pilgrim trade, and from the wealthy patrons who founded and endowed monasteries there; quite apart from her foundations, Melania herself sent fifteen thousand gold *solidi* to Palestine. The church of Jerusalem was richly endowed even by the mid-fourth century, and the city itself became a busy cosmopolitan centre, whose urban hustle Jerome later deplored (*Ep.* 58.4.4, to Paulinus of Nola). Egeria notes that the services at Jerusalem were conducted in Greek but with interpreters for the Aramaic-speaking local population and Latin translations provided by bilingual monks and nuns; the same applied at Bethlehem. Jerusalem and the Holy Land reached the height of their prosperity in the fifth century, with the reign of Theodosius II and the patronage of the Empress Eudoxia.

There are also signs of the early stages of the population growth that characterizes the eastern provinces in the fifth and sixth centuries. Archaeological surveys of particular regions, especially Judaea, the Golan and the Negev, show an increased density of settlement during this period, followed by a sharp falling off after the Arab conquest in the seventh century. Rehovot, the second largest town of the Negev, experienced a revival in the late Roman/ Byzantine period, probably beginning in the late fourth century; during this period the valleys of the central Negev were irrigated and intensively cultivated, so that they were able to sustain a larger population than at any period until recent times. Whereas many of the troops had been withdrawn from the forts in the eastern frontier areas of southern Palestine by the mid-sixth century, the cities on the coast were flourishing. Gaza was extremely prosperous in the late fifth and sixth centuries, partly thanks to trade with the inland settlements, which exported wine of famous quality. A similar settlement pattern has been observed in northern Mesopotamia near Edessa, while parts of northern Syria supported a prosperous economy in the same late Roman period. Around Bostra in the Hauran, and the area of the Decapolis, near the Sea of Galilee, the trend can be easily traced for the fifth and sixth centuries, though less easily for the fourth. The reasons for these trends are likely to vary from area to area; it is clear for instance that irrigation systems, especially in the Negev, played a substantial role in allowing intense cultivation, including olives and vines, though not exclusively. There is still much uncertainty both about the evidence and about its interpretation in particular cases. All estimations of population size in antiquity suffer from lack of statistical evidence, and the vulnerability of arguments based on literary sources, settlement archaeology or the size and number of churches; underlying trends about the movements of population are only very imperfectly understood. By the later sixth century the effects of the great plague epidemic which hit the east in AD 541 must have been felt. But until that happened, there is enough solid evidence about the large number of settlements in the east in this period to show that earlier views of universal demographic decline as a factor responsible for the decline of antiquity simply do not work.

At risk of over-generalization, one can therefore draw a contrast between east and west not only in terms of stability of government and vulnerability to barbarian inroads, but also of economic organization. Where the great estates with their villa economies cluster in the west (Chapter VIII), in the eastern provinces there is more evidence in this period of small peasants and a village economy, with large villages, smaller than a 'city', and without its legal status (though some 'cities' were very small by modern standards), but showing evidence of social organization and diversification. There were great divergences of size even within the latter definition, from the rich villages near Antioch to much smaller settlements in Asia Minor and elsewhere. Furthermore, a village might exist within a large estate. Such communities had 'leading men', attested on inscriptions and in literary sources, and might make offerings at local shrines or build their own churches or synagogues. One such simple village church from the mid-fourth century is that at Qirk Bizze, east of Antioch, built in local style not unlike that of the houses of the same period. By the end of the fourth century such foundations were becoming larger and more elaborate, itself an indication that the villages were prospering. A precious series of papyri from Nessana in the Negev, where there was also a garrison, allows us to glimpse something of the complications of land-holding in such communities at a slightly later period. Though there are still many problems to be solved, the continuity of such settlements until the sixth and seventh centuries, and in many cases their decline thereafter, remains one of the most striking features of the eastern provinces in late antiquity. It was this, rather than the existence of major cities, which enabled the eastern empire to escape the fragmentation suffered by the west; moreover, when the signs of population decline begin to show themselves from the later sixth century on, they have as much to do with external factors such as plague and renewed warfare as with causes exclusive to the eastern provinces themselves.

The relation between the cities, and still more, the government, and rural communities is not easy to define. The tax collector and the soldier were the figures who were most immediately familiar; in contrast to these, the governor was very far away indeed. In time, the bishop also came to play a social role, but when we have good evidence for this, as in the letters of Theodoret of Cyrrhus in northern Syria (d. 466) an interesting picture emerges of a man who, surely having had a thorough classical grounding as well as a religious education, behaved much like an upper-class patron, making Cyrrhus into a worthy episcopal centre by his building activity and writing letters to the governor and other officials. Theodoret was one of the leading Christian controversialists of his day, and was formally anathematized for heresy by the Council of Chalcedon (AD 451); he was also a voluminous writer. But he was highly conscious of the rural society around him, and his *Historia Religiosa*, a collection of lives of monks, contains many vivid anecdotes about rural society in Syria. In the second half of the fourth century Basil lived in religious retirement near Neocaesarea in the Pontos before he was appointed, in AD 370, bishop of Caesarea in Cappadocia, where he built a whole complex of buildings for ecclesiastical purposes, including provision for tending the sick and the poor. Though Basil himself had been educated at Athens, he provided in his monastic *Rule* for schools to be attached to monasteries where children could get a religious education. Something also comes through from the *Life of Macrina* by Basil's brother Gregory of Nyssa, also in Cappadocia, of the relation between large estates and local people in fourth-century Asia Minor. The family's estates were in Pontos, at Annisa, on the Iris and Ibora rivers, not far from the Black Sea coast, though the mother of the large family to which Basil, Macrina and Gregory belonged came from Cappadocia. Basil's place of retirement and that of another brother, Naucratius, were near each other, while the convent founded by Macrina and her mother and a men's monastery were located on the other bank of the river Iris. Though possessing great talent, and presumably education, Naucratius chose a hermit's life at the age of twenty-two, and lived

> far away from the hassle of city life, far away from the time-consuming duties of the imperial service or pleading in the lawcourts.

He used to tend with his own hands some poor and sick old men, for whom he would procure food by making use of his skill in hunting, which at the same time provided an outlet for his youthful energies. Naucratius lived in this way for five years, until he was tragically killed in a hunting accident while looking for food for these same old men. His retreat seems to have been only three days' journey from the family home, and he was accompanied in his retirement by his servant Chrysaphius, who brought the news to his mother (*Life of Macrina*, 8–9).

Theodoret was a major theologian and exegete of the 'Antiochene' school, whose hallmark was a more literal and historical approach, as against the allegory and symbolism deployed by its traditional rival, Alexandria. The condemnation of Arianism at the Council of Nicaea in AD 325 had not solved the problems of Christian unity; on the contrary, it led to continued disagreements during the fourth century about the nature of Christ ('Christology'), out of which there developed two positions known as Monophysitism and Nestorianism, both of which were condemned at the Council of Chalcedon in AD 451. The first argued that Christ had one nature, the divine, while the second, identified with Nestorius (made bishop of Constantinople in AD 428 and deposed by the Council of Ephesus in AD 431), insisted on separating the two natures, human and divine; the difficulty lay in justifying the doctrine of orthodox Christianity whereby Christ's nature was single and indivisible, both human and divine at the same time, which inevitably posed great problems of definition. A good many personal and local issues, not least the supremacy of one episcopal see over another, were also involved in these disputes, which were debated from the late fourth century on. One of the preliminaries was the controversy surrounding the third-century Christian thinker Origen, from Caesarea in Palestine, who was held in Antiochene circles to have carried Alexandrian allegorizing of the Scriptures to excess, as well as to have erred in other doctrinal matters. One of the chief protagonists of the controversies of the fifth century was Cyril of Alexandria, a clever politician who was already bishop when the pagan philosopher Hypatia, the teacher of Synesius, was lynched by a Christian mob in Alexandria in AD 415. While many contemporaries, from John Chrysostom to Jerome, were involved in the Origenist affair, it is no accident that the two great Christological councils of the fifth century took place in the east. They were and are recognized as binding by the church; nonetheless, it is significant that the controversies which had given rise to them originated in the eastern empire.

Basil, Gregory of Nyssa, their friend Gregory of Nazianzus, and Theodoret all wrote in Greek, but Theodoret's native language may have been Syriac, and the majority of the rural population of his diocese were non-Greek speakers. He is one of our main sources for Syrian asceticism, yet he describes his north Syrian holy men and women within the categories of Greek biography, perhaps 'normalizing' them somewhat in the process. The relation between Greek (or 'Hellenic') and local cultures in the eastern provinces is very difficult to establish; Syriac Christianity is a case in point, often being presented not simply as exotic and strange, but also more genuine and authentic where the 'Hellenic' influences are fewest. During the fourth century itself the very word 'Hellene' as used by Greeks themselves came to mean, as well as 'Greek' in the cultural sense, simply 'pagan', a usage to which Gregory of Nazianzus objected strongly (*Or.*IV.5.79–81). There is certainly something in the distinction between the language of culture (Greek) and the language of the people; Greek was the language not only of the traditional education (*paideia*), but also of the administration (though Latin continued to be used, especially for the army and the law until the sixth century). But inscriptions reveal that both the Greek language and Greek cultural influences had also penetrated far into rural society. Theodoret's Cyrrhus was not typical either of central and southern Syria or of Palestine, where Greek continued to be used by ordinary people in their funerary inscriptions until as late as the seventh century. Even at Edessa in Osrhoene, ruled by an Arab dynasty and the centre of Syriac Christian culture, Greek influence in the form of Platonism, and Greek mythological themes such as that of Orpheus were to be found in the third century; further west, excavations have shown the extent of Greek culture in the mosaics of Apamea, another great Syrian city, which, as we have seen, was a main centre of Neoplatonism in the fourth century. A further sign of the actual mingling of Greek and local elements can be found in the assimilation of Greek and local deities; Greek polytheism even influenced pre-Islamic Arab paganism. The early sixth-century Syriac author Jacob of Serug inveighed against a range of pagan cults in Syria, Greek and Aramaic names of deities mingled together, and wrote indignantly of the Greek mythological stories enacted at theatrical shows throughout the Syrian cities.

Egypt is a somewhat different story, both because outside Alexandria it lacked the network of cities possessed by Syria and Palestine and because the literature of Egyptian monasticism itself presents considerable problems of interpretation. Anti-intellectualism had been a feature of Egyptian monasticism since Antony, even though some of the monks as we have seen (above and Chapter V) were men of education themselves. The travel accounts of visits to these Egyptian hermits all present the phenomenon as seen from the outside and with a certain degree of tendentiousness which makes the works difficult to use for historical purposes. Many of the solitaries described seem to have been illiterate local people, but by no means all. Palladius records a monk called Cronius who had been Antony's interpreter in Greek and Coptic (*Lausiac History*, 21); the same man told the story of a certain Eulogius from Alexandria who had been well educated before becoming a monk. There were many visiting monks from elsewhere, even in Antony's day, and Cronius told how Antony would ask whether they were Egyptian or from Jerusalem; if the former, he would simply have them fed, but if the latter, he would engage them in conversation. There was a good deal of posturing involved in some cases: a certain 'Sarapion the loincloth', an Egyptian by birth who wore only a loincloth, sold himself as a servant to some Greek actors, whom he converted, and travelled to Greece, where he begged for money from some 'philosophers' in Athens, converted a Manichaean at Sparta and then went to Rome, where he tried unsuccessfully to persuade a pious virgin to walk naked through the city to prove that she really was as dead to the world, as she claimed (*ibid.*, 37). This literature does not tell us much about the culture of Egyptian villages, but even if we discount a good deal as consisting of colourful stories, it does at the very least indicate the cosmopolitanism and the opportunities for travel in the fourth-century east. It also sometimes strikes a personal note. One man whom Palladius mentions is Posidonius the Theban, who had lived as a solitary in the Porphyrites district of Egypt for a year, but whom Palladius knew in Bethlehem; Palladius attributes to him an observation about Jerome's extreme bad temper and the prophecy that Jerome's friend Paula would die first and be freed of him (*ibid.*, 36).

Not all Egyptian monks were solitaries, or living in small groups; some also lived in large organized communities, which were provided with the apparatus of economic existence – cisterns, bakeries, oil-presses, workshops and stables, and might be walled for security. The monks of such establishments could easily make themselves independent in practice of the local bishop, and their abbots were sometimes powerful characters, such as Shenute, *higumen* (abbot) of the White Monastery near Sohag in the late fourth and early fifth centuries. But papyrological evidence shows close connections between such monasteries and the local village, whether economic or in relations with the local priest. Though many of the monks spoke only Coptic, in the fifth century and later, Panopolis in Upper Egypt still produced a series of Greek poets, rhetoricians and historians who in some cases gained patronage in high places and made highly successful careers outside Egypt.

We also know a great deal from the later papyrological evidence about the great estates which have been seen as a major feature of the Egyptian economy in the early Byzantine period. The best known is that of the Apiones, a family based at Oxyrhynchus, but with separate land-holding scattered over a very wide area. However, even in the sixth century, their relations with their tenants seem not to have been as oppressive as might be expected; moreover, they employed craftsmen and played a considerable role in trade. There was also still a place for skilled craftsmen, who were organized into trade guilds. On a much smaller scale, a town list of land-holdings in the Hermopolite *nome* (administrative district) in the fourth century shows a concentration of land in the hands of a few, while many of the other holdings are extremely small. Life for these independent smallholders could be very difficult, especially when unforeseen circumstances arose. But production was highly diversified, and an individual might support his family in a variety of different ways. There is still a good deal of evidence for money transactions and small-scale commerce during our period, for instance from the early fourth-century papyrological archive of Aurelius Isidorus, which demonstrates the existence of a 'diverse and monetized peasant economy' (Rathbone); the inevitable complaints about taxation and poverty are balanced by the equally large amount of evidence for flourishing, if small-scale, economic life.

In general, similar economic pressures on the broad front exerted themselves on the eastern provinces as on the western, and the heavy hand of imperial government, together with the corruption of its many employees, was felt in the east too. But a great deal of surviving evidence, literary, epigraphic and papyrological, allows us to see how individuals lived and even flourished under such conditions. It should therefore warn us against putting too much emphasis on general theories. One of the most spectacular Syrian Christians, St Symeon the Elder, lived for forty years, from AD 419 to 459, on top of a pillar in the desert north-east of Antioch. When he died his body was taken to Antioch in procession by seven bishops and by the *magister militum* of the east with an escort of six hundred soldiers, followed by a mass of individual pilgrims. Such a juxtaposition shows how society really worked.

XII

Conclusion

THE FALL OF THE Roman empire is conventionally dated to AD 476; thereafter there were no more Roman emperors in the west. Equally conventionally, it is usually pointed out that the line continued in the east, based at Constantinople, until the conquest of the city by the Turks under Mehmet the Conqueror in AD 1453. The year AD 476 itself is more of a convenience for historians than anything else for, as we have already seen, the fifth-century emperors had been weak even before that, in many cases not much more than tools in the hands of the generals who held the powerful position of Master of the Soldiers. It was the last of these, Odoacer, who deposed the young Romulus Augustulus, emperor for less than a year, and declared himself *rex* ('king'), a title traditionally hated at Rome since the overthrow of the kings and the establishment of the Roman republic in 510 BC. By the early sixth century several barbarian kingdoms had come into existence and were in some cases the eventual forerunners of the western medieval states. Among them the most important were the Ostrogoths in Italy, under their king Theodoric (AD 493–526), the Franks (also called the Merovingians), whose kingdom came into being with the victory of Clovis at the battle of Vouillé in AD 507, and the Visigoths, who, despite their defeat in that battle and later reverses at the hands of the Franks, established a unified kingdom in Spain in the mid-sixth century.

Even after these kingdoms were in place, so many Roman traditions and institutions continued that they are sometimes referred to as 'sub-Roman' societies. In particular, Roman landowning families, with their strong cultural traditions, provided many of the powerful bishops in the period, and Latin continued to be used as the language of administration and culture. The last chapter showed how, in the east, there were already signs in the late fourth, and certainly in the fifth century, of the prosperity and population growth which is so marked a feature of the eastern provinces in the early sixth century, and the divide between east and west widened to such an extent that the Emperor Justinian (AD 527–65) could even launch a series of military actions aimed at reasserting imperial control in the west. The 'reconquest' was successful for a time, even though Justinian also had to deploy his troops against Persia on the eastern frontier, but there had been too much change over too long a period for a lasting imperial restoration, and Justinian's successors found it difficult even to maintain adequate forces on the eastern front. After the Persian invasions of the early seventh century and the Arab conquests which took place shortly afterwards, west and east were driven still further apart.

Augustine spent some thirty-five years as bishop of Hippo on the coast of North Africa, just within the Algerian side of the border between modern Algeria and Tunisia, dying just as the Vandals had crossed into North Africa from Spain and begun their conquest of the province. The *City of God* is one of his later works, written over a period of about fourteen years and finished in AD 427. Some of the aristocratic Christians from Rome had fled to North Africa when Rome was sacked by Alaric in AD 410; they needed an answer to pagan taunts that God had allowed this disaster to happen even though Rome was a Christian city. Augustine's reply extended to twenty-two books of sustained and often difficult argument. He sought both to show that pagan culture was inadequate and based on error, and to convince the educated Christians who formed his audience for such a work that they too were in error if they imagined that merely being Christian guaranteed earthly prosperity and happiness. Rather, the heavenly city, Jerusalem as distinct from Athens, was a spiritual concept, existing within us and in the life to come. The last book goes into considerable detail about the kind of life which the virtuous can expect in Paradise, after the judgement which will separate believers and unbelievers. But the *City of God* is also a great work of political theory, which surveys and interprets the history of Rome from its traditional foundation in 753 BC to Augustine's own day. Augustine wished to demonstrate that the world was run according to a Christian providential scheme; thus he had to explain the pagan past of Rome to Christians and to refute the pagan argument that the sack of the city in AD 410 disproved the doctrine of Christian providence.

Thus Augustine, a man steeped in classical culture himself, argued that pagan Rome was based on error; even more, the Rome of Cicero and Livy did not even fulfil Cicero's definition of a state in the *De Republica*; this was so, in Augustine's view, because the Roman state was not based on justice, which means giving God his due as well as men. A large proportion of the *City of God* is in fact devoted to the great Latin classical writers, especially Cicero and Virgil, for Augustine himself knew the pull of their work, and the hold they exercised on educated people. The lengthy passages about Plato and his recent devotees, the Neoplatonists, also reflect Augustine's own intellectual attachments, while addressing the chief intellectual alternative to Christianity. Nevertheless, Augustine is quite firm – Plato and Platonism may represent the highest form of philosophy, but they fail, because they have not identified the true God. Overall, the pagan past was misguided, while the Christian empire is part of God's plan for mankind. However, Christians cannot expect automatic happiness and success on earth. God will continue to test and try them; moreover, human beings are inherently sinful, and must struggle to do right with God's grace – the just will receive their rewards only in heaven.

The *City of God* consists of history, philosophy, political theory and theology, all rolled into one vast work. But just as it rejects the ultimate validity of that classical culture which Augustine had spent his early life teaching, so it rejects the value of the Roman past and its history in comparison with the Christian present, and denies critical inquiry by insisting on the providence of God in directing history. In such a conception, the first duty of a Christian ruler is to enforce the true faith. Augustine provides a justification, explicitly stated, for Christian persecution.

The *City of God* was written because Rome was sacked; its focus is on Rome, the Roman past and Roman authors. Easterners did not read Augustine, either in his own lifetime or later, and even if his own Greek was better than some scholars have allowed, he was not at home in it. A very important aspect of Augustine's legacy lay in his teaching on sin, which was to be fundamental to the ideas of western Christians in the Middle Ages and later. He believed that men and women were inherently sinful and in need of God's grace for forgiveness, and argued fervently against the emphasis placed by the British monk Pelagius on free will. Augustine can be surprisingly modern in his psychology and his philosophical understanding of language, and his *Confessions* mark a landmark in the development of autobiography. But it was his stress on the frailty of man and the dependence of history on the will of God which had such a tremendous influence on the later medieval west. So great indeed is his stature that it tends to be overlooked that the eastern church escaped his influence in this matter as in others, and indeed still rejects his insistence on original sin.

The poignancy of Augustine's own situation, as his biographer Possidius also points out, was that even after he had formulated his Christian interpretation of history in the *City of God*, he lived to see his own province invaded, churches desecrated and Christians killed or imprisoned. Some bishops were inclined to leave their sees for safety, but Augustine stated firmly that it was a bishop's duty to stay with his flock. He was however spared the destruction of Hippo: he died late in AD 430, a year before the town was evacuated and partly burnt. The Roman army in North Africa had become so weakened that it offered no real defence against the Vandals, and what had been one of the most prosperous and secure provinces entered a period of Arian Vandal rule that lasted until Justinian's general Belisarius arrived with a Byzantine army in AD 533.

North Africa vividly illustrates the collapse of the imperial system in the west; the Vandals effectively walked in, with their wives, baggage and dependants – not even a very large force in all – and met little or no resistance, either from Roman troops or from the local population. Recent research has shown that the reasons here have more to do with the progressive weakening of the centre and the general problems affecting the Roman army than with local economic decline, for the North African cities and the North African economy were flourishing in the late fourth century.

This brings us back to the inescapable question of why the

Roman empire in the west 'declined' or 'fell' in the fifth century. Old-fashioned moralizing explanations are no longer acceptable (though they still abound), and it is too simplistic to lay all the blame on the barbarian invasions (though what might have happened had there been no barbarian invasions is an interesting hypothetical question). A more recent theory juxtaposes the fall of the Roman empire with that of other major cultures in world history and provides an explanation in terms of the collapse of complex societies. Roughly, on this view, as a society grows, it becomes more and more socially differentiated and more complex and simply in order to maintain itself its needs correspondingly increase. There comes a point however when the 'marginal return' from strategies of maximization such as conquest or taxation diminishes, under pressure of 'continued stresses, unanticipated challenges and the costliness of sociopolitical integration'. A period of difficulty (economic stagnation, political decline, territorial shrinkage) typically follows, which will be followed by effective collapse unless new factors intervene. In the case of the Roman empire, the unexpected challenges included long-term pressure from real and potential invaders, a problem which the empire did not succeed in managing or containing. There is much that is familiar in this analysis, even though it rests on the questionable assumption that the historical development of societies is itself in some sense historically determined. At least it allows Roman historians to look more objectively at their own field, and to see that the problems which the late Roman government faced were not unique, any more than were its often ineffective attempts to find solutions. We should add to the equation in this particular case the relative lack both of economic understanding and of economic structures, and the inability of the centre even after Diocletian to ensure the economic well-being of the empire as a whole. The Roman empire had always been in precarious balance between centre and periphery, and its survival had depended not only on external peace but also on a high degree of internal goodwill. In the late fourth and fifth centuries all these factors were endangered.

Considerations like these provoke comparisons with the modern world, which can help in understanding the ancient world, so long as we take care to compare like with like. In the course of this book we have seen that behind the standard generalizations about late

Roman society lie a great range and diversity of phenomena. Late antiquity was a time of rapid change, which showed itself differently in different areas. This is also an important part of the explanation for the survival of the east after the collapse of the west. Certainly the east had a more even distribution of wealth, and was much more successful in turning away the threat from northern barbarians (to the detriment of the west). Moreover, a kind of balance of power prevailed through this period between the eastern empire and its major rival, Sasanian Persia; however painful or expensive a given episode might be, neither side seriously tried to destroy the other. But it was the countless small and local variables which made up the total picture. Moreover, though it goes far beyond the scope of this book, none of these explanations accounts for the obstinate survival of Byzantium through the catastrophic losses it suffered in the seventh century and later, when that balance was shattered, right up to the establishment of the Ottoman empire.

The sense of the broad sweep, or *longue durée*, of history also lies behind a somewhat different approach to these questions. Rather than emphasizing the divisions and the breaks both the eastern and the western empires can be seen as belonging to the longer history of Europe and the Mediterranean. This kind of approach also has the advantage of taking our minds away for a while from the over-debated question of the end of classical antiquity and enabling us instead to look at issues like settlement, climate, exchange and political organization over a much longer period. The emphasis of modern historians also has a good deal to do with the evidence they have used – the literary sources lead us to focus on a limited set of questions, among which the relation with the classical past is very prominent, whereas a broader study based more on archaeological, and especially survey evidence, allows rather different issues to come forward. Viewed from this much broader perspective, while there were certainly substantial political changes at certain points (the 'third-century crisis', followed by the reforms of Diocletian, the fragmentation of Roman government in the west, the Arab invasions in the east), none of these in itself fundamentally changed the status quo. Indeed, some parts of the eastern empire had reached a peak of settlement at the time of the Arab conquests, while the effect of the latter was initially much more limited than is usually supposed. Rather, these political turning points represent stages in a much longer evolution, at the end of which the emphasis shifted towards northern Europe, and the development of the conditions leading to expansion and growth in the High Middle Ages was underway. In the east, the movement of the Islamic capital from Damascus to Baghdad in the mid-eighth century was not only crucial in determining the character of Islamic rule thereafter, but also finally put an end to the beneficial effects of the long late Roman investment in the Near East.

In the west, Roman imperial government was replaced by successor kingdoms in which many existing features were kept. Similarly, in the east, life in the conquered provinces was not immediately or totally transformed by the Arab conquests. Wherever we place it chronologically, the 'fall' of the Roman empire was not a single, dramatic event which changed the shape of Europe or the Mediterranean.

This book has been mainly about the fourth century AD. During that period we can see both the resilience of the Roman imperial system and the inertia of pre-modern society. The 'third-century crisis' did not result in revolution, but neither in the end did the fourth-century emperors succeed in surmounting the obstacles which lay in the way of effective rule. During the same period Christianity gained official support, while its powerful institutional network was strengthened by legal and economic advantages. Constantine unwittingly created a church which for centuries would rival the power of the state. No fundamental economic transformation took place in the later empire: indeed, the church now absorbed much of the surplus revenue, just as external pressures increased the difficulties of maintaining an adequate army to such a level that the western government effectively gave up the struggle.

The political, economic and military problems experienced in this last phase of the Roman imperial system were certainly therefore very great, and they are naturally often reflected in the sources. Culturally, however, late antiquity was very unlike what this model suggests. Diverse, changing, innovative, contradictory – all these epithets can be fairly applied to the tumultuous world of Ammianus Marcellinus. In some ways it is a world like our own, with its rapid change and accompanying sense of dislocation. It is not the familiar classical world, but then that is its very attraction.

Date Chart

West	East
	224 Sasanian dynasty begins
	241–72 Shapur I
253–60 Valerian	
253–68 Gallienus	
259–74 'Gallic empire'	
272 Aurelian takes Palmyra	284–305 Diocletian
	301 Edict on Maximum Prices
306 Constantine proclaimed at York	
312 Battle of Milvian Bridge	
	313 'Edict of Milan'
314 Council of Arles	
	324 Constantine defeats Licinius
	325 Council of Nicaea
	330 Dedication of Constantinople
	337 Death of Constantine
350–3 Magnentius in Britain	350–3 Gallus Caesar
357–9 Julian Caesar in Gaul	359 Shapur II captures Amida
	361–3 Reign of Julian
	362–3 Julian's Persian expedition
364–75 Valentinian I	364 Jovian cedes Nisibis
	364–78 Valens
	378 Battle of Adrianople

West

382	Theodosius settles Goths as federates
384	Gratian orders removal of Altar of Victory from Senate House
392	Revolt of Eugenius
394	Battle of R. Frigidus; suicide of Nicomachus Flavianus
395	Honorius rules west
395–430	Augustine bishop of Hippo
408	Fall and death of Stilicho
410	Alaric and Visigoths take Rome
429	Vandals cross into Africa
430	Death of Augustine

East

379–95	Theodosius I
381	Council of Constantinople
387	Riot of Statues at Antioch
395	Arcadius rules east
398	John Chrysostom bishop of Constantinople
403	First exile of Chrysostom
404	Chrysostom deposed

List of Emperors

The names in square brackets are those of usurpers, i.e. those not regarded as legitimate; not all are included. Note that overlapping dates indicate joint reigns.

Gordon I 238
Gordian II 238
Balbinus 238
Pupienus 238
Gordian III 238–44
Philip the Arab 244–9
Decius 249–51
Trebonianus Gallus 251–3
Volusianus 251–3
Valerian 253–60
Gallienus 253–68
[Postumus] 259–68
[Victorinus] 267–8
[Tetricus] 270–4
Claudius II Gothicus 268–70
Quintillus 270
Aurelian 270–5
Tacitus 275–6
Florianus 276
Probus 276–82
Carus 282–3
Carinus 283–5
Numerianus 283–4
Diocletian 284–305

Maximian 286–305, 307–10
[Carausius] 286–93
[Allectus] 293–6
Constantius I Chlorus 305–6
Galerius 305–11
Severus 306–7
Constantine I, s. of Constantius I 306–37
Licinius 308–24
Maximin, nephew of Galerius 308–13
Constantine II, s. of Constantine I 337–40
Constans, s. of Constantine I 337–50
Constantius II, s. of Constantine I 337–61
[Magnentius] 350–3
[Vetranio] 350
[Nepotianus] 350
Julian 361–3
Jovian 363–4
Valentinian I 364–75
Valens, brother of Valentinian I 364–78
[Procopius] 365–6
Gratian, s. of Valentinian I 367–83
Theodosius I 379–95
[Magnus Maximus] 383–7
[Eugenius] 392–4
Arcadius, s. of Theodosius I 383–408
Honorius, s. of Theodosius I 393–423
Theodosius II, s. of Arcadius 408–50

Primary Sources

AMBROSE, bishop of Milan, AD 374–97, formerly governor of Aemilia-Liguria. Author of many exegetical writings, works on the sacraments, on the duties of clergy, on virginity, sermons, hymns and letters. Translation, Fathers of the Church, Nicene and Post-Nicene Fathers, 2nd ser., X and Library of Christian Classics V, also in Fathers of the Church.

AMMIANUS MARCELLINUS, historian, author of the *Res Gestae*, in Latin, finished in Rome in the early 390s and covering the period AD 96–378 (only the part from AD 354 survives). There is an excellent translation (abridged) available in Penguin paperback, which has a very good general introduction; otherwise text and translation in Loeb Classical Library. The most important secondary work on Ammianus is by John Matthews, *The Roman Empire of Ammianus* (London, 1989); on his language and mental outlook see Robin Seager, *Ammianus Marcellinus. Seven Studies in his Language and Thought* (Columbia, Miss., 1986) and R. L. Rike, *Apex Omnium: Religion in the Res Gestae of Ammianus Marcellinus* (Berkeley and Los Angeles, 1987).

ANONYMUS VALESIANUS, *pars prior* (= *Origo Constantini imperatoris*), short biography of Constantine, basically late fourth century, written by a pagan with additions based on the Christian history of Orosius. Translation in Loeb edition of Ammianus, vol. III.

AUGUSTINE, bishop of Hippo, North Africa, AD 395–430. Author of the *Confessions* (c. AD 400, 13 books), of which the translation with notes by Henry Chadwick (Oxford, 1991) is recommended; *City of God* (AD 413–26, 22 books), and many letters, sermons and treatises, including the *De Doctrina Christiana* (finished AD 426). Translations: *Confessions* and *City of God* are in Penguin; *City of God* is also in Everyman, see also Loeb Classical Library. Augustine's works as a whole are translated in several series, e.g. the Library of the Fathers, Library of Christian Classics, Fathers of the Church and Ancient Christian Writers. See Peter Brown, *Augustine of Hippo* (London, 1967) (with date charts of Augustine's writings and notes of translations); Henry Chadwick, *Augustine* (London, 1986).

AUSONIUS, *c*. 310–93/4, rhetor from Bordeaux, tutor to the young Gratian, and subsequently Praetorian Prefect and consul. Author of many poems in classical metres, including the *Mosella* (on the River Moselle) and a set of poems commemorating the professors of Bordeaux, his friends and colleagues. Works translated in Loeb Classical Library. There are selections from Ausonius, Claudian and Prudentius in *The Last Poets of Imperial Rome* (Penguin). Major critical edition with notes and introduction, but no translation, by R. Green, *The Works of Ausonius* (Oxford, 1991); see also H. Sivan, *Ausonius of Bordeaux* (London, 1993).

BASIL, brother of Gregory of Nyssa and Macrina, friend of Gregory of Nazianzus, studied at Caesarea, Constantinople and Athens, bishop of Caesarea in Cappadocia, AD 370–9. Author of homilies on *Hexaemeron* (six days of creation), ascetic works including rules for monastic life, *On the Holy Spirit*, *Address to the Young on how they might Benefit from Greek Literature*, letters. Translations in Loeb Classical Library, Fathers of the Church, Nicene and Post-Nicene Fathers II, VIII.

CALENDAR OF AD 354, known only through a lost Carolingian copy, valuable source for public festivals and iconography. See M. R. Salzman, *On Roman Time. The Codex-Calendar of 354 and the Rhythms of Urban Life in Late Antiquity* (Berkeley and Los Angeles, 1991).

CLAUDIAN, Latin poet from Alexandria, panegyrist of Stilicho and author of hexameter poems on imperial occasions and political events, as well as of invectives against the eastern ministers Eutropius and Rufinus. Translation in Loeb Classical Library; see also W. Barr, *Claudian's Panegyric on the Fourth Consulship of Honorius* (1981), and see under Ausonius. See in general Alan Cameron, *Claudian* (Oxford, 1970).

Codex Theodosianus (CTh.), collection of imperial laws made in Constantinople under Theodosius II. English translation by Clyde Pharr (Princeton, 1952). See Tony Honoré, 'The Making of the Theodosian Code', *Zeitschrift der Savigny-Stiftung für Rechtsgeschichte* 103, röm. Abt. (1986), 133–222.

De Rebus Bellicis, anonymous Latin treatise on military matters in the form of a letter to the reigning emperors, probably Valentinian and Valens, AD 368. The MSS. contain illustrations of the ingenious inventions recommended by the author. Translation and discussion in M. W. C. Hassall and R. I. Ireland, eds., *De Rebus Bellicis* (Oxford, BAR, 1979); see also E. A. Thompson, *A Roman Reformer and Inventor* (Oxford, 1952).

DESERT FATHERS, collections of saying and lives of the eastern ascetics, easily accessible through the translation by Benedicta Ward, *The Sayings of the Desert Fathers* (London, 1975) and *The Wisdom of the Desert Fathers* (Oxford, 1975), see also Helen Waddell, *The Desert Fathers* (New York, 1936). See also under Palladius.

EPHREM THE SYRIAN, *c.* 306–73, Syriac Christian writer and theologian from Nisibis, who later moved to Edessa; author of *Carmina Nisibena*, *Hymns against Julian* and many other works in Syriac, of which a high proportion were soon translated into Greek. Translations by S. P. Brock, *The Harp of the Spirit. 18 Poems of St. Ephrem* (London, 1983) and Kathleen McVey, *Ephrem the Syrian, Hymns*, Classics of Western Spirituality (New York, 1989). The *Hymns against Julian* I–IV are included in S. N. C. Lieu, ed., *The Emperor Julian. Panegyric and Polemic*, TTH (2nd ed., Liverpool, 1989). See R. Murray, *Symbols of*

Church and Kingdom. A Study in Early Syriac Tradition (Cambridge, 1975).

EUNAPIUS, pagan Greek historian from Sardis, AD 349–*c*. 404. Author of *Lives of the Sophists* (Loeb Classical Library) and a history from AD 270 to 404, in two editions, later used by Zosimus, but surviving only in fragments; both the nature of the two editions and whether Ammianus may have used Eunapius or Eunapius Ammianus are disputed. Translation and discussion, R. C. Blockley, *The Fragmentary Classicising Historians of the Later Roman Empire* I–II (Liverpool, 1981–3).

EUSEBIUS, bishop of Caesarea in Palestine, biblical scholar and historian of Constantine, d. AD 338/9. Author of *Church History* (Penguin edition); *Tricennalian Oration*, trans. and comm. by H. A. Drake, *In Praise of Constantine* (Berkeley and Los Angeles, 1976) ; *Life of Constantine*, translated in Nicene and Post-Nicene Fathers I, Averil Cameron and Stuart Hall (Oxford, forthcoming); *Chronicle*, surviving only in Syriac translation, but translated into Latin by Jerome; also apologetic works (*Preparation for the Gospel, Demonstration of the Gospel, Theophany*). See T. D. Barnes, *Constantine and Eusebius* (Cambridge, Mass., 1981).

GREGORY OF NAZIANZUS, son of bishop of Nazianzus in Cappadocia, highly educated like Basil, resisted ordination and was later unwillingly raised to be bishop of Sasima by Basil, and was bishop of Constantinople in 380; later resigned, died *c*. 390. Highly accomplished rhetorician, author of funeral orations on Basil, his sister Gorgonia and his parents, theological writings (including *Five Theological Orations*), letters and poems, some autobiographical. Select orations and letters in Nicene and Post-Nicene Fathers II, VII.

GREGORY OF NYSSA, younger brother of Basil and Macrina, bishop of Nyssa, deposed for incompetence and restored, continues Basil's theology and becomes leading ecclesiastic after Basil's death, died *c*. AD 394. Author of theological, mystical and ascetic works including *Catechetical Orations, On Virginity, Life of*

Moses, trans. E. Ferguson and A. J. Malherbe (New York, 1978), *Life of Macrina*, English trans. by V. Woods Callahan, *Saint Gregory of Nyssa. Ascetical Works*, Fathers of the Church 58 (Washington, DC, 1967). Translations of many of his works in Nicene and Post-Nicene Fathers II, V.

Historia Augusta, collection of often scurrilous imperial biographies up to the reign of Diocletian, starting with Hadrian, supposedly composed by six different authors writing under Constantine. Now generally thought to be the work of one author in late fourth-century Rome. Penguin translation (*Lives of the Later Caesars*), with A. Birley's article in T. A. Dorey, ed., *Latin Biography* (London, 1967), 113–38; text and translation in Loeb Classical Library. See R. Syme, *Ammianus and the Historia Augusta* (Oxford, 1968); T. D. Barnes, *The Sources of the Historia Augusta* (Brussels, 1978), and for computer analysis, I. Marriott, 'The authorship of the Historia Augusta: two computer studies', *JRS* 69 (1979), 65–77.

IAMBLICHUS, Neoplatonist philosopher at Apamea in Syria under Constantine, author of *On the Pythagorean Life* (translation with notes by Gillian Clark, Translated Texts for Historians (Liverpool, 1989); *On the Mysteries*, trans. T. Taylor (2nd ed., London, 1895).

JEROME, AD 342–419. Monk, ascetic and scholar, in Rome 382–4, later set up monastery at Bethlehem. Prolific author and translator of Greek works, including works by Origen and Eusebius's *Chronicle*, also of the Hebrew Bible (Jerome's version is known as the Vulgate); author of exegetical and dogmatic works, often polemical in tone, *On Famous Men*, homilies, *Lives* of the hermits, letters. Selected letters translated in Loeb Classical Library. See J. N. Kelly, *Jerome* (London, 1975).

JOHN CHRYSOSTOM, pupil of Libanius, priest at Antioch and bishop of Constantinople, AD 398, twice deposed, and finally exiled AD 404, d. 407. Perhaps the greatest of Christian preachers, and author of many sermons as well as biblical commentaries and other works. Some sermons trans. by S. Neill, *Chrysostom and his*

Message (London, 1962); works in Nicene and Post-Nicene Fathers I, IX–XIV. *Address on Vainglory and the Right Way for Parents to Bring up their Children*, trans. in M. L. W. Laistner, *Christianity and Pagan Culture in the Later Roman Empire* (New York, 1951). See generally F. Young, *From Nicaea to Chalcedon* (London, 1983), 143–59.

JULIAN, emperor (AD 361–3), author of speeches and other works in Greek, including *Against the Galilaeans*, *Caesares*, *Hymn to King Helios*, *Misopogon* ('Beard-hater', on which see Maud Gleason, 'Festive satire: Julian's *Misopogon* and the New Year at Antioch', *JRS* 76 (1968), 106–19). Julian's works are available in the Loeb Classical Library; see also R. Browning, *The Emperor Julian* (Berkeley and Los Angeles, 1976) and G. W. Bowersock, *Julian the Apostate* (Cambridge, Mass., 1976) , with Gore Vidal's novel, *Julian* (London, 1964). S. C. Lieu, *The Emperor Julian. Panegyric and Polemic*, 2nd ed. (Liverpool, 1989), is a useful collection of sources about Julian in translation.

LACTANTIUS, Christian convert and former rhetor at Nicomedia, later tutor to Constantine's eldest son Crispus. For his work, *On the Deaths of the Persecutors* (*De Mortibus Persecutorum, DMP*), perhaps written *c*. AD 314, see the translation and commentary by J. Creed (Oxford, 1984).

LIBANIUS, (AD 314–93), pagan rhetor from Antioch, taught at Antioch, Constantinople and elsewhere and had both Christian and pagan pupils. Author of many orations; see A. F. Norman, ed., *Libanius's Autobiography (Or.* 1) (Oxford, 1965), and Loeb Classical Library (selections).

MARK THE DEACON, *Life of Porphyry of Gaza*, life of Porphyry, Bishop of Gaza, AD 396, surviving in Greek (ed. with French trans. by H. Grégoire and M-A. Kugener, Paris, 1930) and in Georgian translation from Syriac. Some scholars believe that the original was written in Syriac and at a much later date than the events it describes, but see P. Chuvin, *A Chronicle of the Last Pagans* (Cambridge, Mass., 1990), 76–8, 89–90 and notes.

MELANIA THE YOUNGER, *c.* AD 385–439, rich Roman aristocrat, granddaughter of Melania the Elder, wife of Pinianus, convert to asceticism; subject of *Life* in both Latin and Greek versions; see Elizabeth A. Clark, *The Life of Melania the Younger* (intro., trans. and commentary) (New York, 1984).

Notitia Dignitatum, official list of civil and military offices and establishments, the eastern part dating from *c.* AD 395, the western from *c.* AD 430, ed. O. Seeck (no English translation exists). See R. Goodburn and R. Bartholomew, eds., *Aspects of the Notitia Dignitatum* (Oxford, 1976) ; J. H. Ward, 'The Notitia Dignitatum', *Latomus* 33 (1974), 397–434. For some of the splendid manuscript illustrations, see Tim Cornell and John Matthews, *Atlas of the Roman World* (Oxford, 1982),202–3.

OPTATUS, bishop of Milevis in North Africa, wrote a history of the Donatist schism, AD 365, attaching an Appendix of documents from the reign of Constantine. English translation by O. R. Vassall-Phillips (London, 1917).

OROSIUS, author of *Historia adversus Paganos*, covering the period from Adam to AD 417, an apologetic history of Rome, emphasizing the disasters that had taken place under pagan rule.

PALLADIUS, author of *Lausiac History*, monastic collection in Greek made *c.* AD 420, English translation by R. T. Meyer, Ancient Christian Writers 34 (1965).

Panegyrici Latini, a collection of mainly anonymous Latin panegyrics made in Gaul, which includes Pliny's panegyric to Trajan (AD 100), but otherwise covers the period from Diocletian to Theodosius I. French translation in Budé edition, and see the English translation of Pacatus's panegyric on Theodosius by C. V. Nixon, Translated Texts for Historians (Liverpool, 1987).

PAULINUS OF NOLA, b. Bordeaux, *c.* AD 355, pupil of Ausonius, renounced his property and settled at Nola, where he became bishop *c.* AD 410, d. 431. Author of poems (some trans. J. Lindsay, London, 1948) and letters (trans. in Ancient

Christian Writers, 35–6). See W. H. C. Frend, 'The two worlds of Paulinus of Nola', in J. W. Binns, ed., *Latin Literature of the Fourth Century* (London, 1974), 100–133.

PORPHYRY, Neoplatonist philosopher and pupil of Plotinus, late third century, whose work *Against the Christians* was destroyed by order of Constantine. Author of a *Life of Plotinus*, translated in Loeb ed. of Plotinus, a *Life of Pythagoras*, trans. M. Hadas and M. Smith, *Heroes and Gods. Spiritual Biographies in Antiquity* (London, 1965), *Letter to his wife Marcella*, trans. with notes by Kathleen O'Brien Wicker (Atlanta, Georgia, 1987).

RUFINUS, b. AD 345 at Aquileia, translator of Greek authors including Origen, Basil, Gregory of Nazianzus; translated *Historia Monachorum* from Greek original; translated and continued the *Church History* of Eusebius, basing the latter part on the lost work by Gelasius of Caesarea. Translation, Ancient Christian Writers 20, Nicene and Post-Nicene Fathers III.

SIDONIUS APOLLINARIS (*c*. AD 430–80), b. in Aquitaine, local landowner, became bishop of Auvergne in Clermont-Ferrand. Author of poems in classical metres, and nine books of letters; translation in Loeb Classical Library.

SOCRATES, lawyer and church historian in Constantinople, 440s, author of a church history in seven books continuing Eusebius. Translation in Nicene and Post-Nicene Fathers II.

SOZOMEN, like Socrates, lawyer and church historian in Constantinople, 440s, author of a church history in nine books continuing Eusebius. Translation in Nicene and Post-Nicene Fathers II.

SYMMACHUS, Q. Aurelius Symmachus, b. *c*. AD 345, leading pagan senator, procos. of Africa, AD 373–4, prefect of the city of Rome and consul. Author of speeches and ten books of letters. Translation of *Relationes* dealing with the Altar of Victory, AD 384, in R. H. Barrow, *Prefect and Emperor* (Oxford, 1973); there is no

English translation of the letters, but see the Budé ed.; there is an Italian commentary underway. See J. F. Matthews, 'The Letters of Symmachus', in Binns, ed., *Latin Literature of the Fourth Century*, 58–99.

SYNESIUS (*c.* AD 370–*c.* 413), landowner from Cyrenaica, pupil of Hypatia in Alexandria, later became bishop of Ptolemais, *c.* 410. Author of (Greek) letters, hymns and treatises, some semi-philosophical: *De Regno, De Providentia, Dion, On Dreams*, and a speech *On Baldness*. Translation by A. Fitzgerald (1926, 1930). See in general Jay Bregman, *Synesius of Cyrene: Philosopher-Bishop* (Berkeley and Los Angeles, 1982); Alan Cameron and Jacqueline Long, with Lee Sherry, *Barbarians and Politics at the Court of Arcadius* (Berkeley, 1992); however, the dates and the interpretation of some of Synesius's works are much disputed.

THEODORET, bishop of Cyrrhus in northern Syria, AD 423–66, and Christian controversialist. Author of many letters (Eng. trans. in Nicene and Post-Nicene Fathers II, III, repr. 1979); R. M. Price, *A History of the Monks of Syria by Theodoret of Cyrrhus* (Kalamazoo, 1985); *Ecclesiastical History*, trans. in Nicene and Post-Nicene Fathers II, III.

VEGETIUS, author of *De Re Militari* ('On military affairs'), late fourth century. Trans. by J. Clark (1944). See W. Goffart, 'The date and purpose of Vegetius, *De re militari*', *Traditio* 33 (1977), 65 ff.; T. D. Barnes, 'The date and identity of Vegetius', *Phoenix* 33 (1979), 254 ff.

ZOSIMUS, pagan historian, writing in the late fifth or early sixth century, author of a *New History*, up to the year AD 410, closely dependent on the lost history of Eunapius and the fifth-century historian Olympiodorus of Thebes. English translation with short notes by R. Ridley (Canberra, 1982).

Further Reading

In English, A. H. M. Jones, *The Later Roman Empire. A Social, Administrative and Economic Survey*, 2 vols. (Oxford, 1964) (shorter version: *The Decline of the Ancient World*, London, 1966) is fundamental; for an introduction see also (on a very different scale) Peter Brown, *The World of Late Antiquity* (London, 1971). G. Alföldy, *The Social History of Rome*, Eng. trans. (London, 1985), gives a very highly coloured picture of the later Roman empire. Roger Collins, *Early Medieval Europe 300–1000* (London, 1991), provides a military and political narrative in a short compass. Vol. XIII of the revised *Cambridge Ancient History* covers the period AD 337–425. In German there is now an extremely full reference work on the later empire by A. Demandt (*Der Spätantike*) in the series known as *Müllers Handbuch des Altertumswissenschaft* (Munich, 1989). Strongly recommended for pictures and orientation is Tim Cornell and John Matthews, *Atlas of the Roman World* (Oxford, 1982) (much more of an illustrated history than its title implies); also useful is Clive Foss and Paul Magdalino, *Rome and Byzantium* (Oxford, 1977).

I INTRODUCTION: THE THIRD-CENTURY BACKGROUND

Third-century crisis: the most sensible introduction is by F. Millar, *The Roman Empire and its Neighbours*, 2nd ed. (London, 1981), Chapter 13. For very negative views see M. I. Rostovtzeff, *Social and Economic History of the Roman Empire*, 2nd ed., rev. P. Fraser (Oxford, 1957), Chapter 10, and G. Alföldy, *The*

Social History of Rome, Eng. trans. (London, 1985, rev. 1988), Chapter 6 'The crisis in the Roman Empire and structural change in society', with his article, 'The crisis of the third century as seen by contemporaries', *Greek, Roman and Byzantine Studies* 15 (1974), 89 ff. R. MacMullen, *Roman Government's Response to Crisis, AD 235–337* (New Haven, 1976) also deals with this period. On the difficult questions of coinage and inflation see Michael Crawford, 'Finance, coinage and money from the Severans to Constantine', *ANRW* Prinzipat II.2 (Berlin, 1975), 560–93. D. Sperber, *Roman Palestine 200–400, Money and Prices*, 2nd rev. ed. (Bar-Ilan, 1991) uses the evidence of rabbinic sources for prices in the third century. On the broader economic issues as well as on the Egyptian evidence, see D. Rathbone, *Economic Rationalism and Rural Society in Third-Century A.D. Egypt. The Heroninos Archive and the Appianus Estate* (Cambridge, 1991).

On the 'Gallic empire' see J. Drinkwater, *The Gallic Empire. Separatism and Continuity in the North-Western Provinces of the Roman Empire* (Stuttgart, 1987).

For 'insecurity' and increased religiosity in the third century see E. R. Dodds, *Pagan and Christian in an Age of Anxiety* (Cambridge, 1965), and see Peter Brown, *The Making of Late Antiquity* (Cambridge, Mass., 1978).

For the continued vitality of paganism see R. Lane Fox, *Pagans and Christians* (Harmondsworth, 1986), and on Christianity and Christianization see R. Markus, *Christianity in the Roman World* (London, 1974); id., *The End of Ancient Christianity* (Cambridge, 1991). Averil Cameron, *Christianity and the Rhetoric of Empire* (Berkeley and Los Angeles, 1991), and (for a sceptical view) R. MacMullen, *Christianizing the Roman Empire AD 100–400* (New Haven, 1981).

II THE SOURCES

There are several collections of sources in translation: N. Lewis and M. Reinhold, *Roman Civilization* II (New York, rev. ed. 1966) ; R. P. Coleman-Norton, *Roman State and Christian Church* I-II (1966); A. H. M. Jones, *A History of Rome through the Fifth Century II: The Empire* (London, 1970); J. Stevenson, *A New Eusebius*, (London, 1957 and later eds.) and J. N. D. Kelly, *Creeds, Councils and Controversies* (London, 1966 and later eds.). On special topics see also the source-books by Brian Croke and Jill Harries, *Religious Conflict in Fourth-Century Rome* (Sydney, 1982) and S. C. Lieu, *The Emperor Julian: Panegyric and Polemic*, Translated Texts for Historians (2nd ed., Liverpool, 1989). For reference on the careers of individuals, consult A. H. M. Jones, *Prosopography of the Later Roman Empire I, AD 260–395* (Cambridge, 1971), a biographical dictionary of office-holders; however, only those Christians who held public office are included.

For general information on Latin authors, see Robert Browning, 'The Later Principate', in *Cambridge History of Classical Literature* II (Cambridge, 1982) (also published separately). F. Young, *From Nicaea to Chalcedon* (London, 1983) contains discussion and bibliographies on the main Christian writers in Greek.

On education, see H-I. Marrou, *A History of Education in Antiquity*, 3rd ed., Eng. trans. (Madison, 1982) and see R. Kaster, *Guardians of Language. The Grammarian and Society in Late Antiquity* (Berkeley and Los Angeles, 1988), and see further Chapter 10. In general, see A. Momigliano, *The Conflict between Paganism and Christianity in the Fourth Century* (Oxford, 1963) and B. Croke and A. Emmett, eds., *History and Historians in Late Antiquity* (Sydney, 1983).

III THE NEW EMPIRE: DIOCLETIAN

The main sources for Diocletian and the tetrarchy are *SHA, Life of Carus*; Lactantius, *De Mortibus Persecutorum*; Eusebius, *Church History* VIII; Aurelius Victor, *Caesares* and *Epitome*; Eutropius, *Breviarium*; *Panegyrici Latini* nos. II(10) (AD 289); III(11) (AD 291); IV (8) (AD 297); V(9) (AD 298). The account of Diocletian's reign in Zosimus, *New History* is unfortunately missing. See in general S. Williams, *Diocletian and the Roman Recovery* (New York, 1985), for a traditional account; T. D. Barnes, *The New Empire of Diocletian and Constantine*

(Cambridge, Mass., 1982) collects the evidence for known personnel in both reigns including emperors and many kinds of office-holders; see also Jones, *LRE*, I, Chapter 2. R. MacMullen, *Corruption and the Decline of Rome* (New Haven, 1988), paints a black picture of the late Roman administrative system. Finance, coinage etc.: M. Hendy, *Studies in the Byzantine Monetary Economy c. 300–1450* (Cambridge, 1985) (essential for the whole period).

Parts of Diocletian's Edict on Maximum Prices have been found in several different places, and a consolidated edition of the immensely long Latin text which results is given by Joyce Reynolds in C. M. Roueché, *Aphrodisias in Late Antiquity* (London, 1989), no.231; there is a translation in Lewis and Reinhold II, no. 129, Jones, *History of Rome through the Fifth Century* II, 308 ff. The Latin text of Diocletian's Currency Revaluation edict is also included in Roueché, op. cit., no.230; for partial translation see Crawford, 'Finance, coinage and money' (see above), 589 ff. Diocletian's laws were not included in the Theodosian Code and are to be found in the *Codex Justinianus*, part of the *Corpus Iuris Civilis*, and other collections.

On the religious aspects of Diocletian's reign see R. MacMullen, *Roman Government's Response to Crisis* (New Haven, 1976); J. H. W. G. Liebeschuetz, *Continuity and Change in Roman Religion* (Oxford, 1979) and G. E. M. de Ste Croix, 'Aspects of the Great Persecution', *HThR.* 47 (1954), 75 ff. For the army reforms of Diocletian see the further reading given for Chapter 9; for the size of the army (not more than about 400,000) see especially R. MacMullen, 'How big was the Roman army?', *Klio* 62 (1980), 451–60, and on P. Beatty Panop. 2, R. Duncan-Jones, 'Pay and numbers in Diocletian's army', *Chiron* 8 (1978), 541–60 (revised version also in his *Structure and Scale in the Roman Economy* [Cambridge, 1990], 105–17).

IV THE NEW EMPIRE: CONSTANTINE

The main sources for Constantine are Eusebius, *Church History* (Penguin), bks. IX–X; *Life of Constantine*; *Tricennalian Oration*; Lactantius, *De Mortibus Persecutorum*; the letters and documents on Donatism included in Optatus's *Appendix*; Anon. Vales.;

Zosimus, *New History* II. 9–39; *Pan. Lat.* nos. VI (AD 307); VII
(AD 310); VIII (AD 312); IX (AD 313); X (AD 321). For the coinage
see *Roman Imperial Coinage (RIC)* VI (ed. C. H. V. Sutherland)
and VII (ed. P. Bruun), introductions. A newly discovered Latin
text from Pisidia relating to Maximinus's renewal of persecution in
AD 312 is published by S. Mitchell, *JRS* 78 (1988), 105–24. For
Constantine's religious policies and the church see the source book
by J. Stevenson, *A New Eusebius* (London, rev. ed., 1987);
S. G. Hall, *Doctrine and Practice in the Early Church* (London,
1991) is a useful companion to Stevenson, *A New Eusebius* and
Creeds and Councils (see under Chapter 5).

The most detailed and comprehensive book on Constantine is
T. D. Barnes, *Constantine and Eusebius* (Cambridge, Mass.,
1981), which should be supplemented by his *New Empire of
Diocletian and Constantine* (Cambridge, Mass., 1982). See also
Jones, *LRE*, I, Chapter 3. There are many shorter books, e.g.
R. MacMullen, *Constantine* (New York, 1969); A. H. M. Jones,
Constantine and the Conversion of Europe (London, 1948, repr.
1978). N. Baynes, *Constantine the Great and the Christian Church*
(1929, 2nd ed., 1972) is still useful. See also R. MacMullen,
Christianizing the Roman Empire. AD 100–400 (New Haven, 1984)
and 'What difference did Christianity make?' *Historia* 35 (1986),
322–43. R. Krautheimer, *Rome. Profile of a City, 312–1308*
(Princeton, 1980) discusses Constantine's Roman churches, but
his account of Constantinople in *Three Christian Capitals*
(Berkeley and Los Angeles, 1983) attributes more to Constantine
than the sources allow.

V CHURCH AND STATE: THE LEGACY OF CONSTANTINE

F. G. B. Millar, *The Emperor in the Roman World* (London,
1977), 580–607, sets Constantine's dealings with the church, and
especially with the Donatists, in the perspective of established
imperial procedures in secular matters. For the continuance of
Donatism W. H. C. Frend, *The Donatist Church* (Oxford, 1971) is
still well worth reading, especially for its emphasis on the
archaeological evidence, although its characterization of Donatists
as 'rural' and Catholics as 'urban', and the idea of Donatism as a

'nationalist' movement, have been shown to be much too sweeping: see the various essays by Peter Brown, in his *Religion and Society in the Age of St Augustine* (London, 1972), and for Augustine and Donatism, Brown's biography, *Augustine of Hippo* (London, 1967).

For doctrinal and other controversies after Constantine see the source book edited by J. Stevenson, *Creeds, Councils and Controversies* (London, rev. ed., 1989), and see Hall (above, Chapter 4); for Rome, see also Brian Croke and Jill Harries, eds., *Religious Conflict in Fourth-Century Rome* (Sydney, 1982). For Eusebius's political theory see F. Dvornik, *Early Christian and Byzantine Political Philosophy*, 2 vols. (Washington, DC, 1963). On Arianism see R. Gregg and D. Groh, *Early Arianism. A View of Salvation* (Philadelphia, 1981), and especially R. L. Williams, *Arius, Heresy and Tradition* (London, 1987); older ideas of a canonical norm, from which 'heresy' is a deviation, are questioned in some of the essays in Rowan Williams, ed., *The Making of Orthodoxy* (Cambridge, 1989). G. A. Kennedy, *Greek Rhetoric under Christian Emperors* (Princeton, 1983), gives a good introduction to the public oratory of the great Greek bishops of the period. For the continuance of paganism see P. Chuvin, *A Chronicle of the Last Pagans* (Cambridge, Mass., 1990); see also G. Fowden, 'Bishops and temples in the eastern Roman empire 320–425', *Journal of Theological Studies* n.s.29 (1978), 53–78. For Christians and Jews see F. Millar, 'The Jews of the Graeco-Roman diaspora, AD 312–438', in J. Lieu, J. North and T. Rajak, eds, *The Jews among Pagans and Christians in the Roman Empire* (London, 1992), 97–123; R. L. Wilken, *John Chrysostom and the Jews* (Berkeley and Los Angeles, 1983); A. Linder, *The Jews in Roman Imperial Legislation* (Detroit and Jerusalem, 1987) (sources in translation). Christianization: R. MacMullen, *Christianizing the Roman Empire*, AD 100–400 (New Haven, 1984); 'What difference did Christianity make?', *Historia* 35 (1986), 322–43; Christianization of the Roman senate: Peter Brown, 'Aspects of the Christianization of the Roman aristocracy', *JRS* 51 (1961), 1–11 (also in his *Religion and Society in the Age of St. Augustine*, 162–82). For the late Roman aristocracy, and especially Symmachus and the Altar of Victory, see J. F. Matthews, *Western Aristocracies and Imperial Court AD 364–425*

(Oxford, 1975, rev. 1991), and more generally, see A. Momigliano, ed., *The Conflict between Paganism and Christianity in the Fourth Century* (Oxford, 1963).

For Roman women and asceticism see Elizabeth A. Clark, *Ascetic Piety and Women's Faith* (Lewiston, NY/Queenston, Ont., 1986), and her *The Life of Melania the Younger* (Lewiston, NY, 1984). Peter Brown, *The Body and Society. Men, Women and Sexual Renunciation in Early Christianity* (New York, 1988) sets out in detail the evidence for the development of asceticism, and see also G. Gould, 'Women and the Fathers', in W. J. Shiels and D. Wood, eds., *Women in the Church*, Studies in Church History 27 (Oxford, 1990), 1–13; M. R. Salzman, 'Aristocratic women: conductors of Christianity in the fourth century', *Helios* 16 (1989), 207–20; Gillian Clark, *Women in Late Antiquity* (Oxford, 1993). For the development of monasticism see Philip Rousseau, *Pachomius* (Berkeley and Los Angeles, 1975) and D. Chitty, *The Desert a City* (Oxford, 1966). The social penetration of Christianization: R. Markus, *The End of Ancient Christianity* (Cambridge, 1990); Peter Brown, *Politics and Persuasion in Late Antiquity* (Madison, Wisc, 1992). Christian writing and use of language: Averil Cameron, *Christianity and the Rhetoric of Empire* (Berkeley and Los Angeles, 1991).

VI THE REIGN OF JULIAN

A useful translation of sources otherwise not easily acccessible is provided by S. C. Lieu, *The Emperor Julian. Panegyric and Polemic* (Translated Texts for Historians, Liverpool, 2nd ed., 1989), containing the Latin panegyric on Julian by Mamertinus (AD 362), part of John Chrysostom's homily on S. Babylas and the Syriac hymns against Julian by Ephrem Syrus. Libanius's writings on Julian are contained in the Loeb edition, vol. I. Gregory of Nazianzus is also important, as are the ecclesiastical historians Rufinus, Socrates, Sozomen and Theodoret. For the Syriac letter about the rebuilding of the Jerusalem Temple see S. P. Brock, 'A letter attributed to Cyril of Jerusalem on the rebuilding of the Temple', *Bull. School of Oriental and African Studies* 40 (1977), 267–86.

There are many books available on Julian, among which J. Bidez's *La vie de l'empereur Julien* (Paris, 1930) remains a classic: in English see especially R. Browning, *The Emperor Julian* (Berkeley and Los Angeles, 1976) and G. W. Bowersock, *Julian the Apostate* (Cambridge, Mass., 1978). Diana Bowder, *The Age of Constantine and Julian* (London, 1978), is written for a less scholarly audience, while P. Athanassiadi, *Julian* (London, 1992, rev. ed., first published as *Julian and Hellenism*, Oxford, 1981) focuses on Julian's interest in and relation to Greek culture. Julian has caught the imagination of generations, and Gore Vidal's novel, *Julian* (London, 1964) is well worth reading in order to find out why.

For the conservative attachment of several authors of the period to the ideal of the independence of cities in relation to central authority, see the long article by G. Dagron, 'L'empire romain d'orient au IVème siècle et les traditions politiques de l'hellénisme: le témoignage de Thémistios', *Travaux et Mémoires* 3 (1968), 1–242; for the gradual encroachment of central government on city administration see Fergus Millar, 'Empire and City, Augustus to Julian: obligations, excuses and status', *JRS* 73 (1983), 76–96. An interesting picture of a single city and its urban elites in the fourth century, demonstrating the value of using archaeological evidence, is given in P. Cartledge and A. Spawforth, *Hellenistic and Roman Sparta. A Tale of Two Cities* (London, 1989), Chapter 9. For Ammianus's assessment of Julian (XXV. 4 and generally) see R. C. Blockley, *Ammianus Marcellinus. A Study of his Historiography and Political Thought* (Brussels, 1975).

VII The Late Roman State: Constantius to Theodosius

See in the first place Jones, *LRE*, I, Chapters 5, 15–16; on the rebellion of Procopius and the question of legitimacy, Matthews, *The Roman Empire of Ammianus*, 191–203, and *ibid.*, Chapters 11–12 on the office of emperor and the character of government, with R. MacMullen, *Corruption and the Decline of Rome* (New Haven, 1988), especially Chapter 2. The late Roman bureaucracy is discussed in detail by Demandt, *Die Spätantike*, with charts to show its structure.

For Ausonius, and the value placed on rhetoric as a means of social advancement: K. Hopkins, 'Social mobility in the Late Roman Empire: the case of Ausonius', *Class. Quart.* 11 (1961), 239–300, with Alan Cameron, *Claudian* (Oxford, 1970); compare R. Kaster, *Guardians of Language. The Grammarian and Society in Late Antiquity* (Berkeley and Los Angeles, 1988), on the influence of *grammatici*, the teachers who passed on these skills in the schools. The heavy penalties in the lawcourts are discussed by R. MacMullen, 'Judicial savagery in the Roman empire', *Chiron* 16 (1986), 43–62.

On patronage and dependent social relations, and for comparison with other periods in the ancient world, see Andrew Wallace-Hadrill, ed., *Patronage in Roman Society* (London, 1989), with MacMullen, *Corruption and the Decline of Rome*, Chapter 2; Peter Garnsey and Greg Woolf, 'Patronage of the rural poor in the Roman world', in Wallace-Hadrill, ed., *Patronage in Roman Society*, 153–67, discuss pagan and Christian patronage at 162–7. Carlo Levi's account of his internment in southern Italy in the 1930s, *Christ stopped at Eboli,* gives a vivid picture of a rural society dependent on patronage in action. Generally on the differences between pre-industrial and 'modern' societies, see Patricia Crone, *Pre-Industrial Societies* (Oxford, 1989).

For the traditional ideas of a 'caste-system' and late Roman 'totalitarianism' see A. H. M. Jones, 'The Roman colonate' and 'The caste-system in the later Roman empire', in *The Roman Economy*, ed. P. Brunt (Oxford, 1974), Chapters 14 and 21, with M. I. Rostovtzeff, *Social and Economic History of the Roman Empire*, Eng. trans., rev. P. M. Fraser (Oxford, 1957), Chapter 12, 'The oriental despotism'; these are however overstated, for the reasons given in the chapter. Further critique in J-M. Carrié, 'Le "colonat" du Bas-Empire', *Opus* 1 (1982), 351–70; *id.*, 'Un roman des origines: les généalogies du "Colonat du Bas-Empire"', *ibid.*2 (1983),205–51; A. Marcone, *Il colonato tardoantico nella storiografia moderna (dal Fustel de Coulanges ai nostri giorni)* (Como, 1988). R. MacMullen, 'Social mobility and the Theodosian Code', *JRS* 54 (1964), 49–53 discusses the question of how to interpret the evidence of the law codes. Further evidence of actual social mobility is given in K. Hopkins, 'Elite mobility in the later Roman empire', *Past and Present* 32 (1965), 12–26; and see his 'Eunuchs in politics in the later Roman empire', *Proc.*

Cambridge Philological Society 189 (1963), 62–80. On decurions see MacMullen, *Corruption*, 46–9. On the difficult question of late Roman slavery and the olonate see C. R. Whittaker, 'Circe's pigs: from slavery to serfdom in the later Roman world', *Slavery and Abolition* 8 (1987), 88–123, and G. E. M. de Ste. Croix, *The Class Struggle in the Ancient Greek World* (London, 1981), with R. MacMullen, 'Late Roman slavery', *Historia* 36 (1987), 359–82; D. Rathbone, 'The ancient economy and Graeco-Roman Egypt', in L. Criscuolo and G. Geraci, eds., *Egitto e storia antica dall'ellenismo all'età araba* (Bologna, 1989), 159–76, esp. 161–7.

VIII LATE ROMAN ECONOMY AND SOCIETY

See in general C. E. King, ed., *Imperial Revenue, Expenditure and Monetary Policy in the Fourth Century AD* (Oxford, BAR, 1980). M. Hendy, *Studies in the Byzantine Monetary Economy c. 300–1450* (Cambridge, 1985), more on coinage, money and fiscal policy than on the general economy, is difficult to use because of the way it is arranged, but valuable for its description of late Roman finance and banking. On the bronze coinage see R. A. G. Carson, P. V. Hill and J. P. C. Kent, *Late Roman Bronze Coinage AD 324–498* (1972), and for the gold, J. P. C. Kent, 'Gold coinage in the later Roman empire', in R. A. G. Carson and C. H. V. Sutherland, eds., *Essays in Roman Coinage presented to Harold Mattingly* (1956), 190–204.

Mining: J. C. Edmondson, 'Mining in the later Roman Empire and beyond: continuity or disruption?', *JRS* 79 (1989), 84–102. Coinage and metals: Jones, *LRE*, 438–48; Hendy, *Studies in the Byzantine Monetary Economy*, 284–333. Large estates: see C. R. Whittaker, 'Late Roman trade and traders', in Peter Garnsey, Keith Hopkins and C. R. Whittaker, *Trade in the Ancient Economy* (London, 1983), 163–80. The villas at Carthage and Mungersdorf are illustrated in Foss and Magdalino, *Rome and Byzantium*, 41; see also John Percival, *The Roman Villa* (London, 1976) ; Edith Wightman, *Roman Trier and the Treveri* (London, 1970).

On slavery, see the items listed under Chapter 7, and

M. I. Finley, *The Ancient Economy*, 2nd rev. ed. (London, 1985). Some of the most important recent work on the late Roman economy has been done by Andrea Carandini and his school; see A. Giardina, ed., *Società romana e impero tardoantico*, III (Rome, 1986) , and for a review, C. Wickham, 'Marx, Sherlock Holmes and late Roman commerce', *JRS* 78 (1988), 183–93. For the corn-doles, see B. Sirks, *Food for Rome* (Amsterdam, 1991); J. Durliat, *De la ville antique à la ville byzantine* (Rome, 1990). On cities, C. Lepelley, *Les cités de l'Afrique romaine au Bas-Empire*, 2 vols. Paris, 1979) demonstrates the prosperity of late Roman cities in North Africa, while the relations between Antioch and its hinterland are discussed in the study by J. H. W. G. Liebeschuetz, *Antioch. City and Imperial Administration in the Later Roman Empire* (Oxford, 1972).

There are several important articles relevant to the fourth-century economy in C. Morrisson and J. Lefort, eds., *Hommes et richesses dans l'Empire byzantin I, IVe–VIIe siècle* (Paris, 1989), for example by C. Lepelley, P. Leveau, C. Abadie-Reynal and C. Panella. E. Patlagean's book, *Pauvreté économique et pauvreté sociale à Byzance (4e–7e siècles)* (Paris, 1977), provides an enormous amount of information on population growth and general economic conditions in the eastern provinces, while arguing that one of the consequences was an increase in the numbers of urban poor; see Chapter 11, and see also the review by Averil Cameron, *Past and Present* 88 (1980), 129–35. [Note that unlike most British historians, French scholars often classify the fourth century as part of Byzantium.]

Pilgrimage: J. Wilkinson, *Egeria's Travels* (London, 1971); E. D. Hunt, *Holy Land Pilgrimage in the Later Roman Empire* (Oxford, 1982). The story about Arsenius is quoted from Benedicta Ward, trans., *The Sayings of the Desert Fathers* (London, 1975), 14. For pilgrim souvenirs, see G. Vikan, *Byzantine Pilgrimage Art* (Washington, D.C., 1982). On Christian building, see Bryan Ward-Perkins, *From Classical Antiquity to the Middle Ages. Urban Public Building in Northern and Central Italy AD 300–850* (Oxford, 1984) (Appendix 2 lists church building in the period in Rome, Ravenna, Pavia and Lucca) and Patlagean, *Pauvreté économique*, 196–203. Literary evidence for Christian art: see the collection of sources by C. Mango, *The*

Art of the Byzantine Empire 312–1453 (Englewood Cliffs, 1972), and see further, Chapter 10.

The development of Christian charity is an important theme: see Patlagean, *Pauvreté économique*, 188–96; Judith Herrin, 'Ideals of charity, realities of welfare: the philanthropic activity of the Byzantine church', in R. Morris, ed., *Church and People in Byzantium* (Manchester, 1991), 151–64; J. Harries, '"Treasure in heaven": property and inheritance among the senators of late Rome', in E. Craik, ed., *Marriage and Property* (Aberdeen, 1984), 54–70; see also Garnsey and Woolf, *art. cit.* (Chapter 8) and Chapter 11 below. The late Roman family has been studied by Brent Shaw, 'The family in late antiquity: the experience of Augustine', *Past and Present* 115 (1987), 3–51, and see his 'Latin funerary epigraphy and family life in the later Roman empire', *Historia* 33 (1984), 457–97. For misogyny, virginity and sexuality in the thought of the church fathers, see R. Radford Ruether, 'Misogynism and virginal feminism in the Fathers of the Church', in Ruether, ed., *Religion and Sexism* (New York, 1974), 150–83; Elaine Pagels, *Adam, Eve and the Serpent* (London, 1988) and Averil Cameron, 'Virginity as metaphor', in Cameron, ed., *History as Text* (London, 1989), 184–205. Ascetic ideas were not confined to Christianity – see also the interesting book by Aline Rousselle, *Porneia* (Paris, 1983, Eng. trans. Oxford, 1988), and on Neoplatonic asceticism, *Iamblichus: On the Pythagorean Life*, trans. Gillian Clark (Liverpool, 1989), with the source-book by V. Wimbush, ed., *Ascetic Behavior in Greco-Roman Antiquity* (Minneapolis, 1990). On private life, see the section by Peter Brown on late antiquity in P. Ariès and G. Duby, eds., *A History of Private Life I. From Pagan Rome to Byzantium*, ed. P. Veyne (Eng. trans., Cambridge, Mass., 1987). The quotation is from G. Alföldy, *The Social History of Rome*, rev. Eng. trans. (London, 1988), 210, 217.

IX MILITARY AFFAIRS, BARBARIANS AND THE LATE ROMAN ARMY

Sources: Peter Heather and John Matthews, *The Goths in the Fourth Century* (Liverpool, 1991) (translated sources); for Jordanes's *Gothic History* see the translation by C. C. Mierow (repr. Cambridge, 1966) ; Pacatus's panegyric is translated by C. E. V. Nixon, *Pacatus, Panegyric to the Emperor Theodosius* (Liverpool, 1987); the fragments of Olympiodorus are translated by R. C. Blockley, *The Fragmentary Classicising Historians of the Later Roman Empire* II (Liverpool, 1983), and see I (Liverpool, 1981), 27–47.

On the early history of the Germans, see F. Millar, *The Roman Empire and its Neighbours*, Chapter 17, and E. A. Thompson, *The Early Germans* (Oxford, 1965). See generally on the Goths E. A. Thompson, *The Visigoths in the Time of Ulfila* (Oxford, 1966) ; H. Wolfram, *History of the Goths* (Eng. trans., London, 1988); T. S. Burns, *A History of the Ostrogoths* (Bloomington, 1984); Peter Heather, *Goths and Romans, 332–489* (Oxford, 1991). Huns: O. Maenchen-Helfen, *The World of the Huns* (Berkeley and Los Angeles, 1973); E. A. Thompson, *A History of Attila and the Huns* (Oxford, 1948).

For the battle of Adrianople see T. S. Burns, 'The battle of Adrianople: a reconsideration', *Historia* 22 (1974), 336–45 and Wolfram, *History of the Goths*, 117–39; Heather, *Goths and Romans*, Chapter 4. For its effects on the Roman army, see J. H. W. G. Liebeschuetz, *Barbarians and Bishops. Army, Church and State in the Age of Arcadius and Chrysostom* (Oxford, 1990), Chapters 1–2. Ulfila and the Gothic Bible are discussed in Heather and Matthews, Chapters 5 and 6. On the treaty of AD 382 see Heather, *Goths and Romans*, Chapter 5.

On *hospitalitas* (quartering), see W. Goffart, *Barbarians and Romans AD 418–584* (Princeton, 1980), though this is not accepted by all. For subsidies to barbarians see Heather and Matthews, 23–5. The evidence of Synesius and John Chrysostom is important for the politics of Constantinople in the years around AD 400: see Liebeschuetz, *Barbarians and Bishops*, and for Stilicho's policies, see Alan Cameron, *Claudian* (Oxford, 1970). Britain: M. Todd, *Roman Britain 55 BC–AD 400* (London, 1981); S. Johnson, *Later Roman Britain* (London, 1980).

B. Isaac, *The Limits of Empire* (Oxford, 1990), especially Chapters 4 and 5, is important for the Persian wars and the eastern frontier, on which M. H. Dodgeon and S. C. N. Lieu, *The Roman Frontier and the Persian Wars AD 226–363* (London, 1991) provides annotated and translated sources. F. Millar, 'Empire, community and culture in the Roman Near East: Greeks, Syrians, Jews and Arabs', *Journal of Jewish Studies* 38 (1987), 143–64 puts the case for the shift of balance towards the east. The theory of 'defence-in-depth' is stated by E. Luttwak, *The Grand Strategy of the Roman Empire* (Baltimore, 1976), but see J. C. Mann, 'Power, force and the frontiers of the empire', *JRS* 69 (1979), 175–83 and (against the idea of 'grand strategy') F. Millar, 'Emperors, frontiers and foreign relations, 31 BC to AD 378', *Britannia* 13 (1982), 1–23, with Isaac, *Limits of Empire*, Chapter 4.

For the desert frontier see also S. T. Parker, *Romans and Saracens. A History of the Arabian Frontier* (Winona Lake, 1986); id., *The Roman Frontier in Central Jordan. Interim report on the Limes Arabicus Project, 1980–85*, 2 vols. (Oxford, BAR Inst. ser., 340 i–ii, 1987) and D. Kennedy and D. Riley, *Rome's Desert Frontier from the Air* (London, 1990) (beautiful pictures and useful historical survey); on Rome's use of Arab allies see M. Sartre, *Trois études sur l'Arabie romaine et byzantine* (Brussels, 1982), 132–53; G. W. Bowersock, *Roman Arabia* (Cambridge, Mass., 1983), 138 ff.; I. Shahid, *Byzantium and the Arabs in the Fourth Century* (Washington D.C., 1984).

The army in cities: R. MacMullen, *Soldier and Civilian in the Later Roman Empire* (Cambridge, Mass., 1963); Isaac, *The Limits of Empire*, Chapter 6. The Roman army in general: Jones, *LRE*, Chapter 17; D. Hoffmann, *Das spätrömischen Bewegungsheer und die Notitia Dignitatum* (Düsseldorf, 1969); A. Ferrill, *The Fall of the Roman Empire. The Military Explanation* (London, 1986) (but see my remarks in the chapter). Isaac, *The Limits of Empire*, 208 ff. and 'The meaning of "limes" and "limitanei" in ancient sources', *JRS* 78 (1988), 125–47, argues against the older interpretation of *limitanei* as a peasant-militia. For barbarian federates, see Heather, *Goths and Romans*, 109 ff.; Constantinople and the fall of Gainas, see Liebeschuetz, *Barbarians and Bishops*, especially Chapters 4–5, 10, 16, and for the aftermath of the Gainas affair *ibid.*, Chapters 11–12.

X CULTURE IN THE LATE FOURTH CENTURY

For the educational system see P. Lemerle, *Byzantine Humanism*, Eng. trans. (Canberra, 1986), Chapter 3, and R. Kaster, *Guardians of Language. The Grammarian and Society in Late Antiquity* (Berkeley and Los Angeles, 1988), and on literacy in the late empire see W. V. Harris, *Ancient Literacy* (Cambridge, Mass., 1985), Chapter 8.

There are a number of standard works on Christian and pagan culture, including C. N. Cochrane, *Christianity and Classical Culture* (Oxford, 1940), M. L. W. Laistner, *Christianity and Pagan Culture in the Later Roman Empire* (Ithaca, NY, 1951) (with a translation of John Chrysostom, *On Vainglory*) and W. Jaeger, *Early Christianity and Greek Paideia* (Cambridge, Mass., 1962). There is a valuable chapter on John Chrysostom's preaching in Liebeschuetz, *Barbarians and Bishops* (Chapter 15); see also Young, *From Nicaea to Chalcedon*, 154–8.

The essential arguments against the idea of a 'pagan reaction' have been put in various articles by Alan Cameron: see especially 'Paganism and literature in late fourth-century Rome', in *Christianisme et formes littéraires de l'antiquité tardive en occident*, Entretiens Hardt 23 (Vandoeuvres, 1977), 1–30; 'The Latin revival of the fourth century', in W. Treadgold, ed., *Renaissances before the Renaissance* (Stanford, 1984), 42–58, 182–4, and see also R. Markus, 'Paganism, Christianity and the Latin classics in the fourth century', in J. W. Binns, ed., *Latin Literature of the Fourth Century* (London, 1974), 1–21. For the idea of a 'classical revival' in late fourth-century art see E. Kitzinger, *Byzantine Art in the Making* (Cambridge, Mass., 1977). The Proiecta casket is discussed by Kathleen Shelton, *The Esquiline Treasure* (London, 1981), and see the exchange of arguments as to date between Shelton and Alan Cameron in *American Journal of Archaeology* 89 (1985). Many individual objects of Christian, Jewish and pagan art in late antiquity are illustrated and described in the catalogue edited by K. Weitzmann, ed., *The Age of Spirituality* (New York, 1979), which also gives a very good impression of the sheer range and vitality of art in this period. There are many books on early Christian art: for a general survey, see R. Milburn, *Early Christian Art and Architecture* (Berkeley and Los Angeles, 1991), and for literary evidence about art, see C. Mango, *The Art of the Byzantine Empire 312–1453* (Englewood Cliffs, 1972), Chapter 2 (translated sources).

Trials for magic and treason: see Matthews, *The Roman Empire of Ammianus*, 209–25. On Neoplatonism and its importance, see A. H. Armstrong, ed., *Cambridge History of Later Greek and Early Medieval Philosophy* (Cambridge, 1970); R. T. Wallis, *Neoplatonism* (London, 1972). Chuvin, *Chronicle of the Last Pagans*, Chapter 8, gives an idea of the continued vigour and importance of the philosophical schools in the fifth century.

There is a good brief introduction to Syriac Christianity and the Syriac literature of late antiquity in Sebastian P. Brock and Susan Ashbrook Harvey, *Holy Women of the Syrian Orient* (Berkeley and Los Angeles, 1987), 1–12; see also R. Murray, 'The characteristics of the earliest Syriac Christianity', in N. Garsoian, T. Mathews and R. Thomson, eds., *East of Byzantium* (Washington, D.C., 1982), 3–16.

XI CONSTANTINOPLE AND THE EAST

The best books on Constantinople in the fourth century are both in French: G. Dagron, *Naissance d'une capitale* (Paris, 1974), and C. Mango, *Le développement urbain de Constantinople (IVe–VIIe siècles)* (Paris, 1985, rev. 1992). On the development of the Byzantine traditions about the origins of the city see also the brilliant book by G. Dagron, *Constantinople imaginaire* (Paris, 1984). R. Krautheimer, *Three Christian Capitals* (Berkeley and Los Angeles, 1983), makes attractive reading (the three capitals are Rome, Constantinople and Milan), but is insufficiently critical about Constantine's actions and intentions in Constantinople. For Ephesus, see Clive Foss, *Ephesus after Antiquity* (Cambridge, 1979). Antioch: G. Downey, *A History of Antioch in Syria* (Princeton, 1961), Chapters 12–15, and see for the riots of AD 387 R. Browning, 'The riot of AD 387 in Antioch: the role of the theatrical claques in the later empire', *JRS* 42 (1952), 13–20.

Public entertainments, and the political confrontations which often took place there, are the subject of Alan Cameron, *Circus Factions* (Oxford, 1976) (see especially Chapters 7, for the earlier history, and 8, especially 201–29 on chariot racing). J. Humphrey, *Roman Circuses* (London, 1986) gives a synthesis of the large amount of archaeological evidence for circuses (Greek 'hippodromes') in late antique cities. On the development of acclamation, see C. M. Roueché, 'Acclamations in the later Roman empire: new evidence from Aphrodisias', *JRS* 74 (1984), 181–99, and on claques and acclamations in the later empire see Cameron, 237 ff. and Liebeschuetz, *Antioch, City and Administration in the Later Roman Empire*, 210 ff. C. M. Roueché, *Performers and Partisans* (London, 1992), presents new epigraphic material about entertainments, and contains a new discussion of their organization; see also her article on the theatre at Aphrodisias, 'Inscriptions and the later history of the theatre', in R. R. R. Smith and K. T. Erim, eds., *Aphrodisias Papers* 2 (Ann Arbor, 1991), 99–108. Monks as 'stormtroopers': Cameron, *Circus Factions*, 290 f. For John Chrysostom in relation to public entertainments, see Liebeschuetz, *Barbarians and Bishops*, 181–8. There is much relevant discussion in Patlagean, *Pauvreté économique et pauvreté sociale*, especially Chapter 5, e.g. 179 ff. (population), 203 ff. (urban poor), 208 f. (churches as theatre), 210 ff. (theatres and hippodromes and urban violence), and on 'the poor' see Peter Brown, in Ariès and Duby, eds., *A History of Private Life* I, 277 ff.

Prosperity of Jerusalem and the Holy Land: Hunt, *Holy Land Pilgrimage in the Later Roman Empire*, especially 138–54 and Chapter 10. Patlagean, *Pauvreté économique et pauvreté sociale*, 310–11, gives comparative tables of late antique and other settlements in Palestine; see also the figures for rural churches (312–13) and monasteries (326–7); continuity of villages: *ibid.*, 236–340. Much of the important work in Syria has been done by French archaeologists; for a recent report on northern Syria see G. Tate, in *Hommes et richesses* (see Chapter 8), 69–71, 74–5. For Israel, see for instance D. Urman, *The Golan* (Oxford, BAR Int. ser. 269, 1985); Carol A. M. Glucker, *The City of Gaza in the Roman and Byzantine Periods* (Oxford, BAR Int. ser. 325, 1987).

Antiochene and Alexandrian Christianity: D. S. Wallace-Hadrill, *Christian Antioch. A Study of Early Christian Thought in the East* (Cambridge, 1982). Origenism, Councils of Ephesus and Chalcedon: see Young, *From Nicaea to Chalcedon*, 141 ff. and Chapter 5. Death of Hypatia (unedifying from the Christian point of view): Socrates, *HE* VII. 13–15, on which see Chuvin, *Chronicle of the Last Pagans*, 85–90. Syrian asceticism: S. P. Brock, 'Early Syrian Asceticism', *Numen* 20 (1973), 1–19, repr. in Brock, *Syriac Perspectives on Late Antiquity* (London, 1984); see also Peter Brown, 'The rise and function of the holy man in late antiquity', *JRS* 61 (1971), 80–101, repr. in Brown, *Society and the Holy in Late Antiquity* (Berkeley and Los Angeles, 1982), 103–52. Hellenism in relation to local cultures: see G. W. Bowersock, *Hellenism in Late Antiquity* (Cambridge, 1990). Egyptian monasticism: D. Chitty, *The Desert a City* (Oxford, 1966); Young, *From Nicaea to Chalcedon*, Chapter 1; Rousseau, *Pachomius*. For Egyptian churches and monasteries see Milburn, *Early Christian Art and Architecture*, 145–52, and Alan K. Bowman, *Egypt after the Pharaohs* (Berkeley and Los Angeles, 1986), especially 190–202. Large estates in Byzantine Egypt: see J. Gascou, 'Les grands domaines, la cité et l'état en Egypte byzantine', *Travaux et Mémoires* 9 (1985), 1–90, questioning the traditional view.

XII CONCLUSION

Peter Brown's biography of Augustine (*Augustine of Hippo*, London, 1967) should be read by all students, if only in part. Not only do Augustine's writings throw great light on his age, but he is also one of the few figures from antiquity whom we can hope to know as an individual. The key work on North Africa in late antiquity is the book by C. Lepelley (see above, on Chapter 8).

For complex societies, see J. A. Tainter, *The Collapse of Complex Societies* (Cambridge, 1988), especially Chapter 5, where the late Roman empire is taken as a test case, and Chapter 6 (general conclusions). Any attempt by a general theorist to deal with a specialized area or topic is liable to attract criticism from professional specialists, and the fact that Tainter's analysis relies on a variety of modern works without for the most part attempting to differentiate between their reliability inevitably undermines his credibility in detail. Yet as a general model it offers a new way of thinking about an old problem. For the broad sweep, seen through archaeological evidence, see K. Randsborg, *The First Millennium*

AD *in Europe and the Mediterranean* (Cambridge, 1991); for the 'end of the Roman empire', see especially 166–85. See also C. Wickham, 'The other transition: from the ancient world to feudalism', *Past and Present* 103 (1984), 3 ff.

The period from AD 395 to *c*. 600 is treated in Averil Cameron, *The Mediterranean World in Late Antiquity*, Routledge History of Classical Civilization (London, 1993); the student is referred to that for further reading.

Index

Ablabius, 55, 77
Acacius, Bishop of Beroea, 128
Adrianople, Battle of (AD 378), 85, 116, 136–7, 173
Aedesius of Pergamum, 89, 95
Agathias, 34, 147
Alamanni, 30, 90, 134, 136
Alaric the Visigoth, 22, 83, 138–9, 149–50, 188
Alexander Severus, 3
Alexandria (Egypt), 75, 182; Serapaeum, 75, 87
Allectus, usurper, 32
Alypius, 155
Ambrose, Bishop of Milan: writings, 13, 25, 78; on dedication of Church of Holy Sepulchre, 62; building, 72; and Gratian's removal of altar from senate, 73; refuses communion to Theodosius I, 75; on conversion, 78, 153; influence, 102; Milan basilica, 126; influence on imperial policy, 156, education, 166; negotiates freeing of captives, 177
Amiens, 9
Ammianus Marcellinus: on army, 35; style, 46, 106; and Constantine, 64; on Constantius II, 65; and religion, 73–4; on Serapaeum, 75; on Roman aristocracy, 79; on nuns; 83; on Julian, 20, 64, 86, 89, 91, 93, 95, 97; on Valentinian and

Valens, 99; praises Theodosius I, 101; and decline, 108; on rich landowners, 115; on military campaigns against barbarians, 133–7, 145; on Arabia, 142; on 'Saracens', 143; on class conflicts and education in Rome, 156–9; on treason trials, 163–4; on Antioch, 173; *Res Gestae*, 13, 19–21, 85–7, 194
Amphilochius of Iconium, 128
angareia (military transport), 6, 147
Anicii (Roman family), 159
annona militaris (army supplies), 6, 7, 36–7, 116, 122, 146–7
Antes (mythical giant), 170
Antioch: status, 8, 174; damaged, 9, 173–4; Julian in, 91–2, 95–6; population, 123; welfare, charity, 126, 177; captured by Shapur I, 141; trials for magic, 164; development, 173–5; entertainments, 175–6; 'school' of, 182
Antiochus, Bishop of Ptolemais, 128
Antony (Egyptian hermit), 23, 25, 82, 184
Apamea (Syria), 131, 173, 183
Aper (praetorian prefect), 31
Aphrodisias (Caria), 75, 176
Apiones (Egyptian family), 185
Apollonius of Tyana, 22
Aproniani (Roman family), 159
Apronianus, literary patron, 158
Aquileia, 43, 90

Arabs, 142–4, 188, 192
Arcadius, Emperor, 1, 74, 76, 99, 102, 149, 172
archaeology: as evidence, 28–9
Arianism, 69–71, 182
Arius, 59–60, 69–70
Arles, Council of (AD 314), 67
army (Roman): reforms, 5, 7, 33–6, 146; payments to, 5–7, 116; supply, 6–7, 36–7, 146–7; size, 34–5, 113, 147–8; and campaigns against barbarians, 133–6; cost, 146; effectiveness, 148
Arsenius (monk in Egypt), 125, 131
art: as historical evidence, 28–9; and Christianity, 159–63
ascetics and desert fathers, 82, 154, 184
Athanaric, Gothic leader 135
Athanasius, Bishop of Alexandria, 60, 70; (attrib.) Life of Antony, 23, 25, 82
Athens, 9, 11, 165
Attila the Hun, 140; death, 145
Augustine, Bishop of Hippo: writings, 13; on God's kingdom, 69; education, 72, 152–3, 155, 158, 168; commends attacks on pagans, 76; and conversion, 78; attracted to Neoplatonism, 81, 165, 189; on slaves, 120; on family life, 128–9; betrothal, 129; on poor and uneducated, 130, 154; communal living, 155; and Manichaeism, 166; death, 188, 190; teachings, 188–90; City of God (De Civitate Dei), 22, 83–4, 139, 188–90; Confessions, 23–5, 78, 83, 128, 155, 165, 190; De Doctrina Christiana, 153; De Magistro, 153
Aurelian, Emperor, 4, 5, 30, 42
Aurelius Isidorus, 185
Aurelius Victor: De Caesaribus, 18, 87
Ausonius of Bordeaux, 14, 102, 152

Babylas, St, 96–7

Baghdad, 193
barbarians: threats and invasions, 112, 132, 133–41, 191; Roman attitude to, 140; recruitment as troops, 102, 139–40, 148–50; influence on education and learning, 167
Basil, Bishop of Caesarea: writings, 13; family background, 24; founds monastery, 82; and education, 94, 152–5, 181; Latin translations, 158; in religious retirement, 181
Baynes, Norman: Constantine the Great and the Christian Church, 48
Belisarius, general, 190
bishops, 71–3, 121, 166–7
Blesilla, 81
Britain: Romans leave, 140
Brown, Peter: The World of Late Antiquity, 1
buildings, 8–9, 131; see also cities and towns
Burckhardt, Jacob, 48
Byzantium, 2, 192; see also Constantinople
Byzas (mythical giant), 170

Caesarius, Bishop of Arles, 168
Calcidius, 165
Cameron, Alan, 158, 161
Caracalla, Emperor, 9, 33
Carausius, Augustus, 31–2
Carinus, Emperor, 31
Carnuntum, 43, 113; Conference of (AD 308), 50
Carthage, Council of (AD 411), 66
Carus, Emperor, 31
Cassiodorus, 168
Cassius Dio, 175
Ceionius Rufius Albinus, 54
Chalcedon, 176; Council of (AD 451), 181–2
charity, 126–8, 177–8; see also patronage
Choricius of Gaza, 175
Chosroes I, Sasanian king, 141, 145
Christian Church: fortunes, 10–12, 84, 193; education and learning,

14, 153–6, 159, 166–7; historians, 15–16; persecution, 43–5, 51; imperial attitudes to, 66–7, 73–4, 77; heresies and disputes, 69–70, 182; wealth and power, 71–2, 115, 124; and pagans, 74–6, 78, 80; and Jews, 76–7; ascetic practices, 81–3; under Julian, 94–7; and charity, 126, 177–8; and art, 159–63; and superstition, 164; and Neoplatonism, 164–6; literature, 168; festivals, 175–6; *see also* Constantine I

Chrysaphius, 182

Chrysopolis, Battle of (AD 324), 52

Cibalae, Battle of (AD 316), 52

Cicero: *De Republica*, 189

Cirta (Numidia), 44

cities and towns: buildings and fortifications, 8–9, 131; Julian and, 93–4; development of, 170–5; in eastern empire, 179–80

citizenship (Roman), 9

civil service and officials, 107–8

claques and acclamations, 176

class (social), 10, 130–1, 156; *see also* ranks and titles

Claudian, 14, 152

Claudius Gothicus, Emperor, 49

Clovis, 187

Codex Gregorianus, 26

Codex Hermogenianus, 26

Codex Theodosianus (Theodosian Code), 26, 39, 109, 114, 176

coinage: debasement of, 3, 5–6, 36, 38, 115–16; as source, 28; gold, 53, 115

Cologne, 134

coloni, 45, 106–7, 110–11, 120

Constans, Emperor, 55, 70, 85

Constantia (wife of Licinius), 51, 61

Constantine I, Emperor: reign, 1, 47–65; adoption of and support for Christianity, 1–2, 11–12, 45, 47, 53, 55–61, 66, 193; administrative system, 3, 5, 8, 12, 14, 40, 53–5,

112; taxes, 6, 37, 39, 110, 114; and Senate, 8, 54–5, 103; and Edict of Milan, 15, 44; historians on, 15–17, 20, 47–8, 52, 53, 64–5; military campaigns, 16, 48, 50, 52, 133; public spending, 26; and law codes, 27–8, 110; and Diocletian, 31–3, 46, 53–4; ends tetrarchy, 31, 49; titulature, 32; army reforms, 35, 53; and Constantinople, 43, 48, 63, 170–1; accession, 46, 48; birth and career, 48–52; Arch of (Rome), 50–1; legislation, 54–5, 58; and Donatists, 56, 59, 66–7; baptism, 57, 70; and Council of Nicaea, 59–61, 68; church building, 61–3; image, 64; and church controversy and heresy, 68–70; forbids sacrifice, 74; removes penalties on celibacy, 83, 128; and ranks, 103, 105; fiscal measures, 115; inheritance law, 124; mausoleum, 126, 171; law on divorce, 128; conflict with Licinius, 133; and Persia, 143; and frontier defences, 146; statue and column, 170–1; and claques, 176; *Oration to the Saints*, 57

Constantine II, Emperor, 70, 85

Constantine, usurper, 139–40, 149

Constantinople: founding and development, 1–2, 43, 63–4, 170–2; bishopric, 68; Council of (AD 381), 71, 154; rise as capital, 112; senators in, 118; free food supply, 122, 172; mausoleum of Constantine, 126, 171; statue and column of Constantine, 170–1; Nika revolt (AD 532), 174; emperors in, 187

Constantius I Chlorus, Emperor, 31–2, 43–4, 48, 101

Constantius II, Emperor: Julian's relations with, 15, 87–91; and Christianity, 65, 70, 74; exiles Hilarius, 71; and sacrifices, 74; as sole emperor, 85; Ammianus on, 87–8; death, 89, 91; military cam-

paigns, 133, 135, 141; and con-
version of Goths, 136; and trials
for magic, 164
Constitutio Antoniana (AD 212), 9
Coptic language, 10
Crispus (son of Constantine), 17, 57
Cronius (hermit), 184
currency *see* coinage
Cyprian, Bishop of Carthage, 10
Cyril, Bishop of Alexandria, 182
Cyril, Bishop of Jerusalem, 68, 97
Cyrrhus (Syria), 181, 183

Damascus, 193
Damasus, Pope, 126, 156, 162
Daphne (near Antioch): Temple of
Apollo, 92, 95–6; taverns, 125
Decius, Emperor, 4, 10–11
De Rebus Bellicis (anon.), 25, 116,
145
de Ste Croix, G.E.M., 112
desert fathers *see* ascetics and desert
fathers
Dexippus, P. Herennius *see* Herennius Dexippus, P.
Didius Julianus, 101
Diocletian, Emperor: accession, 1, 3,
30–1; tetrarchic system and
reforms, 3, 8–9, 12, 14, 31–2, 42,
45; army reforms, 5, 7, 33–7, 142;
taxes, 6, 36–7, 45–6, 110, 113;
persecutes Christians, 10–11, 45;
court ceremony and titulature, 12,
42–3, 45; and contemporary
histories, 15; law collections, 26;
Edict on Maximum Prices, 27–8,
38–9; Revaluation Edict, 28;
administrative reforms, 39–43, 53–
4, 112, 193; abdication and death,
46, 48; financial measures, 113,
115; 'state factories', 113; marriage
laws, 129; and Mesopotamia,
141; defence against barbarians,
146
Dodds, R. E., 11
Dominate, The, 2

Donatism and Donatists, 47, 56, 59,
66–7, 69
Donatus, 59
Dracontius, 168
dress, 131–2

Edessa, 167, 183
education, 152–5, 167
Egeria (Spanish nun), 124–5, 178
Egypt, 23, 82, 184–5
Elvira, Council of (AD 305), 67
Ennodius, Bishop of Pavia, 168
entertainments, 175–6
Ephesus, 172, 176; Councils of
(AD 431), 130, 172; (AD 449),
172
Ephrem Syrus, 93, 97–8, 167–8
Epiphanius, Bishop of Constantia
(Salamis), 128, 154; *Panarion*, 69
Eros Monaxius, 70
estates: management, 119–21; *see
also* landowners
Eudoxia, Empress, 72, 179
euergetism, 8, 126
Eugenius, 22, 75–6, 80, 87, 156
Eulogius, 184
Eunapius, 64, 76, 89, 149; *Lives of
the Sophists*, 165
Eusebia (wife of Constantius II),
87, 89–90;
Eusebius, Bishop of Caesarea: writings, 15–18, 23, 47, 52, 56, 60,
137; on Constantine, 47–8, 52–4,
56–8, 60, 64, 68, 74, 84, 91, 133,
143; and Council of Nicaea, 59–61;
and building of Church of Holy
Sepulchre, 62; on Constantinople,
63, 171; on Christian asceticism,
83; on senatorial order, 103;
speeches, 152
Eusebius, Bishop of Nicomedia, 70,
88
Eustochium, 81–2, 131
Eutropius, 87, 102, 149–50; *Breviarium*, 18
Evagrius Ponticus, 82, 154

exchange (market), 121–2; see also monetary system

Fabiola, 127
Fabius Titianus, 54
Fausta (wife of Constantine I), 49, 57
Faustus of Riez, 168
Ferrill, A., 148
Finley, Moses I.: The Ancient Economy, 123
Firminus, 155
Flavian, Bishop of Antioch, 73, 174
Flavianus, Virius Nicomachus see Nicomachus Flavianus, Virius
Flavius Aetius, 145
Franks (Merovingians) 134, 136, 187
Frigidus, River, Battle of the (AD 394), 22, 76

Gainas, Gothic leader and rebel, 139, 148–50
Galerius, 15, 31, 44–5, 48–9, 51
Gallienus, Emperor, 4, 7, 30
Gallus, Caesar, 85–6, 88–90, 95
Gaul (and Gallic empire), 4, 9–10, 133–4, 145
Gerontius: (attrib.) Life of Melania the Younger, 24
Gervasius (martyr), 126
Gibbon, Edward, 2, 21
gold: tax payments in, 6, 53, 115; coins, 53, 115; mining, 114
Gothic alphabet, 168
Goths, 4, 135–8, 147, 149–50
Gratian, Emperor, 14, 73, 100, 102, 109, 135, 138; death, 137
Greek language and culture, 14, 158, 167–9, 183
Grégoire, Henri, 48
Gregory the Great, Pope, 68
Gregory, Bishop of Nazianzus: writings, 13; oratory, 72; opposes Julian, 93, 95; education, 94; visits shrine of St Thecla, 125; on father's monument, 126; attends Council of Constantinople, 154; Latin translations, 158; and Neo-

platonism, 165; on term 'Hellenic', 183
Gregory, Bishop of Nyssa, 13, 83, 126, 128, 155, 165; Life of Macrina, 24, 181
Gregory, Bishop of Tours: History of the Franks, 168
Hadrian, Emperor, 172
Hannibalianus, 86
Helena (mother of Constantine I), 61–2, 124
Hellene, Hellenic, 183
Heraclius, Emperor, 4, 145
Herennius Dexippus, P., 11
heresies, 69; see also Christian Church
Heruli, 9, 11
Hilarion (hermit), 23
Hilarius, Bishop of Poitiers, 71
Hippo, 177, 190; see also Augustine, Bishop of Hippo
Historia Augusta, 11, 20–2, 157
Historia Monachorum, 82
Holy Land: pilgrimages to, 124–5; prosperity and population growth, 178
Honorius, Emperor, 1, 14, 74, 76, 99, 140, 149
Huns, 136, 140, 145, 148
Hypatia, 182

Iamblichus of Apamea, 95, 131, 165; Chaldean Oracles, 165; On the Mysteries, 165; On the Pythagorean Life, 166
Imru'l-quais, son of 'Amr, 144
inflation see prices
inheritance, 124
Isaac, Benjamin, 142–3
Islam, 193; see also Arabs

Jacob of Serug, 183
Jerome: writings, 13, 25; translations, 23, 168; and paganism, 78; and women 81–3, 127, 131; on Huns, 136; on sack of Rome, 139; reading, 153, 158; on ascetic life-

Jerome *(cont.)*
style, 162; deplores growth of Jerusalem, 178; and Origen, 182; temper, 184
Jerusalem, 62, 68, 92, 97, 178
Jesus Christ: disputes over nature of, 182
Jews, Judaism, 76–7
John Chrysostom, Bishop of Constantinople: writings, 13, 25; preaching, 72; commends attacks on pagans, 76; homilies against Jews, 77; attitude to Julian, 93, 96–7; warns pilgrims, 125; puritanism, 131, 155, 175; and Gainas, 150; and education and culture, 155, 166; in Constantinople, 172; on Antioch, 174; and Origen, 182
John the Lydian, 107
Jones, A. H. M., 40–1, 45, 107, 146–7, 167; *History of the Later Roman Empire*, 1, 28, 37
Jovian, Emperor, 91–2, 99–100
Jugurtha (North African prince), 106
Julian, Emperor: paganism, 14–15, 61, 71, 74–5, 79, 89, 91–2, 94–6, 98, 131, 156; writings, 14–15, 86–7, 95; Ammianus and, 20, 64, 86, 89, 91, 93; and Themistius, 73; birth, upbringing and career, 85, 88–90; death, 86, 91–2, 98, 100; grudge against Constantius II, 87–8; reign and administration, 91–5; Persian campaign, 92, 97–8, 135; qualities, 92–3, 95, 98, 103; attitude to Christians, 94–7; campaign in Gaul, 134; and education, 153; and Neoplatonism, 165; in Constantinople, 172; *Caesares*, 58, 95; *Misopogon* ('The Beard-Hater'), 15, 92
Julius (Carthaginian villa-owner), 119
Julius Constantius, 85
Justina (wife of Valentinian I), 100, 102

Justinian, Emperor, 26, 129, 171, 188
Juvenal, 158

Lactantius: attacks Diocletian, 33, 35, 38–9, 46, 47; as rhetor in Nicomedia, 43; praises Constantine, 47, 49, 56; on death of Galerius, 49; *On the Deaths of the Persecutors*, 15, 44, 52
landowners: wealth, 115, 117–19, 121; in Egypt, 185
Laodicea, 174
Laterculus Veronensis (Verona List), 39
Latin language, 14–15, 158, 168–9, 183, 188
Latin Panegyrics, 47
law, 26–7, 107–12
Leo (henchman of Valentinian), 163
Libanius: oratory, 72; paganism, 74, 76, 89, 93; and Ammianus, 87; influence on Julian, 89, 95; teaches Christians, 94; on death of Julian, 98; on protection systems, 107; and public duty, 109; in Constantinople, 172; on Antioch, 174–5; on the poor, 177; *Antiochikos*, 173
Liber Pontificum (Book of the Popes), 124
Licinius, Emperor: and Edict of Milan, 15, 44; wars with Constantine I, 16–17, 47, 50–2, 56, 63, 133; at Pannonia, 43; Christian sympathies, 57
Liebeschuetz, W., 150
Limigantes, 135
Livy, 189
Luttwak, Edward, 35, 142

Macarius the Great, 82
MacMullen, R., 107
Macrianus (Alamannic chief), 135
Macrina (sister of Gregory of Nyasa). 24, 83, 155, 181
Macrinus, Emperor, 175

Macrobius, 165; *Saturnalia*, 157, 160
magic: trials for, 163–4
Magnentius, 74, 85, 113
Magnus Maximus, usurper, 100, 135
Mani and Manichaeans, 81, 155, 166
Mann, J. C., 142
Marcella, 81, 128
Marcellus, Bishop of Apamea, 75
Marcian, Emperor, 145
Marcus Aurelius, Emperor, 4–5, 10, 33, 91, 100
Marius Maximus, 158
Marius Victorinus, 78–9, 94, 165
marriage, 128–30
Mary, Virgin, 130
Mavia (Mawiya), Queen, 144
Maxentius, Emperor, 16, 46, 48–51, 56–7, 91, 170
Maximian, Emperor, 31, 42, 44, 46, 48–9
Maximin (Maximinus Daia), Emperor, 49, 51
Maximin (henchman of Valentinian), 163
Maximus of Ephesus, 89, 95, 164–5
Maximus, Bishop of Turin, 177
Mehmet the Conqueror, 187
Melania the Elder, 127, 154
Melania the Younger, 24, 81, 83, 117, 119, 124, 126, 177–8
Mesopotamia, 133, 135, 141, 144
Milan, 43, 63, 79, 126; Edict of (AD 313), 15, 45, 51
Milvian Bridge, Battle of the (AD 312), 16–17, 48, 50, 56, 91
mining, 113–14
monasticism and monks, 82–3, 184–5
monetary system, 116–17; *see also* coinage
Monica (Augustine's mother), 128
Monophysitism, 182
Moses, hermit of Sinai, 144
Mungersdorf (villa, near Cologne), 119

Naissus (Nis), 43, 91
Naqsh-i-Rustam, 4

Naucratius (brother of Basil), 181–2
Nazarius, 56, 133, 152
Nebridius, 155
Nectarius, Patriarch of Constantinople, 128
Negev, 179–80
Neocaesarea (Pontos), 181
Neoplatonism, 80–1, 89, 95, 155–6, 164–6, 189
Nessana (Negev), 180
Nestorianism, 182
Nestorius, Bishop of Constantinople, 182
Nicaea, Council of (AD 325), 17, 59–61, 68–70, 182
Nicomachi (Roman family), 159–60
Nicomachus Flavianus, Virius, 75, 79, 156, 158, 160; *Annales*, 22
Nicomedia (Izmir), 8, 42–3
Nisibis: ceded to Persia, 92, 99, 141–2, 167
Nola (Campania), 124
North Africa: urban growth, 9; grain production, 122; trade, 123; Vandals in, 145, 188, 190
Notitia Dignitatum, 25–6, 33–4, 113, 147
Numerian, Emperor, 31

Odenathus, King of Palmyra, 4
Odoacer, 187
Olympus, 83, 126, 128
Olympiodorus, 117
Optatus, Bishop Milevis, 43, 47, 66
Origen, 44, 158, 182
Orosius: *Historia contra paganos*, 139
Ossius, Bishop of Cordoba, 61
Ostrogoths, 136–7, 140, 187
Oxyrhynchus, 185

Pacatus, 138, 152
Pachomius, 82
paganism, 74–6, 78–80, 89, 94–5
Palladius, 119, 184; *Lausiac History*, 82
Palmyra (Syria), 4, 9; *see also* Odenathus, Zenobia

Pamphilus, 44
Panopolis (Egypt), 185
Paphos (Cyprus), 131
Paris, 9
Patricius (Augustine's father), 128
patronage, 106–8, 121, 127–8; *see also* charity
Paul (hermit), 23
Paula, 81–3, 125, 127, 184
Paulina, Fabia Aconia, 79
Paulinus, Bishop of Nola, 72, 124, 127, 177
Pelagius (monk), 190
Perperna, 101
Persia: Julian's campaigns in, 92, 97, 135; Constantine's war in, 133; conflicts with, 141–4, 188, 192
Pescennius Niger, 101
Petronius Probus, 73, 117
Philostratus, 22; *Life of Apollonius of Tyana*, 158
pilgrimages, 124–5, 178
Pinianus, 24, 81, 117, 177
plague, 10
Plato *see* Neoplatonism
Plotinus, 11, 81, 165
Pollentia, Battle of (AD 402), 139
poor, the, 106, 130, 154, 177–8
population: increases in, 114, 123, 179, 188
Porfyrius, Publilius Optatianus, 133
Porphyry, neoplatonist, 81, 165–6
Porphyry, Bishop of Gaza, 127, 173
Posidonius the Theban, 184
Possidius, 190
Postumus, Emperor, 4
Praetextatus, Vettius Agorius, 79, 156–7, 164, 171
praetorian prefects, 39–40, 53
Praxagoras, 18
prices: and coinage, 5–6; Diocletian's Edict on, 27, 38–9; and inflation, 113
Primuliacum (Gaul), 124
Principate, The, 2

Probus, Emperor, 30–1; diptych, 163
Procopius, usurper, 101
Procopius of Caesaraea, 93
'Proiecta casket', 160–2
Protasius (martyr), 126
Prudentius, 80
Pulcheria, Augusta, 78
Pythagoras, 166

Quadi, 135
Qirk Bizze (near Antioch), 180

ranks and titles, 103–6
ransoms, 177
Rehovot (Negev), 179
rhetoric, 152–3, 167
Romanianus, 155
Rome: status, 8, 63–4, 68; sacked (AD 410), 83–4, 139, 189; iconography, 103; development, 112; free food supplies, 122–3, 174; church building, 126; class and learning in, 156, 158–9; artistic patronage in, 159–60; and development of Constantinople, 170; Augustine on, 189; decline of empire, 191
Romulus Augustulus, Emperor, 187
Rostovtzeff, M. I., 12
Rufinus, 102
Rufinus (writer), 18, 82, 137

sacrifices, 74, 95
Ste Croix, G.E.M. de *see* de Ste Croix, G.E.M.
'Saracens', 143–4
Sarapion 'the loincloth', 184
Sarmatians, 135
Sasanians, 4, 9, 133, 141, 192; *see also* Persia
Scythopolis, 164
Senate and senators: status and role, 7–8, 41–2, 54–5, 103; wealth, 117–18
Septimius Severus, Emperor, 5, 33, 171

Serena (wife of Stilicho), 126
Servius, 157, 160, 165
Severian, Bishop of Gabala, 128
sexuality, sexual relations, 129–30
Shapur I, Sasanian king, 4, 141
Shapur II, Sasanian king, 135, 143
Shelton, Kathleen, 161
Shenute, *higumen* (abbot) of the White Monastery, near Sohag, 185
Sidonius, Apollinaris, 168
Silvanus, 134
silver *see* coinage
Singara: ceded to Persia, 99, 142
Sirmium (Pannonia), 43, 90, 135
slavery, 118–21; *see also coloni*
Socrates (historian), 18, 149
Sofia (Serdica), 8, 42
Sopater, 171
Sozomen, 18, 58, 144, 149
Split, 8, 43, 46
Stilicho, Vandal general, 14, 102, 126, 139–40, 148–50
Strasbourg, Battle of (AD 357), 90, 134
Strata Diocletiana (road), 35
Sulpicius Severus, 124, 127
Syme, R., 22
Symeon the Elder, St, 186
Symmachi (Roman family), 159–61
Symmachus, Q. Aurelius, 13, 73, 75, 79–81, 117, 120, 156–7, 160
Synesius, Bishop of Ptolemais: *De Providentia*, 150
Syria, 183
Syriac language, 10, 167–8, 183

Tacitus, 10
taxation, 3, 6; in gold, 6, 53, 115; under Diocletian, 36–8, 45–6, 110, 113; under Constantine, 37, 53–4, 110; under Julian, 94; collection, 114; and army, 146–7
Tervingi, 136
tetrarchic system, 3, 8–9, 12, 14, 31–2, 42–3, 45–6
Tetricus, 30
Thagaste, 177

Thecla (Seleucia, Isauria), 125
Themistius, 14, 73, 93, 138, 152
Theodoret, Bishop of Cyrrhus, 181–3
Theodoric the Ostrogoth, 187
Theodosian Code *see Codex Theodosianus*
Theodosius I, Emperor: death, 1, 76, 99; funeral oration, 13; defeats Eugenius, 22; calls Council of Constantinople (AD 381), 71–2; and Christianity, 73, 75, 80; and sacrifices, 74; accession, 100; reign, 101; and Ambrose, 102; and protection systems, 107; marriage laws, 129; recruits Goths, 137–8; Ephesus, frieze of, 172
Theodosius II, Emperor, 26, 77, 105, 150, 152, 171–2; *see also Codex Theodosianus*
Theophilus, Patriarch of Alexandria, 125
Theophylact Simocatta, 18
Thesssalonica, 42
theurgy, 164–5
Ticinum, 133
travel *see* pilgrimages
Tribigild, 148–9
Trier, 8, 43, 63, 119
Turcii (Roman family), 162

Uldin, or Uldes, 148–50
Ulfila, Bishop among the Goths, 136
Ursicinus, 134

Valens, Emperor: defeat and death, 19, 116, 136–7; proclaimed co-emperor, 99–100; war with Procopius, 101–2; and guilds, 109; military campaigns against barbarians, 135, 136–7, 147; trials under, 163–4; builds Constantinople aqueduct, 172; and development of Antioch, 173
Valentinian I, Emperor: Ammianus on, 21, 74; reign, 99–100; and Valens, 99; and guilds, 109; and

Valentinian I (*cont.*)
  coinage, 116; military campaigns,
  135; trials under, 163
Valentinian II, Emperor, 73, 100,
  102, 135
Valerian, Emperor, 4, 11, 141
Vandals, 84, 141, 145, 188, 190; *see
  also* Stilichus
Vegetius, 137
Venantius Fortunatus, 168
Verecundus, 155
Verus (adopted brother of Marcus
  Aurelius), 100
villages: in East, 180

Visigoths, 136–7, 145, 177, 187
Volusianus, Rufius, 54

women: lives of, 23–4; independence
  and achievements, 127–8, 160;
  treatment of and laws on, 128–30;
  asceticism and learning, 154–5,
  158

Zenobia, independent ruler of
  Palmyra, 4, 9, 30
Zosimus: *New History*, 15, 19, 35,
  47, 53, 63–4, 87, 137–8, 146, 149,
  171